Guide to the Successful Thesis and Dissertation

BOOKS IN LIBRARY AND INFORMATION SCIENCE

A Series of Monographs and Textbooks

1. Classified Library of Congress Subject Headings: Volume 1, Classified List, *edited by James G. Williams, Martha L. Manheimer, and Jay E. Daily*
2. Classified Library of Congress Subject Headings: Volume 2, Alphabetic List, *edited by James G. Williams, Martha L. Manheimer, and Jay E. Daily*
3. Organizing Nonprint Materials, *Jay E. Daily*
4. Computer-Based Chemical Information, *edited by Edward McC. Arnett and Allen Kent*
5. Style Manual: A Guide for the Preparation of Reports and Dissertations, *Martha L. Manheimer*
6. The Anatomy of Censorship, *Jay E. Daily*
7. Information Science: Search for Identity, *edited by Anthony Debons*
8. Resource Sharing in Libraries: Why · How · When · Next Action Steps, *edited by Allen Kent*
9. Reading the Russian Language: A Guide for Librarians and Other Professionals, *Rosalind Kent*
10. Statewide Computing Systems: Coordinating Academic Computer Planning, *edited by Charles Mosmann*
11. Using the Chemical Literature: A Practical Guide, *Henry M. Woodburn*
12. Cataloging and Classification: A Workbook, *Martha L. Manheimer*
13. Multi-media Indexes, Lists, and Review Sources: A Bibliographic Guide, *Thomas L. Hart, Mary Alice Hunt, and Blanche Woolls*
14. Document Retrieval Systems: Factors Affecting Search Time, *K. Leon Montgomery*
15. Library Automation Systems, *Stephen R. Salmon*
16. Black Literature Resources: Analysis and Organization, *Doris H. Clack*
17. Copyright–Information Technology–Public Policy: Part I–Copyright–Public Policies; Part II–Public Policies–Information Technology, *Nicholas Henry*
18. Crisis in Copyright, *William Z. Nasri*
19. Mental Health Information Systems: Design and Implementation, *David J. Kupfer, Michael S. Levine, and John A. Nelson*

20. Handbook of Library Regulations, *Marcy Murphy and Claude J. Johns, Jr.*
21. Library Resource Sharing, *Allen Kent and Thomas J. Galvin*
22. Computers in Newspaper Publishing: User-Oriented Systems, *Dineh Moghdam*
23. The On-Line Revolution in Libraries, *edited by Allen Kent and Thomas J. Galvin*
24. The Library as a Learning Service Center, *Patrick R. Penland and Aleyamma Mathai*
25. Using the Mathematical Literature: A Practical Guide, *Barbara Kirsch Schaefer*
26. Use of Library Materials: The University of Pittsburgh Study, *Allen Kent et al.*
27. The Structure and Governance of Library Networks, *edited by Allen Kent and Thomas J. Galvin*
28. The Development of Library Collections of Sound Recordings, *Frank W. Hoffmann*
29. Furnishing the Library Interior, *William S. Pierce*
30. Cataloging and Classification: A Workbook, Second Edition, Revised and Expanded, *Martha L. Manheimer*
31. Handbook of Computer-Aided Composition, *Arthus H. Phillips*
32. OCLC: Its Governance, Function, Financing, and Technology, *Albert F. Maruskin*
33. Scientific and Technical Information Resources, *Krishna Subramanyam*
34. An Author Index to Library of Congress Classification, Class P, Subclasses PN, PR, PS, PZ, General Literature, English and American Literature, Fiction in English, and Juvenile Belles Lettres, *Alan M. Greenberg*
35. Using the Biological Literature: A Practical Guide, *Elisabeth B. Davis*
36. An Introduction to Automated Literature Searching, *Elizabeth P. Hartner*
37. The Retrieval of Information in the Humanities and the Social Sciences: Problems as Aids to Learning, *edited by Thomas P. Slavens*
38. The Information Professional: Survey of an Emerging Field, *Anthony Debons, Donald W. King, Una Mansfield, and Donald L. Shirey*
39. Classified Library of Congress Subject Headings, Second Edition: Part A–Classified List; Part B–Alphabetic List, *edited by James G. Williams, Martha L. Manheimer, and Jay E. Daily*
40. Information Technology: Critical Choices for Library Decision-Makers, *edited by Allen Kent and Thomas J. Galvin*
41. Structure and Subject Interaction: Toward a Sociology of Knowledge in the Social Sciences, *Stephen Bulick*
42. World Librarianship: A Comparative Study, *Richard Krzys and Gaston Litton*
43. Guide to the Successful Thesis and Dissertation: Conception to Publication: A Handbook for Students and Faculty, *James E. Mauch and Jack W. Birch*
44. Physical Disability: An Annotated Literature Guide, *edited by Phyllis C. Self*

45. Effective Online Searching: A Basic Text, *Christine L. Borgman, Dineh Moghdam, and Patti K. Corbett*
46. Easy Access to DIALOG, ORBIT, and BRS, *Patricia J. Klingensmith and Elizabeth E. Duncan*
47. Subject and Information Analysis, *edited by Eleanor D. Dym*
48. Organizing Nonprint Materials: Second Edition, *Jay E. Daily*
49. An Introduction to Information Science, *Roger R. Flynn*
50. Designing Instruction for Library Users: A Practical Guide, *Marilla D. Svinicki and Barbara A. Schwartz*
51. Guide to the Successful Thesis and Dissertation: Conception to Publication: A Handbook for Students and Faculty, Second Edition, *James E. Mauch and Jack W. Birch*
52. The Retrieval of Information in the Humanities and the Social Sciences: Problems as Aids to Learning, Second Edition, *edited by Thomas P. Slavens*
53. Manheimer's Cataloging and Classification: A Workbook, Third Edition, Revised and Expanded, *Jerry D. Saye*
54. Electronic Printing and Publishing: The Document Processing Revolution, *Michael B. Spring*
55. Guide to the Successful Thesis and Dissertation: A Handbook for Students and Faculty, Third Edition, Revised and Expanded, *James E. Mauch and Jack W. Birch*
56. Library Information Technology and Networks, *Audrey N. Grosch*
57. Using the Biological Literature: A Practical Guide, Second Edition, Revised and Expanded, *Elisabeth B. Davis and Diane Schmidt*
58. Guide to the Successful Thesis and Dissertation: A Handbook for Students and Faculty, Fourth Edition, Revised and Expanded, *James E. Mauch and Jack W. Birch*
59. Manheimer's Cataloging and Classification: Fourth Edition, Revised and Expanded, *Jerry D. Saye*
60. Using the Biological Literature: A Practical Guide, Third Edition, Revised and Expanded, *Diane Schmidt, Elisabeth B. Davis, and Pamela F. Jacobs*
61. Using the Agricultural, Environmental, and Food Literature, *edited by Barbara S. Hutchinson and Antoinette Paris Greider*
62. Guide to the Successful Thesis and Dissertation: A Handbook for Students and Faculty, Fifth Edition, *James E. Mauch and Namgi Park*

ADDITIONAL VOLUMES IN PREPARATION

Becoming a Digital Library, *edited by Susan J. Barnes*

Guide to the Successful Thesis and Dissertation

A Handbook for Students and Faculty

Fifth Edition

James E. Mauch
University of Pittsburgh
Pittsburgh, Pennsylvania, U.S.A.

Namgi Park
Kwangju National University of Education
Kwangju, Republic of Korea

MARCEL DEKKER, INC. NEW YORK • BASEL

Although great care has been taken to provide accurate and current information, neither the author(s) nor the publisher, nor anyone else associated with this publication, shall be liable for any loss, damage, or liability directly or indirectly caused or alleged to be caused by this book. The material contained herein is not intended to provide specific advice or recommendations for any specific situation.

The previous edition was published as *Guide to the Successful Thesis and Dissertation: A Handbook for Students and Faculty, Fourth Edition, Revised and Expanded,* by James E. Mauch and Jack W. Birch.

Library of Congress Cataloging-in-Publication Data
A catalog record for this book is available from the Library of Congress.

ISBN: 0-8247-4288-5

This book is printed on acid-free paper.

Headquarters
Marcel Dekker, Inc., 270 Madison Avenue, New York, New York 10016, U.S.A.
tel: 212-696-9000; fax: 212-685-4540

Distribution and Customer Service
Marcel Dekker, Inc., Cimarron Road, Monticello, New York, New York 12701, U.S.A.
tel: 800-228-1160; fax: 845-796-1772

Eastern Hemisphere Distribution
Marcel Dekker AG, Hutgasse 4, Postfach 812, CH-4001 Basel, Switzerland
tel: 41-61-260-6300; fax: 41-61-260-6333

World Wide Web
http://www.dekker.com

The publisher offers discounts on this book when ordered in bulk quantities. For more information, write to Special Sales/Professional Marketing at the headquarters address above.

Current printing (last digit):

10 9 8 7 6 5 4 3 2 1

PRINTED IN THE UNITED STATES OF AMERICA

To our wives, Rebecca and Sungsook

Preface

The first edition of this book grew out of the dearth of written information on the subject for either students or faculty. They told us they needed to know much more about doing or directing theses and dissertations than they found in college catalogues, graduate office instructions, or discussions with those who had experienced the process.

We decided to write about the "how to" aspects of thesis and dissertation study and to emphasize the intellectual effort required of both students and professors.

This book is designed to inform and advise about the thesis and dissertation process, how to get through it and get the most out of it. The fact that half of the students who complete course requirements do not go on to complete the dissertation (in some schools as high as 70%) makes our objective more urgent (Monaghan, 1989).

This fifth edition was prompted by suggestions from students, colleagues, and other users of earlier editions. In response to those helpful recommendations and our own observations, we believe that the book is substantially improved in the following ways:

- Attention is given to the honors thesis as an important and rapidly growing category of student research.
- More attention is given to the use of up-to-date technology, (e.g., computers and software) in the thesis and dissertation (T/D) process, from initial research to writing the final results.
- New suggestions designed to help foreign students are made, with special emphasis on critical points, such as helpful advice for advisors of foreign students.
- A new section on qualitative research has been added to the first chapter.
- The intellectual property aspects of the T/D are given major attention.
- Socially sensitive research is explained and discussed.
- Confidentiality and privacy of Internet communication are presented as critical issues.
- Cautions about the accuracy and trustworthiness of research reported on the Internet are offered.
- A new section has been added concerning the appropriate use of animal subjects.
- The historical background of advanced degrees is summarized in the new Introduction.
- Reorganization, consolidation, and altered sequencing of topics, with an enlarged index enhances use of the book as a reference.
- There are additional suggestions for students and faculty in the academic disciplines, as well as readers in the professional disciplines.
- The forms of dissertation now current in higher education are recognized and acknowledged to be different but equally appropriate ways to assemble data and focus on a problem, depending on the nature of the problem to be addressed.
- A table of contents is offered for both the thesis and the dissertation, as models for student researchers.
- A checklist for theses and dissertations is included to help student researchers in critiquing and revising their own first drafts, as well as the work of others.
- More than twenty operational models have been presented for

dealing with specific problems in the thesis and dissertation process, from topic selection through evaluating the finished product.
- To the best of our knowledge, the bibliography is the most comprehensive one in print on the thesis and the dissertation.

Perhaps the most unusual quality of this book is that it addresses both students and faculty members. Certainly it is aimed primarily at students. Yet we found it necessary to write both to the student and to the thesis or dissertation committee members in order to convey certain concepts like colleagueship and consultation. So one should not be surprised that the student is advised about interactions with committee members at the same time that suggestions are given that committee members might apply in their dealings with students. We hope that our treatment of the subject encourages discussion among those involved in the enterprise.

One of the surprising weaknesses in the thesis or dissertation process is that there is relatively little scholarly literature and a remarkably small number of empirical investigations about it. This is true not only for the professions but also for the arts and sciences and all aspects of the honors thesis.

Comparative and descriptive studies of T/D topics do exist. However, the theoretical articles and the data-based studies one might expect to find about the principles and processes of such an important part of academia are few. That is why we report little hard evidence on most of the issues in thesis and dissertation preparation. In fact, we found it necessary to conduct our own investigations to help us arrive at the viewpoints we present in the various chapters.

To broaden the database more than 100 faculty members were interviewed, each of whom had directed more than five dissertations. The insights they shared during structured and informal interviews averaging considerably more than one hour each afforded us an unparalleled opportunity for learning. The findings from those interviews, supplemented by publications, constituted the raw material from which the various chapters were constructed.

We are grateful to C. Baker, R. M. Bean, D. B. Cameron, R. Dekker, J. T. Gibson, A. K. Golin, T. Hsu, R. D. Hummel, A. Kovacs, L. Pingle, M. C. Reynolds, M. Spring, G. A. Stewart, M. Wang, and

T. Zullo for reading and critiquing the book, for using early drafts of the book in seminars, and for employing it with individual students in graduate research direction and guidance. We appreciate their wise and acute observations on how to improve it. For assistance in building a relevant bibliography we owe thanks to many professors, graduate students, and bibliographers from the University of Pittsburgh and other centers of higher education in the United States and abroad. Special appreciation is acknowledged to Russell Dekker and Allen Kent for helpful counsel and support throughout.

Whatever merit the book has is owed in good part to the thoughtful help we have had from all who aided and advised us along the way.

We are naturally pleased that the response to our work has been both substantial and warm. We hope that the fifth edition will prove even more useful than the previous editions to students and faculty.

James E. Mauch
Namgi Park

Contents

List of Figures

Historical Introduction: The Emergence of Advanced Degrees and Graduate Research

The present college and university degree structure has deep roots in more than 700 years of tradition. The connection of advanced degrees with written theses and dissertations goes back in time almost as far.

EMERGENCE OF ADVANCED DEGREES

The awarding of degrees as evidence of advanced study occurred in a time when skill in argument and appeal to authority were valued highly. The thesis and dissertation (T/D) constituted components of well-reasoned arguments. The successful applicant had to take a position (the thesis), buttress it with logic, and relate it to the earlier conclusions of respected scholars (the dissertation) to the point that it could not be refuted. That concept of the T/D gave rise to a viewpoint that continues to this day, namely that the final act with regard to T/D study is the defense of the study by the student before a group of probing questioners. Historically, successful defense led to advancement of the writer from the status of student first to rank of master, then to doctor, with the rights and privileges that were part of those stations in life.

Artisans and craftsmen had organized to keep their skills from becoming the property of everyone, thus protecting their livelihoods. They systematized the preparation of new specialists by enforcing a sequence of training leading from apprenticeship to the status of master. Preparation of a masterpiece, a work that was judged worthy of the name by a jury of masters, signaled the successful conclusion of training.

As academic centers emerged, and as a sequence of study evolved, the thesis and the dissertation became the capstones of successive levels of achievement. The model, probably borrowed from the guilds of artisans and craftsmen, spread. The masters and the doctorate became identifying symbols. For example, in the early fourteenth century in Bologna, a candidate for the Doctor of Law degree had to take two examinations—a private one and, later, a public one in the cathedal. The private examination was conducted by the faculty of doctors.

SPECIALIZATION APPEARS

A series of knowledge explosions led to differentiation of academic and applied fields. The age of terrestrial exploration greatly expanded human knowledge. Much of the new information and understanding also challenged long-held beliefs. The Industrial Revolution brought another and much higher level of comprehension, particularly about the physical world, triggering the post-Victorian period of technology and science.

Each period brought changes. A major one was the emergence of professional degrees as contrasted with academic degrees.

The Doctor of Philosophy degree, an academic discipline degree, was first offered in the United States at Yale University in 1861. Less than three decades later, in 1890, New York University initiated a Graduate School of Pedagogy, the first graduate school of education in this country. It offered the Doctor of Philosophy plus a Doctor of Pedagogy degree, the latter credited with being the first doctoral level degree in the professional discipline of education awarded in the United States.

The master's degree predated the doctorate. In 1858 the University of Michigan, for example, had courses of study leading to the Master of Arts and the Master of Science degrees. As far as a master's degree in a profession is concerned, probably the first was the Master of Pedagogy, also offered in 1890 by New York University. Incidentally, the Bachelor of Pedagogy degree had a brief period of popularity from about 1900 to 1936 as an indicator of graduation from undergraduate teacher preparation.

The Doctor of Education degree was introduced in 1920 by Harvard University. It was intended for practicing educators. In 1933 another new degree was born at Harvard University, the Master of Arts in Teaching. It was to be administered jointly by the faculty of the Graduate School of Education and by the Faculty of Arts and Sciences.

During the same period, other professions developed masters and doctors degrees that required theses and dissertations. The T/D process in some disciplines developed uniquely. An example is law and jurisprudence. Aspirants to the JD degree face requirements of an extraordinary kind. Most professions, however, employed the familiar M.A., M.S. and Ph.D., adapting them to their purposes but retaining much of the flavor that the degrees originally had in the academic disciplines and simply adding a phrase, as in Master of Arts in the Adminstration of Justice. Several growing professions developed distinctive advanced degrees in addition to the well-established ones.

Some examples are:

Business:	Master of Business Administration
Dental Medicine:	Master of Dental Science
Engineering:	Master of Energy Resources
	Master of Public Work
	Master of Public Work
Library and Information Science:	Master of Library Science
Nursing:	Master of Nursing
	Master of Nursing Education

Psychology:	Doctor of Psychology
Public and International Affairs:	Master of Public and International Affairs
	Master of Public Administration
	Master of Urban and Regional Planning
Public Health:	Master of Public Health
	Doctor of Science in Hygiene
	Doctor of Public Health
Social Work:	Master of Social Work
	Doctor of Social Work

Each of these degrees, like others offered by responsible, accredited universities and professional schools, has legitimacy and indicates attainment worthy of respect. Each also has its unique history.

Other professional degrees emerge each year, and existing degrees attain more and more prominence. Actually, the histories of many degrees have not yet been thoroughly sought out and recorded. (There are still some T/D topics awaiting students!)

Whether in chemistry, psychology, public health, social work or any other academic discipline or profession, students should know the history of the degrees they expect to earn. That background provides a valuable base from which to judge the appropriateness of a potential T/D topic and to represent one's discipline honorably and well.

The material published in university bulletins and elsewhere about degrees usually tells little about the thesis or dissertation requirements. In some cases, they say only that they require a project that is considered equivalent to a T/D study. The scarcity of published data on these matters for many of the academic or professional disciplines shows a need for additional scholarly inquiry into the natural history and the characteristics of the thesis and dissertation.

THE EMERGENCE OF RESEARCH IN THE PROFESSIONS

Every contemporary profession was, in its beginning stages, made up of a number of separate individuals operating with a loosely knit group of common skills, responsibilities, and assumptions. The group was held together only by social sanctions. As each profession's central core of functions crystallized, a body of laws and customs developed that institutionalized the activities of the profession. At the same time, the members usually organized and took steps to define their roles even further, particularly with respect to two considerations: ethical behavior toward their clients and toward each other, and protection of the public from charlatans.

These evolutionary steps had different points of origin for different professions. For law in America the start was in the period 1775–1780. For educators in the United States, professionalization started around 1850. The first call for a school to train social workers arose in 1894. Before then, little theoretical or empirical writing had appeared about the standards, teaching, financing, objectives, and substance of professional education.

During the second half of the 19th century, an empirical base for many of today's professions began to develop. Books, journals, and state and federal publications carried the material. Virtually all investigations, though, dealt with matters that could be approached by the collection of factual data, examining the data in terms of totals, ranges, averages, and percentages. Ideas about professional practice continued to achieve acceptance or rejection on the basis of their logical or emotional appeal to the public and to persons in authority. Not until the new century began did actual field-testing of new concepts start to rival debate in determining the efficacy of professional practices.

The enthusiasm for science that characterized the Western world at the turn of the century had a decided impact. The idea of a scientific base for the professions began to be taken seriously. The science adherents came from a variety of academic disciplines. They had in common a conviction about the paramount importance of seeking quantifiable evidence, deriving principles, and testing the principles by additional investigations.

The investigative procedures advocated by science-minded members of the professions came, naturally enough, from the various academic disciplines in which they had been trained. They added techniques devised to suit the questions they sought to resolve. The additions ranged from the questionnaire, the rating scale, the controlled experiment, and the case study to the complex set of procedures used in surveys of entire societal units (i.e., communities, school systems, cultures, and nations).

Theses and dissertations on topics related more to the professional disciplines than to the academic disciplines grew in number each year. So did the number of practicing professionals familiar with research procedures. But the formal training of individuals for careers in professional research moved forward more slowly.

During the first three quarters of the 20th century, the newly trained professors who elected to work in professional schools became more and more separated from the professors in the academic disciplines, including the disciplines that had generated most of the "profession-oriented" professors. During that same timespan, the training of persons to conduct investigative studies on "professional" topics became largely a function of faculty in the professional schools. More and more often, the professional disciplines found themselves almost completely separated from the main bodies of their parent academic disciplines (e.g., social work from sociology and public affairs from political science).

Certainly, this altered the nature of the T/D work. The investigations of both faculty members and students who recognized their primary engagement in professional preparation edged toward a more operational, practice-oriented mode than the studies conducted by the faculties and students in the arts and sciences. The same trend appeared even in professional preparation programs which often remained housed in university academic departments, such as speech pathology and audiology, clinical psychology, economics, theater, dance, studio arts, music, and journalism.

The widening separation of the professions from the academic disciplines showed in the increasingly pragmatic stances of the former, as contrasted with the more abstract devotion to knowledge for its own sake in the latter. There were exceptions, of course; some leaders managed to straddle the gap. But the rapid growth in the availability of schooling and the public demand for high standards of human services, coupled with accelerated professionalization, exerted powerful socioeducational forces. Among other things, these forces influenced scholarship in professional schools to increase serious efforts to develop professional preparation, with its own theoretical base, and to construct a body of knowledge and practice that would define the profession. The movement accelerated, too, under the influence of the steady and widespread growth in empiricism in most of the Western world's cultures and by increasingly sophisticated utilization of statistical analysis of data in all sectors of society.

The impact of these factors in combination was strong. By mid-century, empirical research methods dominated. Virtually all advanced degrees in the professions required the study of statistical procedures for data analysis. Research departments developed in professional schools not so much to conduct research as to teach graduate students to understand and use designs and data-analysis procedures for empirical studies with the greatest feasible degree of control of variables. Acceptable research came to be identified by the procedures taught by the research departments of their particular schools. The definition of "respectability" in many professional schools was to do a T/D that employed some form of a controlled experimental design and subjected its data to a complex statistical analysis.

RECENT AND CURRENT TRENDS IN T/D INVESTIGATIONS

The late 1950s saw the development of a noticeable negative reaction to the attitude that any professional discipline could build a theoretical and conceptual base securely founded on a narrowly conceived underpinning of research design and research methodology. Some professional-school faculty members had pressed for a broader interpretation all along. Their students carried out surveys, conducted polls and case studies, did retrospective project evaluation, analyzed the impact of laws on practices, studied development processes, and in countless other ways asserted the importance of a wider range of methodologies and technologies of investigation. That reaction appears by now to have approached a balance with the earlier, narrower point of view. Contributions to the different knowledge bases for the various professions are at present welcomed from many directions. Recently added dimensions in investigations are found, for example, in the widespread interest in qualitative research and in the development of systems of evaluation. Today's T/D student in either an academic or a professional discipline has unprecedented latitude in choice of subject and methodology.

Guide to the Successful Thesis and Dissertation

1

Getting Started

QUICK REFERENCE TO ANSWERS TO SPECIFIC QUESTIONS

This book is for

Students looking for practical help with honors and master's theses and doctoral dissertations

Faculty seeking instructional tools to use in seminars on research and with advisees

THE RIGHT BEGINNING

Two precious commodities dare not be wasted in thesis and dissertation (T/D)* work: student time and faculty time. Guidelines in this book emphasize high-quality effort, excellence of product, and minimum loss of time.

*For convenience, T/D means honors and master's theses, dissertations, and other terms used by various colleges and universities to designate the T/D work product. When necessary, distinctions are drawn.

The four essentials for a good start are

1. A clear understanding of the meaning and purpose of student research work.
2. Accurate knowledge of what constitutes an acceptable T/D.
3. A detailed plan of action.
4. The technical skill to implement the plan.

These essentials are interrelated. Serious efforts should be devoted to getting all four well in mind right away.

Special Note: One of the most important changes in thesis and dissertation preparation has been the influence of technology. Two decades ago, many theses and dissertations were still being typed on a typewriter, and students' use of computers to do the research, make statistical calculations, properly cite references in the text, and prepare bibliographies was at a beginning stage. Students today marvel at what was accomplished by students before the advent of computers and relevant software. For current students, computer knowledge and skill are essential. If there remain students who lack such knowledge and skill, now is the time to get up to speed. Throughout this text, we point out the ways computers can help you do a better and more efficient job of research and preparation of your thesis or dissertation.

MEANING AND PURPOSE OF THESES AND DISSERTATIONS

Clarifying the Meaning and Purpose of the T/D

Students who know the *official* answers to the queries below tend to begin the T/D process with more confidence and a good prospect of success.

1. What are the purposes of the T/D according to (a) your university, (b) your school, and (c) your department?
2. If more than one kind of honors or master's or doctoral degree can be earned in your department, which should you aim for and why?

Avoid misunderstandings by talking with your academic or research advisor to get full responses to the above two questions. If answers are not available in writing, take notes on what you are told and by whom. Then, write a summary of your notes and give a copy to your advisor for verification.

Keep a copy of the verified notes. If any doubts linger, recheck your notes with the department chairperson. Here and elsewhere in this book, we advise keeping verified notes. One key reason is that both faculty members and procedures can change during the period of your study, and your verified notes can prevent your progress from being interrupted or delayed by such changes. It helps to use a computer file (see Appendix A) and to maintain a backup.

Distinction Among Honors, Master's, and Doctoral Levels

In the United States, honors programs are typically opted for by outstanding undergraduate students. Honors research normally takes place in the junior and senior years. Common to honors research is the requirement of proof of the student's capacity for independent scholarship, shown by the production, presentation, and defense of a senior thesis. That thesis is held to a standard of quality and depth usually reserved for the graduate level (University of Pittsburgh, 1992). The U.S. honors programs are substantially different from the British honors system, and students from countries that employ the British system (e.g., India, Pakistan, and some African nations) should not confuse the two.

Master's and doctoral degree research expectations are strikingly similar among schools. These statements, for example, are from an engineering school publication (Stuart, 1979).

> The master's thesis must demonstrate the candidate's ability to make use of appropriate research procedures, to organize primary and secondary information into a meaningful whole, and to present the results in acceptable prose. The length of the thesis is not important so long as these ends are fulfilled. (p. 1)

> The doctoral dissertation is expected to represent independent and original research in the field of the candidate's graduate study. It must add, in some fashion, to understanding in the candidate's field. Such contribution to knowledge may result either from the

> critical examination of materials not hitherto dealt with or from the re-examination of traditional materials by means of new techniques or from new points of view. The project undertaken must be of sufficient difficulty and scope to test the candidate's ability to carry on further research [independently] and it must ensure . . . mastering the skills needed for such research. (p. 1)

These quotations illustrate an overarching concept: The T/D is done to provide a demonstration of the candidate's ability to carry out, with substantial independence, a rational investigation that is significant in the field and to report the results in a sensible and understandable fashion. There are marked differences among fields as to what constitutes "independence" and "significant" in the research process and product. Yet, essentially the same principles apply to thesis and dissertation study in all professions and academic disciplines (Council of Graduate Schools [CGS], 1990b).

Thesis and dissertation study is a part of higher learning intended to identify significant problems, investigate them, analyze the findings, relate them to important concepts or issues, and convey conclusions and implications to others in clear, objective prose. In that context, thesis and dissertation study is a stimulating activity carried on by students in an increasingly collegial relationship with faculty members. It is a culminating and synthesizing activity based on prior study, and it should be a launch pad for future independent investigations. Finally, thesis and dissertation work should prepare graduates who become faculty members in colleges and universities to guide students through the same experiences later.

WHAT CONSTITUTES AN ACCEPTABLE T/D?

General statements about the meaning and purpose of T/D work need to be brought into sharper focus to be helpful in particular instances. To accomplish that, students should ask their advisors specific questions.

1. What forms of investigation, if any, are favored by the faculty of the department? What forms of investigation, if any, are unlikely to be approved? Accepted forms of T/D investigation range widely from school to school and even within departments of the

same school. Form is often related to the student's major field of study. For example, studies of ancient bridges might be acceptable in a history department, a seminary, a geology department, or an engineering school. But one can be sure that the *form* the studies would take (i.e., the research question, the data collected and means of collecting it, the analysis of the data, and the definitions of validity and replicability) would vary considerably.
2. Are any topics discouraged or even out of bounds for T/Ds? Are any topics of special interest to the faculty?
3. Does the department have a particular orientation (e.g., the family, public policy, or intercultural concerns) that characterizes much of its student and faculty research and other scholarly work?
4. Is there a published list of departmental faculty with notes about their individual or team research interests?
5. Are computer workstations and software packages available for student use in T/D work? Is the library automated, and are its holdings accessible on line?

Inquiries like these can be used to initiate conversations with one's advisor. Also, it is helpful to talk about such questions with students who have recently completed T/Ds successfully. It is suggested that notes be taken and summaries written after discussions with faculty and students. The more clarification one can obtain at this point, the more likely one is to avoid difficulties in the future.

MAKE A PERSONAL TIME LINE

A realistic time line projection is imperative. It helps keep the project on course, and it encourages disciplined use of time. Moreover, it is a communication tool with the advisor and committee members. It allows an advisor to react to and to be aware of the student's orderly approach. Our stress on the value of using a time line is reinforced by W. G. Bowen and Rudenstine (1992), who urge the use of time lines to help improve the effectiveness and the efficiency of advanced study in general and the dissertation phase in particular.

The T/D time line (Fig. 1-1) can be used as is or adapted. The action points may need minor alterations to make them match the

Student's name: ______________________ Date initiated: ________

Step no.	Action points	Time estimate	Date
1.	Selection of advisor	_____	_____
2.	Submit potential topic(s) to advisor	_____	_____
3.	Tentative approval of topic by advisor	_____	_____
4.	Departmental approval of advisor and topic	_____	_____
5.	Selection of other committee members	_____	_____
6.	Departmental approval of committee	_____	_____
7.	Draft of proposal reviewed by advisor to show committee members	_____	_____
8.	Proposal draft cleared by advisor	_____	_____
9.	Meetings with individual committee members for comment on proposal	_____	_____
10.	Considerations of committee on proposal with advisor	_____	_____
11.	Inclusion of committee and advisor suggestions in proposal	_____	_____
12.	Approval of proposal document by advisor and institutional human subjects review board	_____	_____
13.	Proposal committee meeting	_____	_____
14.	**Final approval of proposal**	_____	_____
15.	Beginning of thesis/dissertation study	_____	_____
16.	Progress reports to advisor and committee	_____	_____
17.	Adjustments in study procedure approved by advisor/committee	_____	_____
18.	Completion of study	_____	_____
19.	First draft of completed thesis/dissertation written	_____	_____
20.	First draft of thesis/dissertation typed in correct style and format	_____	_____
21.	Review of first draft with advisor for corrections	_____	_____
22.	Corrected first draft approved by advisor	_____	_____
23.	Corrected first draft submitted to committee members	_____	_____
24.	Individual interviews with committee members	_____	_____
25.	Discussion with advisor to integrate committee comments	_____	_____
26.	Advisor approval of changes	_____	_____
27.	Final copy of thesis/dissertation to committee	_____	_____
28.	Oral defense meeting	_____	_____
29.	Correction as specified by committee	_____	_____
30.	**Final approval**	_____	_____

Figure 1-1 The thesis/dissertation time line.

specific procedures of a given school, but each of the 30 items appears as an essential step somewhere in the process in most schools. It is helpful to put this T/D time line on your computer and to update it daily.

Start Now to Use the Time Line

First, define present status by checking off those items that are completed and circling the one or two currently under way. This allows a precise answer to questions like: "How is the investigation going? Where are you now?" *Second*, use the time line in planning. Reference to the time line encourages thinking ahead, making appointments with committee members, and scheduling one's own time. *Third*, use the time line to project one's graduation date. Universities commonly require that final approval (Action 30) be certified by the T/D committee by a specified date that falls some weeks prior to the close of the term in which the student intends to be graduated. Ordinarily, the committee-approved final copy of the project must be submitted by that same date. Insert that date at the bottom of the appropriate column and work backward, estimating how many days, weeks, or months it will take to move from one action to the next until the current status is reached. This vital exercise brings into the open any discrepancies between a student's wishful thinking and the actuality of the calendar. Most students find it helpful to enlist their advisor's aid in making time estimates and in gathering information about special considerations related to timing.

TAKE ADVANTAGE OF TECHNOLOGY

Students are familiar with the calculator and the word-processing functions of computers because those functions are most helpful in completing assignments in college and university courses. *But, some may not have had experience with computer use and computer-related technology for the independent kind of research called for in theses and dissertations.*

Today's applications of integrated circuits and their linkages allow research to be done more quickly and more accurately. Investigators can use technological tools profitably in almost every stage of a study, including pinpointing the topic; doing the literature search; selecting the research methodology; collecting, analyzing, and displaying the data; and publishing the results and conclusions.

Probably the computer would come to mind first if one were asked for examples of technological tools rich in research applications. The computer certainly has great value in almost every facet of research. And, it definitely exemplifies high technology.

But not to be overlooked are a number of other devices of real potential utility, too. Here is a partial list:

Tape recorders
PowerPoint presentations
Scanners
Internet providers
Fax machines
Photocopiers
Cell phones
Internal modems
E-mail providers

There is no end in sight so far as the potential for using enabling devices and technologies is concerned. New on-line universities are being created based on the ability to communicate with students using the new telecommunication technology. The University of Phoenix (http://www.gradschools.com) Online is one example. Another is Walden University's (http://www.waldenu.edu) Online Accredited University Degree Program. Older universities are joining in also, by starting courses or programs that eventually lead to degree programs. See the home page (http://www.gradschools.com) for some examples.

Also, many of these devices can be connected to one another at nearby or distant places to bring resources together for the researcher's advantage and to conduct procedures in a matter of seconds that would otherwise take hours or days of the investigator's time. In succeeding chapters, such technological applications are suggested as they might fit the requirements of a particular stage of research.

Electronic Communication Etiquette

The deep absorption in one's problem fostered by the demands of research does not qualify as an excuse for not maintaining normal civility and etiquette. This applies to both students and faculty in their relations with both colleagues and associates.

Increasingly, colleges and universities are publishing policy statements on civility in discourse, debate, and other person-to-person interactions. These have special merit for investigators caught up in the often-intense emotional and pressure-filled atmosphere of T/D work.

Sensible guidelines for electronically mediated interactions are found in the current (18th) edition of *Etiquette, the Blue Book of Social Usage* (Post, 1997). Etiquette continues to be defined as a code of behavior based on thoughtfulness and consideration. Particularly relevant for the modern researcher is Post's section on electronic communication. A coined word, "netiquette," covers appropriate behavior in using the Internet (or any net).

The Terminology of T/D Work Needs to Be Defined

Terminology in higher education is not standardized. The definitions that follow do, however, enjoy common usage.

Thesis: The thesis is the product of a scholarly and professional study at the honors or the master's degree level. It is usually a document* in a format and style specified by the particular university. (Sometimes, "thesis" is regarded as a synonym for "dissertation." That is acceptable, but we elect to link thesis with honors or master's degree studies and dissertation with the doctorate.)

Dissertation: The dissertation is the product of student work at the doctoral level, distinguished from thesis study chiefly by its deeper,

---

*Theses and dissertations are referred to as *documents* in most instances throughout this book since the majority do take that form. It is sometimes the case that the end product of thesis and dissertation study is a musical composition, a painting, or a performance of artistic merit. We respect all of these and documents equally, but we could find no generic expression that would adequately include all forms of the various capstone works in advanced graduate study.

more comprehensive, and more mature professional and scholarly treatment of the subject.

Proposal: A proposal (synonymous with "overview") is a written plan for a thesis or for a dissertation developed by a student for consideration and possible approval by a T/D committee.

T/D Committee: The T/D committee is a group of faculty members, usually at least three for the thesis and four for the dissertation, responsible for assisting the student in planning a proposal, for determining if it is approvable, for guiding the student in the conduct of the study and in preparing the T/D, and for examining the student at the end of the process.

T/D Advisor: The T/D advisor is the faculty member officially designated to chair the T/D committee and to have chief responsibility for the student's guidance in all matters through the process; sometimes also called the research advisor; not necessarily the student's academic advisor.

T/D Chairperson: The chairperson and the T/D advisor may be the same person or they may be two different persons. In the latter case, the chairperson has primary responsibility for convening meetings of the committee, monitoring matters of regulation and protocol that need to be observed, and ensuring that the student's rights and privileges and those of the faculty members are understood and not abridged. Thus, the research advisor has primary responsibility for guiding the student in the conduct of the study and in the preparation of the T/D document.

Graduate Office: The graduate office is the university office with responsibility for issuing, implementing, and interpreting regulations about the T/D, such as forms to be used, time schedule of events, and style guides. This office also usually has record maintenance functions. For the honors thesis, the above functions are usually located in the office of the dean of the honors college.

Academic and Professional Disciplines: There will be occasions to refer to substantive bodies of knowledge in the sciences, humanities, and arts (such as physiology, history, literature, philosophy, chemistry, and music), as well as reasons to refer to such professional fields as education, law, social work, nursing, and engineering. In many lexicons, these bodies of knowledge are called "disciplines." In order to clarify a distinction that is grounded in a real difference, we refer separately to the "academic" disciplines and the "professional" disciplines, as in Fig. 1-2.

The person trained in an academic discipline is master of a large and involved, but unified, body of knowledge and is primarily interested in adding to that body of content. The person trained in a professional discipline, on the other hand, is master of diversified information and concepts that focus on the efficient and effective conduct of some operation, such as teaching, treating an illness, trying a case in court, or designing or directing plays. So, it is reasonable to expect that T/Ds done in the academic disciplines and the professional disciplines would differ.

Examples of academic disciplines	*Examples of professional disciplines*
Art	Accounting
Chemistry	Architecture
Economics	Clergy
English	Education
Geology	Engineering
History	Journalism
Information science	Law
Linguistics	Library science
Mathematics	Medicine
Music	Military
Philosophy	Pharmacy
Physics	Social work
Psychology	Theater arts

Figure 1-2 Examples of academic and professional disciplines.

Characteristic Similarities and Differences Between T/D Research in Professional and Academic Disciplines

Similarities: The same three elements must be present in all acceptable T/D work in both the professional and the academic disciplines: originality, individuality, and rigor. Originality means that the research has not been done before in the same way. It is rare to find a topic that has not been researched before to some extent and by some procedure. So, originality does not mean that the research questions or hypotheses are entirely new. Instead, the originality criterion is met if the student continues to study an unresolved problem in a way that is substantially different from prior approaches and that has a reasonable prospect of adding to an understanding of the problem. Also, replication of prior research meets the originality criterion if features are added to the replication that make it possible to check on the procedures and findings of the earlier study, thus making the replication more meritorious research than that replicated.

Individuality means that the study is conceived, conducted, and reported primarily by the student. Topics may often be suggested by others. Also, advisors may help in thinking through the concepts and the procedures to be used. But, the chief decisions about whether to study the topic, how to study it, and how to report it must be made, rationalized, and defended by the student. When one applies the individuality criterion, it is difficult to accept a T/D that is simply "a piece of" a large research project being carried on by the advisor. If a student's T/D is to be related to the research program of the advisor (and that idea has much to recommend it), special care must be taken to ensure real independence for the student in conceptualizing and conducting the study.

The third element common to T/D work in the academic and professional disciplines is rigor. To attain rigor means to be characterized by strict accuracy and scrupulous honesty and to insist on precise distinctions among facts, implications, and suppositions. Rigor is achieved by sticking to demonstrable facts when reporting procedures and results, by building on a foundation of facts when drawing conclusions, by specifying links to facts when inferring implications, by always bringing forward all relevant data, and by being both self-critical and logical in reporting and when projecting needed research.

The individuality, originality, and rigor criteria are common requisites for investigations in both the academic and professional disciplines, even though research in the two kinds of disciplines may differ markedly otherwise. And, there are real differences both in objectives and in procedures, as elaborated in the next section. Many students and faculty members take up work in professional schools after study and experience in academic disciplines. For them, especially, as well as for T/D students in general, it is valuable to compare and contrast research in the two settings.

Despite overlap in the topics studied, we have found seven points on which there are conceptual or administrative differences (see Fig. 1-3). To make the differences explicit, read item 1 under "Academic Discipline Research" and then item 1 under "Professional Discipline Research." Note the contrast. Then, do the same through the seven-item lists.

These seven comparisons should help students and faculty members to clarify their thinking as well as to recognize and rationalize the differences listed. It should be evident that there is no special quality in any T/D work that does not have its roots in the social-professional mission it is intended to support and foster. Thus, the better one understands the social role and function of a profession or an academic discipline, the better prepared one is to conduct or direct T/D study within it.

Note also that, within a professional discipline, there may be distinctions between "applied or practice-oriented" T/D and "theoretical or concept-oriented" T/Ds. *Now is the time* to ascertain whether your school or department values that distinction and what it might mean for you.

The next section turns to the following questions: What factors go together to make up a high-quality T/D? How can students make those factors operational in getting started on their own work?

CHARACTERISTICS OF HIGH-QUALITY STUDENT RESEARCH

In a thesis or dissertation, it is the integrity and objectivity of the investigator that count most. These criteria prevail regardless of the

Area of difference	Academic discipline research[a]
Purpose of the research	1. The chief purpose is to increase knowledge in a particular disciplinary field.
Nature of the problems researched	2. The topics studied are clearly linked to other problems previously studied within the prescribed and academically recognized bounds of the discipline. Thus, a physicist or philosopher might say of a proposed topic, "Interesting, but it isn't physics (or philosophy)," and fully expect that a great majority of colleagues would agree.
Criteria for assessing the worth of the research	3. The worth of a thesis or dissertation is assessed chiefly on the basis of the amount it advances knowledge, clarifies or adds to a theory, or stimulates further investigation.
Reasons for gathering knowledge through research	4. Knowledge is accrued for its own sake.
Position on the relevance of values	5. Matters of value are deliberately eschewed, except as primary data. The objectivity of the academic scholar is most closely tied to dealing with concepts, ideas, animate or inanimate objects, materials, documents, and events.
Methodology of research acceptable	6. Each academic discipline has certain respected methods, legitimized by the power they have shown in helping uncover or prove matters of importance to the discipline. Witness the controlled experiment in chemistry or the dig plus analysis and documentation in archaeology or physical anthropology.
Who may approve acceptance of a T/D	7. The thesis or dissertation is submitted to judges from within the discipline. The candidate's examination may be relatively public (within the the university community), but its approval or disapproval is in the hands of three or four members of the discipline, perhaps with one additional voting examiner from a closely related discipline.

[a]Compare with like-numbered statements under "Professional discipline research" in second part of figure.

Figure 1-3 Distinctions between research in academic disciplines and professional disciplines.

Professional discipline research
1. The chief purposes are twofold: to increase knowledge about a matter relevant to the practice of the profession and to reinforce the attitude of using objective and systematic approaches to problem solving.
2. The problems studied may range anywhere in the realm of human concerns as long as they also have demonstrated implications for society's professional enterprises.
3. The worth of the T/D is judged mainly by the potential applications of the results and conclusions in professional practice and knowledge.
4. Knowledge is accrued to validate or to bring into question aspects of professional practice, to create better practices, and, generally, to foster and guide the improvement of the profession and its services.
5. Both matters of substance and of value can be legitimate and necessary topics of inquiry; sometimes values are the essential data subjected to study.
6. Methods of investigation used are invented or adapted to suit the problems that need to be probed. Investigators freely borrow procedures from the academic disciplines or from other professional disciplines if they seem to have promise.
7. The acceptability of the thesis or dissertation is judged by members of the profession who have backgrounds consonant with the topic of the investigation. Also, it is prevailing practice to invite the participation of specialists from academic disciplines or other professional disciplines whose competencies bear especially on the topic. Approval is usually by a majority vote of the four or five examining committee members who are also graduate faculty members of the university.

Figure 1-3 (continued)

form of investigation or analysis used. *Integrity* is shown when every component of the study is carried out with scrupulous honesty. The criterion for *objectivity* is met if the investigator recognizes and, as much as possible, sets aside personal interests and desires and maintains a steady state of academic or professional inquiry from the beginning to the end of the project.

For a definitive analysis of these important concepts we recommend three works: *Honor in Science* (Sigma Xi, 1991), *On Being a*

Scientist (National Academy of Sciences, 1989), and "Breaking Faith" (Root-Bernstein, 1989).

Finally, high-quality research should be characterized by publication. Others deserve access to both the findings and the method used in the investigation. We call attention to publication now because we agree with Meloy (2002), who suggests that publication concerns need to be addressed much earlier than they usually are in the T/D research process (see Chapter 10).

What Is High-Quality Dissertation or Thesis Research?

Research cannot take the place of thoughtful reflection and even-handed deliberation. Research can produce facts and ideas that, in turn, can fuel thought. Research can help the investigator to know whether all relevant matters are being considered in the study of a problem. But, research itself does not produce solutions. Human thought—not research—is the sovereign problem solver. Only when thought is applied to the information unearthed by research is it probable that valid, reliable, and operationally useful outcomes can be expected. Thus, the quality of an investigation is a function both of the research that has been done and of the human cognition that has been applied in the process.

Some consider that the term *research* should be applied only to a very restricted form of controlled, experimental scientific inquiry. But, that point of view leaves out many important realities in the professions. Also, the investigations of historians, anthropologists, or sociologists would frequently not qualify for the title research under that rule, nor would many of the studies in the arts and in literature. Those who invent new theories, new psychosocial measures, new techniques of instruction or who design new curricula or do qualitative research would often be excluded, too, despite the fact that they may employ very sophisticated procedures leading to objective evaluations of what they do.

If the term research is to be used meaningfully in the context of T/D study, it must encompass not only controlled experimentation, but also many additional forms of planned, thoughtful, investigative activities. The definition should be broadly inclusive, encouraging full use of the ability and the creativity of the student and the advisor. The following definition of research best accommodates these needs: "Diligent and systematic inquiry or investigation into a subject in order to discover or revise facts, theories, applications, etc." (Flexner, 1987, p. 1219). It is only fitting that the specific nature of T/D work, and how research is defined, should depend on the kinds of problems that need to be investigated to enhance the particular body of knowledge of concern in each discipline.

No one research approach is inherently better than another. Rather, there are research methods that match some problems well and others poorly. For example, morale factors among supervisors probably can be studied more adequately through polling, critical incidents, or case studies than by other methods. If the question is the effectiveness of a new or modified traffic control system, it is probably best attacked through an evaluation procedure. For decisions about long-range building programs, comparative financial projections and analyses may be important contributing studies. Research about changes in motivation or about improvement in human skills may be best undertaken through applied behavior analysis or other forms of controlled experimentation. Researchers need all forms of investigation, need to respect them equally, and need to attempt to link each problem to the research approach that has the best likelihood of helping to apply human thought to solve it.

QUALITATIVE RESEARCH

Students and colleagues have urged us to add content about qualitative research to this edition. Their reasons are the following: They found many associates unfamiliar with that form of research and its potentialities for T/D work; they were concerned about possible misunderstandings between those who used qualitative and quantitative approaches to investigations; and they pointed out the increasing and spreading use of qualitative research beyond the disciplines and professions in which that style of research had its roots.

Those observations seemed to justify devoting added attention to the matter. Moreover, both of us have directed qualitative research for T/Ds and have published qualitative research on our own. Thus, in the following, we call on first-hand experience as well as on research methodology literature.

The Nature of Qualitative Research

Qualitative research represents the general name for a group of investigative procedures with common characteristics. Also, qualitative research is *empirical* in the same sense as other recognized forms of scientific inquiry. It relies on observation. It follows the principle that experience, especially of the senses, forms the primary source of scientific knowledge (Bogdan and Bikler, 1998; Hernandez, 1996; Lancy, 1993; Le Compte et al., 1993; Taylor and Bogdan, 1998).

Qualitative research encompasses several forms of the investigation. They all share this characteristic: The data used do not accommodate readily to quantification, specification, objectification, or classification. Because of that, common statistical procedures cannot be used for data display or analysis. Typical of such data might be reports of participant observation or the texts of in-depth and relatively unstructured interviews.

In qualitative investigations, the researcher strives for understanding of the phenomenon under study, for example, why people like certain foods, how an athlete prepares for optimum exertion, how opinions about political issues are formed, how it feels to be a "senior citizen," or how threats are expressed in Maori culture. The researcher keeps detailed records of events heard, seen, read, felt, or otherwise noticed in respect to the topic or situation under scrutiny. The primary objective is to gain knowledge (data) from the subject's frame of reference.

Securing accurate information about feelings, sensitive behaviors, and other personal experiences is critical in many areas of research. It has been historically difficult to obtain unbiased and full reports from research subjects about, for example, their pain, mood, personal and social history, or dietary habits. Techniques have been developed in the last few decades to improve the reliability and accuracy of self-report and observer report; qualitative research studies often depend heavily on such methods. Such data then contribute to the evaluation of hypotheses or interventions and to the development of theories or prognostic indicators. Many researchers are already knowledgeable about prevailing quantitative methods of investigation. Therefore, a useful way to define qualitative research is to highlight how it compares and contrasts with the more familiar quantitative procedures. In the following, we amplify and extend the distinctions made by Ford (1997, p. 46) in an article aimed at psychologists.

Distinctions Between Qualitative and Quantitative Research

1. Qualitative research relies on deduction. It reaches conclusions by reasoning or inferring from general principles to particulars. Quantitative research relies on induction, arriving at generalizations by collecting, examining, and analyzing specific instances.
2. Qualitative research requires the investigator to engage with the persons, events and ambience studied as an integral part of the study process. Most often, quantitative research calls for the investigator to remain detached.
3. Qualitative research offers particular value in the process of generating new concepts or theories. Quantitative research focuses more on the testing of existing theories of generalizations.
4. Qualitative research seeks to provide full and accurate descriptions of phenomena in all their complexity. The aim of quantitative research is to reveal or establish cause-and-effect relationships in or among experiences or occurrences.
5. Qualitative research attempts to discover and show the assumptions that underlie events or actions. Quantitative research focuses more on testing the operation of assumptions.
6. Qualitative research uses natural settings as primary data. Qualitative studies deal mainly with statements and questions couched in words and with detailed descriptions of settings and events. Quantitative research constructs or controls settings and deals chiefly with amounts and numbers as primary data.
7. Qualitative research begins with broad questions or problems and attempts to narrow them. Quantitative research starts with narrow or specific phenomena and attempts to relate them to others as building blocks to illuminate larger matters.

8. Qualitative research tends to deal with small samples and uniqueness. Quantitative research encourages studying large samples and prizes representativeness.
9. Qualitative research considers the context of words and events an integral part of the primary data. Quantitative research tends to delete context or tightly control it to minimize the influence of affective nuances.
10. Qualitative research depends on thoroughness and depth of reporting to demonstrate significance. Quantitative research utilizes statistical analyses, particularly employing probabilities, to demonstrate significance.

From the above comparisons and contrasts, it becomes evident that qualitative research has a distinctive character. How the unique attributes of qualitative research might best serve the T/D student's purpose should be resolved in discussions with the advisor and others who have the responsibility of guiding student research.

Rigor in Qualitative Research

Investigators using the more conventional forms of research believe that rigor, or strict and scrupulous accuracy and honesty in conducting and reporting, is illustrated in part by several markers. The most common are evidences of validity (both external and internal), reliability, and objectivity. Qualitative research has its own specific procedures that convey similar assurances of rigor.

Using the equivalency formulation put forward by Lincoln and Guba (1985), Ford (1997) draws parallels as follows between meanings of terms from the two types of research:

Qualitative research	Quantitative research
Credibility	External validity
Transferability	Internal validity
Dependability	Reliability
Confirmability	Objectivity

If the conditions implied by the above terms can be firmly built into a qualitative research proposal, it is well on its way to meeting the high standards that T/D work should exemplify.

Pilot Studies

Pilot studies are tools in determining, in a preliminary fashion, the potentialities and perils of almost any research idea. For qualitative research proposals, we strongly agree with Krathwohl (1988) and Meloy (2002) that only the foolhardy begin without a pilot study that suggests how the full-blown study should be constructed. Pilot trials can sharpen the procedures, remind one of the permissions and approvals needed, assay likely costs in time, and check the feasibility of a larger study. Investment of energy in a pilot study (with advisor and committee support) can enhance the quality of a subsequent study and minimize the likelihood of unexpected delays and possible failure.

Applications of Qualitative Research

Qualitative research, sometimes called "naturalistic" or "field" research, has deep roots in the "social" research of the late 1800s. During that time, society's concerns prompted investigations of the life conditions and the views and characteristics of industrial workers, rural families, dock laborers, criminals, and other groups defined by occupation or lifestyle.

At the same time, other beginnings of qualitative approaches to building knowledge came from the academic disciplines of anthropology, geography, and sociology. The naturalistic aspects of qualitative research also attracted attention from journalism and photography and from writers of history, biography, and fiction.

Whenever societal problems—or simply intriguing questions—pressed for dependable answers and scholars found it difficult or impossible to really quantify data firmly, it proved necessary to rely on the observations of thoughtful and careful investigators. Such reports and analyses, whether gleaned from interviews, visual inspection, or other sources, were critiqued and polished by peers. Finally, having survived a gauntlet of skeptical scholars, the observations attained respectable positions in science. Otherwise, we might not have arrived at such scientifically useful notions as the color spectrum of light, biological taxonomies, gravity, or the theory of evolution and bodies of knowledge like etymology and paleontology.

Even the most qualitative and objective sciences sometimes face process questions that can best be studied by qualitative designs. A contemporary example is the ecology of human communities, with special reference to the preservation of environmental quality (i.e., air and water) through application of optimum conservation and civil engineering practices.

Using Qualitative and Quantitative Approaches

Differences between research styles do not necessarily make one better than another. Rather, *one research approach may prove more suited to a given problem than another*. Thus, we reemphasize that, in planning any research, it is essential to choose the investigative approach that best promises to match the problem and its setting and to result in the most believable and dependable solution. In some instances, a qualitative design may well be the approach of choice.

Role of the Research Advisor

Students may encounter faculty members who favor one research style over another. Some professors may seem almost messianic in their conviction that a certain investigative style should be employed. This can occur particularly when the faculty member tries to introduce a form of research not traditional to their academic or professional discipline.

Such advisors can sometimes actually prove helpful because their enthusiasm and commitment extends to students who elect to work with them. Alternatively, such single-mindedness in an advisor can put limits on the flexibility and on the encouragement of independence that best satisfies the needs of the beginning researcher.

For balance, we continue to urge the student to seek a broad range of information before committing to an advisor. Also, we suggest that students remain wary of advisors who let selection of the research method take precedence over the selection of the problem to be studied.

Conclusion

Qualitative research does have much in common with all other research. It calls for a statement of the problem, and a research design must guide the study toward its goal; data are gathered, organized, inspected, analyzed, synthesized in deliberate and replicable ways, and related to other data. For the T/D student, the keys to success in qualitative research appear fundamentally no different from those for success in any other research enterprise.

In the final analysis, the utility and the rigor of the product depend on the researcher's integrity and mastery of the subtleties of the methodology and on a full, honest, and clear description of what occurred in every step of the research protocol.

THE THESIS IN HONORS COLLEGES AND HONORS PROGRAMS

A report of the National Collegiate Honors Council (1997) stated that it included 578 colleges and universities, all of which mount undergraduate honors programs or honors colleges. Such academic units emerged more than 30 years ago and are on the increase.

During the past two decades, a growing number of schools authorized undergraduate degree studies in which the completion of a thesis is required for graduation. Such courses of study are commonly known as honors programs or honors academic units.

Honors academic units vary greatly in structure and in operational characteristics from place to place, but they all are similar in one way: Each aims at locating highly able undergraduates and allowing them to advance in higher education at their own pace. A foremost concern is that students with unusual talent, drive, and curiosity should receive incentives and recognition for achievement with individualized opportunities for intellectual, artistic, and physical challenge, special advising, and demanding and rigorous instruction and content (University of Pittsburgh, 1992).

Generally, a university or college undergraduate honors program provides courses that, so far as intellectual challenge is concerned, match the highest undergraduate or the initial graduate levels. That is consistent with the high academic attainment focus typical of such offerings.

Ordinarily, study under the auspices of an honors faculty calls also for strong evidence of the student's ability to carry out scholarly independent work consistently and in depth. The culminating evidence of that ability is the successful completion of an honors thesis.

All honors units emphasize student research in one or more forms. A large proportion of member schools include a research project similar to the master's thesis in scholarly scope and quality as a standard requirement. Faculty members from all of the academic and professional disciplines are recruited into honors units to teach, to guide, and to evaluate student research.

The procedures employed by students and faculty members in moving toward completing an honors thesis are, in the programs we have reviewed, strikingly similar to those that apply to the master's thesis. In fact, the faculty members who direct or chair honors thesis committees are often the same persons who do so for graduate T/Ds.

An honors program (sometimes called an honors college) is, in short, a distinctive undergraduate course of study that is more than ordinarily demanding academically, that requires consistently high achievement, and that culminates in a thesis, through which the student demonstrates a proven capacity for academic initiative and for independent scholarship. The guidance of the advisor and committee during the thesis preparation and defense is similar to that found in master's degree study.

Because of the common elements in honors thesis and T/D objectives, policies, and procedures, we treat them together, making note, when necessary, of any special considerations.

THE THESIS AS AN ELEMENT IN THE MASTER'S PROGRAM

The master's degree is a highly valued degree that has been increasing both in number awarded and in prestige. The number awarded nearly doubled from 1970 to 1996. Since then, growth has been steady, rising to over 500,000 earned annually, most in the applied sectors like business and nursing (National Center for Education Statistics [NCES], 1999). Master's recipients credit thc degree program with helping to sharpen the ability to connect theory and practice, and to refine critical ability (Clifton, 1993).

In preparing a master's thesis, the graduate student can present evidence of the competencies required to make use of accepted procedures of scholarly inquiry. For instance, the student can combine data from primary and secondary sources into a unified presentation in correct and readable prose. The general objective of the thesis as part of master's degree study has been stated as follows:

> It is reasonable to expect that, in a fifth year of academic work of respectable quality, a student will have had an intellectual adventure which can be described in writing. And such description gives an experience which will be obtained in no other way; by it, one is introduced to the methods employed in the acquisition, preparation and the analysis of material. Depending upon the field and the type of degree for which one is a candidate, this exercise may represent a small piece of research, the solution of a complex problem of design, a critical understanding of a sector of knowledge of considerable dimensions, or critical appreciation or creative work in literature or one of the arts. (Report of the Committee on Graduate Work of the Association of American Universities, quoted in and adapted from the *Style Manual* of the School of Education, University of Pittsburgh, 1981, p. 88)

This statement did not differentiate between professional school and academic discipline master's projects. Note, too, its similarity in substance to the master's research requirement from an engineering school quoted above (Stuart, 1979).

Both the honors and the master's thesis can serve these functions:

1. They can give first-hand experience in conducting investigations and can familiarize the student with the kind of effort and integrity demanded by research. That, in turn, can help to prepare those who aspire to the doctorate.
2. They can make the student expert in at least one aspect of a professional or academic discipline.
3. Either can serve as a capstone for a significant unit of advanced study.

PREFERRED PRACTICES IN STUDENT RESEARCH

Students and faculty alike are probably most interested in which characteristics a T/D should have to merit acceptance. That is what the student wants to know when seeking guidance in the selection of a topic and a procedure to use in studying it. That is what the faculty member wants to know when trying to decide whether to encourage a student to move ahead with a proposed investigation or, later, whether to settle for what the student has produced at the end of a period of study, analysis, and writing.

A landmark national study reported on practices in doctoral study in the more than 100 institutions in the United States that had doctoral programs in the profession of education (Robertson and Sistler, 1971). According to that study, the dissertation "is considered a training instrument in the techniques of scholarly research and of reporting findings; it also represents a contribution to the knowledge of a given field" (p. 183). The Council of Graduate Schools, in 1990, stated that a "Doctor of Philosophy program is designed to prepare a student to discover, integrate, and apply knowledge, as well as to communicate and disseminate it" (CGS, 1990b, p. 1). Thus, scholarly investigation and the presentation of findings to others are a pair of characteristics that has a historical association with doctoral research, whether in professional study or in the academic disciplines. Contemporary writing uniformly reports training in scholarly and research procedures and contributions to knowledge as the chief features the graduate student's research should have (Barzun and Graff, 1985; Cortada and Winkler, 1979; CGS, 1991b; Krathwohl, 1988; Martin, 1980; Sternberg, 1981).

Another feature reported by Robertson and Sistler (1971) was its service as the subject of a final examination for doctoral students. The last examination of the student by the faculty covered only the research project in 85% of the queried institutions. Three-fourths of the time this examination was oral. No institution used only a final written examination of the student's research. Approximately 10% used both, with the written test at certain schools invoked only if students did not perform satisfactorily in an oral interrogation. Less than 10% of doctoral programs had no final examination. The role of the final oral doctoral examination remains essentially the same today (CGS, 199lb).

THESIS AND DISSERTATION OBJECTIVES

Students may well ask, "What is involved in completing T/D work?" "Why should I do this work?" "What will it have to do with my professional and academic competence?" Faculty members, particularly new ones, can be plagued by related questions: "What am I supposed to be conveying to the students whose investigations I direct or on whose committees I serve? What really are the functions served by this phase of graduate study?" "What has this process to do with the purpose of the university?" A core element common to those questions is "Why?" For an answer, we look first at the commonly stated objectives of graduate student research found in institutional publications.

General Objectives

Published objectives, as mentioned above, emphasize evidence of scholarly work, research competence, and contribution to knowledge. These have the validity of academic consensus. Faculties agree that both theses and dissertations should aim at those objectives. Moreover, they agree that those qualities should be easily discerned in acceptable documents submitted by students.

Operational meanings for *scholarly work*, *research competence*, and *contribution to knowledge* are not easy to specify, however. Criteria for judging those three matters are highly individual. They vary from faculty member to faculty member and among the academic and professional disciplines. Our findings from interviews with students, faculty members, and other university institutional representatives, however, indicate that these general objectives are commonly accepted by academics, and scholars feel they can tell us when they are present in theses and dissertations.

Objectives of Students

Student objectives include those that are short range and those that look to the more distant future.

Professional and Academic Standing: Students often find that the qualifications they seek are linked to obtaining the master's or doctoral degree. Thus, the attainment of an advanced degree may be tied to goals like being recommended for qualification as a specialist in teaching, doing research, promotion in rank, supervising, managing, counseling, or a specific realm of practice or administration. Foreign students are often under specific direction from the ministry that provides the scholarship and support (e.g., there is an expectation that a Ph.D. will be earned rather than another doctorate). Hence, it is appropriate that the T/D be recognized as an essential short-range objective, the outcome of which will be evaluated by others along the student's way to some desired position, certification, or licensure.

Completing Course Work at a High-Quality Level: When the student's aim is doctoral study, the master's degree becomes a short-range objective, one that must be reached at an acceptable level of quality before doctoral study can be undertaken.* Some schools set a limit on the residence time, the number of graduate credits, or the particular graduate courses a student may take before completing the thesis, thus operationally defining the thesis as a short-range objective.

Staying Within the Statute of Limitations: Almost all schools put a time limit on the completion of the dissertation, too. Commonly, a statute of limitations reads like this: "The dissertation must be completed within three years of the time the proposal received initial approval." The number of years allowed may vary from school to school, but some time constraint is all but universal, although extensions may be granted for cause.

Finding Good Advisors and Models: Students do detective work, trying to find out what faculty members consider an acceptable T/D. This effort to define what might find favor with potential advisors and committee members can be motivated by a sincere desire to do a worthwhile job because of what it means for self-esteem and to gain added respect from the faculty. In pursuing this objective, students

---

*Some schools permit or encourage students to move from the bachelor's degree directly to the doctorate. Students in those cases, we believe, should be advised to do directed independent study equivalent to master's thesis work along the way to help prepare them for the dissertation experience. Honors thesis students may be at an advantage here.

look for models primarily in the recently completed T/Ds of other students.

Foreign students are often especially dependent on their advisors, so for them the choice of an advisor may also involve affective considerations of empathy, learning styles, and personal relationships. Such considerations, while possibly important to all students, seem to be less an issue when cultural differences between students and faculty are small or well understood by both parties (Mallinkrodt and Leong, 1992; Mauch and Spaulding, 1992; Parr et al., 1992).

Objectives of the Higher Education Institution

Institutional objectives are stated in broad terms. Hence, it would be unusual to find them phrased in language specific to student research. It can be inferred, however, that the T/D elements of a student's advanced preparation are expected to be consistent with the institution's mission. The three statements below represent how a professional school faculty might phrase institutional objectives.

Providing Leadership: Preparation of leaders for the profession for communities, for state and federal agencies, for colleges and universities, and for other components of the public and private sectors.

Expanding Knowledge: Fostering theory building and conducting studies that create new and better approaches to our profession and encouraging and carrying out demonstrations that illustrate and disseminate information about improved practices developed at the university and elsewhere.

Improving Professional Practice: Development of master practitioners who will bring professional and humanistic advances to the fields in which they apply their skills.

These statements say little about T/D activities. Yet, embedded in those objectives are clues to the kinds of proposals that ought to be well received at this particular institution. Students should look for statements of institutional objectives and discuss them with their advisors. Not only will that trigger ideas about possible topics, but also it may help to establish part of the rationale for the selection of a topic.

Objectives of the Faculty

Faculty objectives for T/D activity are to enhance scholarship in the sense of looking for truth, to build on the existing body of knowledge, and to create original works. Steggna (1972) speaks of scholarship as an activity inherent in the mission of a university, one that should be exemplified in the work of the faculty. He calls it a faculty duty to search for the truth, add to knowledge, and produce new cultural materials. That role for scholarship is reemphasized, directly or implicitly, in more recent publications (W. G. Bowen, 1981; Ziolkowski, 1990). Certainly, the faculty efforts devoted to guiding student investigations should contribute to the discharge of that duty to an appreciable degree.

Yet, here we turn to the questions "What is scholarship?" and "What is scholarly work?" The expressions are often used, but seldom defined. This need for definition is more than a matter of intellectual curiosity—-more than an academic question. For example, students who are told that their work will have to be "more scholarly" to be accepted really deserve to be given a definition in operational terms, plus examples. Likewise, assistant professors who have, after due process, been refused tenure because their publications were not sufficiently scholarly should have illustrations for comparison and criteria for reference. Tenure and promotion committees in universities are hard put also to define scholarly in sufficiently specific and objective terms to allow them to develop reasonable standards for the up-or-out decisions they must make. A more behavioral definition is needed. Any one chosen will not be entirely satisfactory. However, the definition below will be useful now, and it may lead to a better definition in the future.

Inculcation of Scholarly Standards

Following is a list of seven features that, in our judgment, characterize scholarly written work. Few scholarly works meet all seven criteria, but a work that meets none of them is almost certain to be in trouble with the scholars. Faculty members try to inculcate these seven scholarly qualities during T/D work.

1. A scholarly work is published in a respected, refereed journal or in book form.
2. It has been available for a sufficient period of time to be subjected to the criticism of other scholars in the same field, and it has stood up successfully to that criticism.
3. It is based on the expert wisdom and literature of the field. The work indicates that the author is familiar with the conventional wisdom of the field, and if it departs in new directions, it presents a sound and rational defense for its departure.
4. It demonstrates the workings of a thorough, careful, critical, and analytical mind, looking at all sides of any proposition, examining and testing hypotheses, setting up and knocking down arguments, and marshaling in a complete and fair way all the facts in the process of critically analyzing the study's findings. A scholar will, of course, believe and support the findings of a careful investigation, but a scholar is not an advocate or a promoter. The scholar is evenhanded and is willing to entertain the possibility that errors can be made by even the most watchful investigator. Scholars should be happy to find error in their own positions when such errors exist, for only in this way can truth be sought.
5. It demonstrates to other scholars that the writer is a competent specialist who understands the theories and concepts of the domain and who has a systematic knowledge of the chosen field rather than a smattering of insights here and there.
6. It is nonpolitical or amoral. It may, of course, be concerned with political and moral judgments and related phenomena as fields of study and specialization, but a scholarly work is not a polemic. It is not selectively cleaned up or toned down or otherwise slanted because it may be popular or unpopular with the contracting agency, the government, the church, the boss, or professional colleagues. An essential ingredient to scholarship is the assumption that politically, socially, and morally unpopular and even repugnant works may be scholarly, and decisions about whether one should work in these areas and about whether or not they should be published, examined, and debated should be based on the scholarship of the work and not its political correctness. Scholars

seem to agree on this, but the point has to be made because everyone at times can find the commitment to free and open scholarship weakening under the various pressures that can be brought to bear so skillfully, subtly, and punitively by defenders of sacred cows.

7. It must be useful, as indicated by how often others cite the work. This also constitutes an index of scholarship. A well-regarded, innovative, or provocative publication will be referred to frequently by others. Thereby, it demonstrates that it has qualities that are of significant value.

Evidence or Promise of Scholarly Work

As one reviews these seven standards, it becomes evident that student research would need to be on public view for some time before it could receive the in-depth testing implied in several of them. Moreover, it would be too much to expect that T/D work by students should match the productions of seasoned and polished investigators.

Therefore, it is *the indications* of and *the promise* of scholarly work, as characterized by the list, that advisors and committee members look for in the productions of their students. There are occasions when student work is qualitatively equal to the best of that of well-established investigators and theorists. But, more often, the faculty member is satisfied to lead students *toward* that level of attainment and to judge by comparison and inference whether students finally reach a respect for and an understanding of scholarship as a concept, internalize it as a goal, and demonstrate by their own work that they show substantial potential for attaining it.

Preparation for the Advisor's Role

In addition to the faculty's objectives that have to do with the student's attainment of a scholarly point of view and the promise of scholarly productivity, there are others. A major one concerns the student's possible future role as an advisor or committee member for others. Faculty members who guide graduate students recognize that their own performances are models for their students—perhaps the only such models the students will ever know so close at hand and with such intensity. It is also plain to those faculty members that they will be both judge and jury in determining the extent to which their graduates are ready to help other students as fledging advisors.

Emphasizing Responsibility and Development

Especially important is balance in assessing graduate research scholarship quality. Above, we noted the blend that needs to be achieved of pragmatic technology and pursuit of knowledge for its own sake. Alfred North Whitehead (1953, p. 199) said, "There is something between the gross specialized values of the mere practical man and the thin specialized values of the mere scholar. . . . What is wanted is an appreciation of thc infinite variety of vivid values achieved by an organism in its proper environment. We want concrete fact with a high light thrown on what is relevant to its preciousness." That can be achieved by guiding students to insist that they be able to demonstrate that their work has relevance for the advancement of their disciplines, while at the same time, to show that it meets the requirements to search out truth, contribute to the sum of knowledge, and produce fresh material for the culture.

SUMMARY

A time line is one of the first essentials for a student who wishes to embark on T/D work. It helps to develop a plan of action. It has increased value, too, when linked to an understanding of modern technology and of the meaning and purpose of graduate student research and to a grasp of the standards for acceptable work.

Students and faculty members, academic and professional, make important contributions through theses and dissertations. There is a historical time line, extending at least to the Middle Ages, that validates such investigations as culminating achievements in advanced study.

In recent years, academic disciplines and professional disciplines have moved to separate paths. The professions have matured, while continuing to acknowledge their roots in the arts and sciences. There are palpable differences now between the T/D in the academic disciplines and in the professions. Also, it is possible to specify some of their special characteristics. Purposes differ, depending on whether they are examined from the viewpoint of the student, the institution, or the faculty. Yet, they have much in common. T/D study is growing. Both students and faculty need and deserve more objective and specific information about the process than they have had available in the past.

2

The Research Advisor

QUICK REFERENCE TO ANSWERS TO SPECIFIC QUESTIONS

The research advisor, who typically also chairs the T/D committee, is the starting point for this discussion. Since the more common practice is to give students some voice in research advisor selection, it is valuable to know what that individual is supposed to do and how to make constructive contact with potential research advisors to assess their interests and comparability. We agree with Allen (1973), who said,

> Since you may be working with this committee for an extended period of time, you should—if at all possible—attempt to influence the selection of a committee that increases your chances of completing a high-quality research paper in the time you have allotted for the task. (p. 30)

Others have since advised or implied the same notion (Krathwohl, 1988; Meloy, 2002).

LEARNING ABOUT ADVISOR FUNCTIONS

The advisor is the most important person in the scholastic life of the student during T/D work. Moreover, university publications repeatedly stress that much of the initiative for finding a research advisor must come from the student. One reason is that faculty members are reluctant to be seen as "selling" students on their specific interests or their particular ideological or research agenda. Another reason is that choosing an advisor tends to be tightly linked to choosing a topic for investigation. That relationship is noted in this chapter, but the details of topic selection are elaborated in Chapter 3.

Starting to Talk with Potential Advisors

The care one should give to the selection of an advisor cannot be overestimated. A mistake here could lead to disaster. Yet, students, perhaps particularly new students, find themselves in a complex social and academic situation with very little experience to guide them. An excellent place to start is with other students, especially those who are experienced in the academic program and perhaps well along in the thesis or dissertation process. Ask the experienced students about advisors, about their strengths and weaknesses, the number of advisees they have, and their record in seeing advisees through to successful completion.

Also, a bit of time in library research can tell you what potential advisors have published and where. Try starting with search strategies that focus on subjects in your academic program area and the research area of interest to you and to potential advisors. The research librarian can be of great help here, of course, but some places to start on your own might be the *Academic Search Elite*, *MLA* (Modern Language Association) *International Bibliography*, *Public Affairs International*, *Science Citation Index*, *Social Citation Index*, and so forth. That tells you something about the areas of expertise, as well as the quality of the work of those scholars cited. Another indication of the quality of the work is how often it is cited by peers, and many of the databases will give you that information. All this information is available in your research library and, in many cases, is available on your home computer through access to the library's on-line resources.

Many faculty members have home pages that will provide a good deal of information about them as potential advisors. Many faculty members, in addition to their academic program or department, are affiliated with a number of other academic centers in the university (e.g., Center for Latin American Studies, the Honors College, or the International Institute for Studies in Education). Investigating these affiliations can yield much information about the background, area of expertise, research interests, and accomplishments of a faculty member. Also, faculty academic backgrounds and fields of expertise are often published by their universities, either in print or on line.

Another way to search for an appropriate advisor is to read theses and dissertations from students who have graduated. Of course, the fact that the students have graduated and completed their theses or dissertations is already a good sign. University libraries usually catalog copies of theses and dissertations. Read them and look for the names of advisors, committee members, and the academic area of the dissertation.

Ordinarily, faculty members are pleased to talk about their interests with students. Such discussions should be started by students soon after admission to advanced study. Records should be kept of interviews. Faculty members not exactly right for research advisor may later prove to be good choices for committee membership or consultation on specific T/D problems.

Before approaching a faculty member, the student should be sure there is something to talk about. That calls for planning a brief agenda. One way to start is by reading one or two of the faculty member's most recent publications. Look for places where the faculty member calls attention to the need for more information or to prior research that did not fully resolve the matter that it attacked. Use those references to open the conversation; ask whether anyone known to the faculty member is doing research to close those knowledge gaps. Suggest that you might try to develop a proposal related to the question or questions if no one else is already doing so. Be ready, too, with a few written first-draft research questions or hypotheses that you have developed on the subject(s), but recognize that neither the student nor the faculty member expects that they are in final form. The most important point is to show that a serious effort has been made to prepare for the interview, and that the student has accepted responsibility for the initiative.

Still a third effective variation on this approach is to study T/Ds recently completed under the faculty member's direction. The majority of academic and professional T/Ds contain sections on implications for further research. Equally important, the faculty members who approved them had already tacitly agreed to the relevance and importance of the proposed investigations. Foreign students may seek advisors who have successfully worked with other foreign students or who have conducted or directed studies having a strong international component.

As part of getting under way on the selection of an advisor, we urge the student to do two other things without delay. One is to obtain, carefully study, and follow any policies, statements, or procedure that the local school or department has about research advisor selection. The other is to commit time to a careful reading of the rest of this chapter and at least to skim the rest of the book to identify areas to be studied later. The suggestions in the book are intended to be useful in making the most of the student's important initial steps.

The Advisor's Role

The role of the research advisor is mainly that of a teacher, but also is that of a guide, mentor, confidant, and senior research colleague. The role definition rests on the premise that the advisor is instructing the student in learning to conduct investigations independently. Successful students and advisors often describe their relationships as respectful and collegial. The advisor, usually older, wiser, and knowledgeable about the ways of the university world, wields a considerable amount of power. The student, typically plagued with anxieties about the ability to do what is expected, looks up to the advisor as someone who has done it and who can teach or impart the needed knowledge and skill.

A general theory of the student-advisor relationship can be illustrated graphically (see Fig. 2-1). In its basic form, the theory holds that the relationship at the outset of T/D study is one to one, with the advisor mainly in thc role of teacher and the T/D candidate in the role

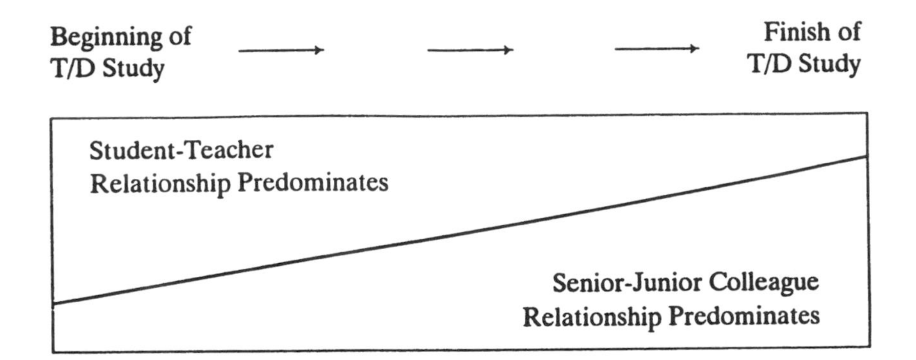

Figure 2-1 Progress of student-advisor relationship.

of pupil. Then, as the work progresses, the relationship moves more and more toward that of a junior colleague working with and maturing as a researcher under the influence of a senior colleague. That theory underlies the discussions and the recommendations about student-advisor interactions in the major contemporary reports on the subject (CGS, 1990a, 1991b; LaPidus, 1990).

Currently, the above theory fits best in fields in which the prevailing model is that of the T/D scholar working, for the most part, alone, with no one else sharing the same or very similar research activities and goals. In some disciplines, though, T/D research projects are typically small components of much larger collaborative studies. In the last case, the vested interest of the advisor in the research may prove to be paramount from the outset, with the result that the advisor takes a larger hand in managing the student's investigation from the very beginning, thus casting the student in the role of junior colleague and collaborator all the way through the T/D experience.

In a policy statement, the Council of Graduate Schools (1991b) says:

> Because of the inherent status differences of the participants, student/faculty collaboration can present opportunities for abuse; when students work on faculty projects, conflicts of interest can arise over ownership of the data and the research results. How is an equitable division of credit achieved for collaborative re-

> search between a doctoral (or master's or honors) student and his or her advisor? (p. 11)

The policy statement goes on to respond:

> Faculty and graduate students alike see a need for some mechanism to identify and evaluate a doctoral (or master's or honors) student's individual contributions to a collaborative research project. . . . Universities should have clear policies governing collaboration among faculty and students and among students. These policies should insure the integrity of the various functions of doctoral (or master's or honors) research and protect all parties' rights in the research results. (p. 11)

We agree with Myers (1993), who says:

> I have never met a student who did not hope to make a personal imprint on his or her dissertation. Often the research idea comes from the student's own experience. Even when this is not the case, there is a strong desire to implant one's self-concept in the work. Of course, there are examples of a student taking a minor spinoff of a sponsor's programmatic research. This is a very efficient way to do dissertation research, but it seldom results in feelings of fulfillment for the student. The internal drive to make it one's own is powerful and pervasive. (p. 334)

Truly, inherent in the T/D process itself, there is collaboration, in the broad sense of willing cooperation, between students and faculty members. But, when collaboration promises to involve the student as one of a number of investigators jointly working on more or less connected aspects of a large research enterprise, the above general theory of student-advisor relationship (Fig. 2-1) needs the protection of clear, written guidelines to ensure that the traditional purposes and goals of the T/D process are never unintentionally subverted, with the real loser being the student.

Students often feel absolutely dependent on the advisor to finish. It can be lonely. The camaraderie of classes, groups, and grades is all but gone. Prior learning now has to be synthesized and actively drawn on in a rigorous fashion to produce something of worth, something that will be open to the critical examination of the advisor and later a committee of learned peers of the advisor.

Although the roles are different, both students and advisors aim for successful completion. The advisor may become anxious if the student falters, if there appears to be a waste of time, fumbling, or indecision. The advisor will chastise, cajole, encourage, reinforce, and perhaps, at times, threaten. All this seems to be tolerated to a remarkable degree when the student respects and trusts the advisor and knows that the advisor is acting out of concern and interest.

There must be, after all, advisor respect for the advisee in order that the thesis or dissertation preparation is a growth experience. Too much direction and hand-holding can stifle creativity and independence, blind both parties to reality, and weaken the selectivity of the program. No matter how humanistic the advisor's concerns, it is difficult to argue that all candidates in an honors, master's, or doctoral program should complete it. The advisor who defends an advisee under any circumstance has gone beyond the bounds of appropriate behavior.

A more appropriate role for the advisor is that of advanced instructor. Here, the advisor presumes that the student is a mature person, possessing the skills and tools of research appropriate to the topic.

A colleague, C. Baker (personal communication, Dec. 18, 1992) has collected statements made by students to advisors; she labeled these "things dissertation advisors hate to hear." These statements were gleaned from years of experience working with graduate students and their advisors:

Things dissertation advisors hate to hear:
"Just tell me what to do and I'll do it!"
"It would be much easier if you gave me a topic to investigate."
"I know it's taken me 6 months to revise my overview, but could you possibly have it read by tomorrow?"
"What rules were in effect when I started the program?"
"You mean that I should have committee members from *my* program?"
"I'll study any topic as long as it doesn't require statistics."

"Don't expect me to know what I'm doing; I've never written a dissertation before."
"You have to sign off on this because I have made arrangements for my family to fly in from across the world for graduation."
"Couldn't you make an exception in my case?"

Advisor advocacy is appropriate, but it has to be accompanied by advisee responsibility with respect to identifying the topic, personally conducting the research, setting reasonable and realistic goals and meeting them, and using clear language in writing. If the student fails in any of these respects, without acceptable cause, it is time for some difficult evaluation and reassessment, with requests for appropriate changes in behavior. The student has the right to know what is expected, to understand and discuss these expectations, and to know the consequences of failing to meet them.

Phases of Faculty-Student Interactions

From experiences related by faculty members, it is possible to identify three sequential phases of faculty-student interaction. First is an *exploratory* phase; the student is given encouragement to look for an area of study. Having been contacted by a student, the advisor throws out leads and gives information about where and how to look for problems in need of investigation, but the student is not directed toward specific problems. The advisor supports the search and offers encouragement to continue it. This is an opportune time for advisor and student to discuss how best to use electronic technology to help accomplish the literature explorations—the browsing—and then to carry out the literature searches that are needed. Advisors can help students learn how to use computer-assisted literature searches to examine what has been reported in a particular "problem area" and to move from that activity to the identification of specific potentially researchable topics within the problem areas being explored. In this phase, also, the advisor informs the student of criteria that can be used to help determine whether a topic is one that would lend itself to T/D work. For discussion purposes, criteria can be grouped in three categories: the student's criteria, the advisor's criteria, and the institution's criteria. The last includes university, school, and departmental criteria. Chapter 9 supplies a suggested checklist of criteria.

The second stage in the advisor-student interaction sequence is one of moving toward *problem focus*. The student settles in on two or three problems in a topical area (sometimes more than one topical area). The problems are described, and a beginning is made on stating their boundaries. Though specific T/D problems have not yet crystallized, there is movement in that direction. The advisor and student have fairly well-defined problem areas to examine. In this stage, a literature search is an important activity. Also, referring to the criteria discussed in the first stage should prove helpful.

The third stage is *generation of research questions or hypotheses*. The student formulates questions or hypotheses and tries them out on the advisor, on friends, and among the other graduate students. Still endeavoring not to be overly directive, advisors tend at this point to lead the students toward a narrower and more precise problem definition. All of that is done, to the extent possible, in a spirit of cooperative helpfulness. Inadvertent discouragement of students at this stage is all too easy for the closer the student comes to defining a T/D problem, the more strongly the criticism is felt.

The Advisor as a Mentor/Tutor

Mentor* refers to a person of competence who volunteers to instruct a junior or less experienced person in an area of mutual interest. The person who finds a mentor will be helped to prepare for a lifetime career without losing a sense of identity. From the relationship comes the confidence to succeed by one's own efforts (Kavoosi et al., 1995). Such a relationship is especially important to foreign students.

Mentoring is probably the most applicable instructional term for the style of faculty-student interaction in T/D work. Unlike a tutor

*Some universities use the term *mentor* as the official designation for the T/D advisor. Fordham is an example. Mentor was Odysseus's trusted counselor, in whose disguise Athena became guardian and teacher of Telemachus, Odysseus's son. Other meanings of *mentor* are adviser and wise one.

devoted to subject matter, the mentor tends to become more sharing and confidential. The student is apt to learn in depth what the advisor thinks about topics of mutual interest. The faculty member who is truly a mentor is liable to learn much about the student's motives, plans, and hopes. The searching and reporting by the student often bring new information and insights to the faculty member, who in turn enriches the contacts with the student (and with classes) by talking about them.

Both students and faculty remark that they learn from each other during graduate study. But, there is little literature that bears directly on the learning experiences accruing from T/D study or advisement (LaPidus, 1990).

Hints as to potentially valuable procedures can be found, however, in the extensive literature on the education of the gifted. Most T/D students are in that category based on conventional definitions (Sellin and Birch, 1980, 1981).

There remains, however, a constant acknowledgment that the advisor has power that the student does not have. Krathwohl (1988, p. 262) urges the student to look for an advisor who, among other qualities, is "secure enough to stand up to others in your defense if she thinks you are right." He suggests asking other graduate students about potential advisors who have that strength and who are respected by fellow faculty members for it.

The Advisor as a Model

The advisor is probably the only faculty member the student will see in action so closely and in such an intense way. Thus, it can be expected that the student, if later in the position to serve as T/D advisor to others, will be greatly influenced by earlier example. The behavior of the advisor is of signal importance, therefore, because it becomes the model for others.

To summarize, the Council of Graduate Schools characterizes the dissertation advisor in this way, and we believe that the same description should hold for the thesis advisor (CGS, 1990b, pp. 7 and 8).

> The principal advisor of a dissertation in particular is a mentor in a special position of influence and trust. Inasmuch as dissertation

> advisors have the most to say about whether the student has done adequate research, and to make employment recommendations for positions after the degree has been completed, they have a most serious responsibility to foster in the student intellectual autonomy, appreciation of the highest academic standards, and a realistic sense of appropriate career options.
>
> At all stages, advising is a reciprocal responsibility. Faculty are expected to be diligent in providing counsel and guidance, and to be available for consultation. They should demonstrate flexibility and critical thinking, a willingness to be challenged and to challenge constructively, and the desire to help the student to become better at research and teaching than they are themselves.

Both research and anecdotal evidence testify that advisors (and committee members) have power over students, and that the power is sometimes exercised inappropriately (Heinrich, 1991; Smallwood, 2002; White, 1991). If a person is sexist, has racial or ethnic biases, enjoys bullying, or has other inappropriate tendencies and attitudes, the student may be understandably intimidated and have few, if any, defenses. Many women students, especially, develop a view of themselves as "victims" in the one-to-one advisor-student relationship (Vartuli, 1982). But, women are not alone in experiencing the unprofessional behavior of certain advisors. Sexual harassment, for example, can occur in a same-sex advisor-student setting. Sexual harassment or harassment of any other kind is reprehensible and not to be tolerated.

Both students and faculty should be made aware that they will be given a fair, objective hearing if there are cases reported of inappropriate advances or insulting or demeaning behavior. For all advisors and committee members, we propose this guiding rule:

> I will never exploit my position of power or status to take advantage of a student-academically, professionally, socially personally, sexually, financially, or otherwise.

Advisors who pledge themselves to this credo have set the foundation for being worthy models.

THE T/D AS A TEACHING DEVICE

The T/D is a teaching device; this is at the heart of its reason for existence. The honors or graduate student research process normally yields more opportunities for faculty and students to interact on a close academic and professional basis than any other institutional situation. Nowhere else in the university is so much individual time devoted to students by faculty, on a one-to-one basis, in examining substantive issues and academic-professional concerns at the edges of current knowledge and practice. The guidance of student research provides the major opportunity for systematic identification and attack on a problem of interest to both faculty advisor and student.

Practicum in Guided Independent Study

Thesis and dissertation study is aimed at increasing the student's ability to work independently on problems and researchable issues, building on existing literature. The ability to work independently on a research problem is one of the qualities that often separate those who finish and those who do not. It is not an easy skill to learn to the proficiency level required by the T/D; it depends very much on one's attitudes toward doing research and toward one's own professional skill. But, it can be strengthened by going through earlier, similar processes successfully several times, thus building confidence. Some useful ways universities have to provide this experience are enrollment for directed study, research papers in courses, and research seminars in specialized fields. These experiences should precede rather than parallel the T/D if they are to be of maximum help.*

Perhaps at no other time is there such opportunity to help students work through questions about the nature of evidence, the nature of scientific investigation, the processes of inductive and deductive reasoning, and the drawing of inferences and generalizing, appropri-

---

*A number of schools use a T/D seminar both as a screen and as an aid to students having difficulty. A typical requirement might read as follows: "Upon or near completion of prerequisite course work, honors or graduate candidates will register for the T/D seminar. There they are expected to develop a T/D proposal that will meet the approval of the seminar faculty. Students who do not prepare approved proposals after two semesters of seminar will meet with the student progress committee to determine future directions of study."

ately or inappropriately, from a body of data (National Academy of Sciences [NAS], 1989). Readings, lectures, examination of examples of good investigations, discussions, and hands-on experience in conducting research are all tools that should be common in the work of the advisors and students. At least the opportunity is there if the university provides faculty with the resources and if the faculty is competent to use the resources.

Long-Range Influences of Guided Independent Study

The impact of seminar research reports and of T/D production on future professional work is not known in detail. There is good reason to believe that such investigative activities do have an influence. Terman (1954, pp. 222–223) reported his own recollection as follows:

> I was a senior in psychology at Indiana University and was asked to prepare two reports for a seminar, one on mental deficiency and one on genius. . . . The reading of those reports opened up a new world to me, the works of Galton, Binet and their contemporaries. . . . Then I entered Clark University where I spent considerable time . . . reading on mental tests and precocious children. . . . By the time I reached my last graduate year I decided to find out for myself how precocious children differ from the mentally backward, and accordingly chose as my doctoral dissertation an experimental study of the intellectual processes of fourteen boys, seven of them picked as the brightest and seven as the dullest in a large city school. . . . The experiment contributed little or nothing to science, but it contributed a lot to my future thinking. . . . My dream was realized in the spring of 1921 when I obtained a generous grant from the Commonwealth Fund of New York City for the purpose of locating a thousand subjects of IQ 140 or higher.

Perhaps not many dissertations presage such monumental contributions as Terman's Stanford-Binet Tests of Intelligence and Genetic Studies of Genius, both active today. Many contemporary leaders in the various professions, however, can identify links between their master's and doctoral investigations and important work they did later.

Teaching Function Involved in All T/Ds

In guiding T/D work, teaching opportunity is constantly available to faculty members, whether in experimental investigations, critical analyses of social problems, health issues, developments in physics or computer technology, analytical study of public policy or practice, or developmental projects such as improving the mathematics curriculum or staff of a school. Studies in the United States and abroad indicate that most students need continued instruction in research skills during the time they are engaged in T/D work (Reynolds et al., 1986; Zuber-Skerritt and Knight, 1986). It cannot be too often emphasized that T/D activities should teach the candidate to (a) identify and examine critically alternative approaches to any question, (b) marshal facts and data systematically to support choices among alternatives, and (c) test the adequacy of these choices against the reality of the professional workplace and the views of one's academic colleagues.

An Exercise in Synthesis

Finally, the T/D should build on a synthesis of all earlier courses, readings, and professional experience that the candidate brings to the task. It is the major opportunity in the scholastic career in which all past experiences can be brought together in a creative independent work of the student's design. The synthesis is not accomplished without help, but is essentially an independent exercise; as such, it is an opportunity for personal, academic, and professional integration unequaled elsewhere in higher education. The *instructional obligation* of the advisor is to set that goal before students and to help them both internalize and achieve it.

SCOPE OF ADVISOR RESPONSIBILITIES

Advisors have responsibilities to a number of people and groups: the advisee, other students, the university, the school and department faculty, the fellow members of the student's T/D committee, the members of their academic field or profession, and the registrar and graduate office. While none of these should be ignored, most advisors set as priorities three main responsibilities: to the student, to the other committee members, and to the university.

Responsibilities to the Student

Advisors ought to be committed deeply to the belief that their first responsibility is to the student. At no other time is the student so vulnerable and so in need of close identification with one faculty member. The advisor ideally should be as involved and interested as the student, within the restrictions of time and competing responsibilities.

The obligation to the student is expressed in part in a consultant relationship. The student should feel free to ask questions, try out new ideas about procedures or substantive issues, and obtain guidance and direction when it is requested. No other faculty member should be as ready to help in the dissertation process as the advisor, specifically with regard to two matters: the topic the two persons have agreed to pursue and the university, school, and departmental rules and processes applicable.

The help of the advisor in choosing a topic is expected. After all, the advisor, too, will have to live with the topic. The position of the advisor is delicate, steering a tight course between giving the student a topic and allowing a completely free choice. The risk with the topic chosen by the advisor is, of course, that the student may have little interest in it and may feel inadequate to tackle it. The possibility of conflict of interest arises, too. Will the study become an article or part of a book for the advisor? Is the topic chosen to perform work that the advisor is unwilling to do? Such suspicions inhibit work and endanger relationships. If the suspicions are confirmed and the activity is allowed to continue, one wonders what the real purpose of the dissertation is in the eyes of the advisor, the faculty, and even the institution. It is still a learning situation for the student, but the model may persuade the observer that it is appropriate to use the university to act in unethical ways if it serves one's purpose and if one can get away with it.

The problem with allowing the student a free choice is no less difficult. It is a shirking of responsibility, putting it all on the student. It provides the perfect faculty excuse for failure at any point in the process: “Well, you chose the topic completely by yourself.” It encourages a minimum commitment on the part of the advisor. It may deny the student the benefit of the experience and the expertise of the research advisor—one of the compelling reasons, presumably, why the university provides this very costly teaching relationship.

It is the research advisor’s responsibility to ascertain that the topic is well thought out, that the student can give cogent arguments as to why the specific topic was chosen, and that these arguments cover all the standard questions in the literature, such as feasibility, efficiency, importance of the topic, competence of the student to attempt the specific topic, and a theory base underlying the student’s understanding of the topic. (These are explored in depth in the next chapter, along with suggestions for satisfying them.)

The student should come to an acceptable topic with the advisor’s sound advice, but not with a dependent or authority-beholden attitude. The student exercises independent judgment within criteria agreed on, analyzed, and discussed with the advisor. Such a process regards both parties as mature human beings capable of being self-directed, but capable also of recognizing and accepting suggestions from each other. Each will understand their mutual concerns and commitments to the topic. Each will understand the problems connected with the topic and will be prepared to help resolve the problems. This process can set the tone for interactions throughout the T/D study period and help to weather many storms along the way.

Unsatisfactory Student Progress: The faculty member who regards little or no progress at the T/D stage solely as student failure does not understand the advisor’s job. Students’ failure to complete graduate research work may ensue mainly from their own errors or failures, but in some ways the advisor, the faculty, and the university may have failed also.

In most university programs, the student signs up for a substantial number of credit hours during the development and writing of the overview, the thesis, and the dissertation. The system is designed to reflect in a general way that the student is taking valuable time, and that time carries with it costs to be paid and credits to be awarded. In many programs, this is a substantial block of time—perhaps one-fourth or more of the total postmaster's credits required for the doctorate. Viewed in this way, it becomes clear that the student has the right to reasonable faculty time and advice and has paid for this right. The advisor, especially, then has the responsibilities of being available for help, advice, and guidance and of offering such advice and guidance on the highest professional and academic level. Failure in the context of this system is seldom entirely one sided.

Ethical Responsibilities: The advisor's professorial responsibility transcends material considerations. Whether the student is contributing directly to the support of the institution or not, one would expect the professional behavior of the advisor to be the same. In fact, this concept is at the heart of the idea of professionalism. Specifically, what are the ethical responsibilities of the advisors?

First, the advisor does what is best for students in all academic or professional situations. Although the principle is easy to state, it is not always easy to know or determine what is best for the students. Conflicting values make life difficult for those who try to maintain high ethical standards. For example, if a student hands in a paper that is not his or her own or cheats on an exam, how does the advisor ascertain what is in the best interest of the student? Faculties face many examples of conflicts of values in what is best for the student, and agreement is not always reached. Nevertheless, there must be at least the sincere attempt to put the student first as a fundamental value of advising. An advisor who operates in this way—working as fairly as possible—is usually perceived so by colleagues and students; that action and perception helps to minimize ethical conflicts.

Second, the advisor avoids using the position for personal gain and refuses to accept the offer of such gain. There are instances when faculty admitted being given valuable gifts by an advisee, instances of lavish entertainment provided to advisors by advisees, and the provision of other personal and professional favors.

If a foreign student proffers a gift and insists that it is considered an insult in his or her homeland to refuse to take it, the advisor can, gently but firmly, point out that they are not in the student's homeland, and that the customs of this land must be applied. The advisor can then explain that here it is considered improper for a student to offer a gift and for an advisor to accept one. It can be suggested by the advisor that the whole matter will be resolved with honor if both the student and the advisor agree to forget the incident entirely and return to their normal relationship.

It can be difficult to draw an exact line between ethical and unethical behavior, but that difficulty is no excuse for failing to try to do so. It is the responsibility of the university as well as the profession to publish codes of ethics and to monitor ethical behavior. In our view, accepting any favors (or the promise thereof), awards, gifts, professional grants, and the like from a dissertation advisee creates an improper and unethical situation. It may prevent the advisor from being critical or objective in evaluation. It creates conditions of expectation by the student. It is unfair to other students who are unable or unwilling to engage in similar behavior. The situation compromises the integrity of everyone it touches, indeed, of the whole institution.

A *third* matter involving professorial ethics is the use of student work as if it were the work of the advisor so that the advisor gains the credit (Smallwood, 2002). Marchant (1997, pp. 3–5) asked five colleagues at different universities this question: "When should dissertation and thesis chairs or other committee members be included as authors on any papers or articles resulting from the dissertation?" Key excerpts from their responses follow:

> A doctoral dissertation should be an independent research contribution by the candidate so . . . the candidate should either be the sole author or the first author.
>
> —Richard Mayer, University of California, Santa Barbara

> Dissertation chairs are not routinely included on a paper derived from a dissertation.
>
> —Angela O'Donnell, Rutgers University

> Students always merit first author's slot on publications that derive from a thesis because they take the lead in conceptualizing, analyzing, and writing up those research projects.
>
> —Phil Winne, Simon Fraser University

> A dissertation ought to be rewritten for publication by the Ph.D. student with the advisor (or other committee members who con-

> tributed to the piece of research beyond the call of their advisor duty) being second author.
>
> —Gavriel Salomon, University of Haifa

> Authorship must recognize . . . professional contributions [which] include developing a research design, a conceptual model, and building theoretical arguments. Tasks such as creating a data file, carrying out analyses specified by the faculty member, and preparing manuscript are not considered professional contributions, but may warrant acknowledgement in a footnote.
>
> —Rick McCown, Duquesne University

All five respondents qualified their answers to account for unusual circumstances. But, all insisted, except for extraordinary conditions, that the T/D student have unquestioned priority as the first author, and that any additional author earn that privilege through having made a significant contribution to the research itself.

If each advisor puts the legitimate work of the student forward, encourages the student to publish, to read papers at professional and academic meetings, to pursue further research, and to do all this under the student's name, there will be little likelihood that the advisor will have to worry about ethical transgressions on this score. Certainly, the contributions of the advisor, when real and substantial and beyond the normal teaching and consulting role of a T/D advisor, should receive due credit. A guide that helps govern such questions is to divide the credits commensurately with the amount of work and time invested by each (Fine and Kudek, 1993; Smallwood, 2002). If that guideline is followed, it is difficult to imagine how an advisor's name could appear at all as a coauthor, much less a senior author, on a publication arising out of a thesis or a dissertation done by a student unless a very substantial amount of additional analysis, interpretation, discussion, and editing is done by the advisor after the T/D has been approved by the final oral committee.

A *fourth* note on ethical behavior concerns competence. Qualitatively, within the narrow confines of one's specialty, the self-examination of competence seldom arises. In fact, however, faculty competence varies a good deal; it is indeed the wise and ethical advisor who is aware of faculty limitations.

A reasonable position regarding competence would be something like this: Be as parsimonious as possible in the selection of research-advising responsibilities; serve only on T/Ds of other advisors when you are sure you have a needed competence and can make a substantial contribution; be willing to admit that there are many dissertation areas for which the best you can do is learn from the student; and finally, lace the committees of your advisees with the most competent experts you can find.

Maintain Competency: One of the important responsibilities of advisors is to maintain their academic and professional competencies. Without this, an advisor is not much good and even may be harmful to the student. A faculty member maintains competency by reading the literature, by keeping up with the latest thought (even though the latest is not always the best), by teaching and keeping in contact with colleagues and students, by taking a meaningful part in conferences and meetings, by listening and discussing, and by speaking and writing. Perhaps no other activity keeps faculty as sharp in doing rigorous research and writing and the subsequent exposure to the critical analysis of colleagues and other experts. After all, one can say or write what one wants, within the bounds of propriety, before a class of students who will be graded on how well they restate it later; it is quite a different experience to address a group of colleagues and experts.

We do not maintain that the best advisors are those who do the most research and writing. The variables associated with excellence in advisors are too complex for such a conclusion. The point is that a given faculty member will probably be a more competent advisor for having personally done research and writing. We, in fact, feel so strongly about this point that we recommend that one of the criteria for the appointment of research advisors from among the general faculty is evidence of high-quality research and writing. We do not believe that such evidence would be as difficult to assess by peers as some may suggest.

Responsibilities to Other Committee Members

Traditionally, the advisor chairs the committee and sets standards of committee behavior. The research advisor sets the climate of expertise and high standards within the committee. No one else is in a position to have such a positive or negative influence on the committee climate for no one else can set the level of expectations for committee behavior. Most faculty will tend to conform to the expectations and leadership behavior of the chairperson of the committee. It is unlikely that the committee will rise above it. Indeed, the accepted (although unstated) rules of committee behavior make it very difficult for members not to conform to the pattern set by the chairperson.

Defining Committee Roles: Many advisors hold a pre-overview work session with the committee to go over and agree to rules for operation. Sometimes, the institution or a professional group has detailed standards for expectations (CGS, 1991b). At many institutions, though, each committee sets its standards under general rules. Indeed, the frequent vague guides for students or faculty are one of the motivating forces behind the preparation of this book.

Useful rules with respect to committee role start *first* from the notion that the committee should know and agree on its expectations for itself. These are best discussed openly and explicitly before individual instances come along to test the limits of the principles. *Second*, rules should enjoin the committee to act always in the highest interest of the student, consistent with maintaining high professional, academic, and institutional standards. Of course, words like "high" and "highest" have to be defined operationally within the institutional context, but agreeing to the principle is a good place to start. *Third*, operating at a professional level implies that committee members consistently treat the student and one another with respect and maintain a collegial atmosphere. Persons can disagree without being disagreeable.

ENCOURAGING COMMITTEE PARTICIPATION

The research advisor has the job of ensuring that the committee members participate throughout the T/D process. The committee is selected for the expertise of each individual, and the student has a right to that expertise. Furthermore, if the members have been taking an active part throughout, there should be no surprises at the final defense.

T/D students queried by Meloy (2002) repeatedly told of being hampered by absence of or delay in response from their committee members. That, plus a seeming lack of interest in their views on the part of committee members, sapped students' confidence in themselves and in their supposed mentors.

The amount of guidance and time to be expected of committee members falls into proper perspective if it is understood that the research advisor has the primary responsibility for guiding the work of the student. The advisor keeps the committee informed of progress and ensures that the student sees the committee members—or attempts to see them—periodically to keep them informed and seek advice. The advisor and student share responsibility to see that committee expertise is used and that committee members are kept involved. Specific ways to seek creative suggestions of members and to follow through on them are spelled out in Chapters 5 and 6.

If the advisor and student sincerely try to involve the committee, the response is usually quite good. At the very least, individual committee members will read the proposal, critique it, be available for consultation when the student asks for consultation, read the document and critique it before a final defense, and attend scheduled overview and defense meetings. Anything more is to be desired and encouraged.

Coordinating Committee Communications:

Some faculty want all communication between the student and other committee members to come through the advisor; others think the student should feel completely free to spend as much time and take as much direction as wanted from committee members. These are probably the two extremes; most research advisors fall between them. It is more important that the advisor and the student talk out and agree on the ground rules than to argue about which procedure is best. Probably any reasonable procedure will work if the rules are agreed on and if the student understands the consequences of alternative kinds of behavior.

Special attention is advisable with foreign students since cultural differences often mean that the nature and frequency of written communication can create difficulties. A discussion can lead to understandings that forestall such problems.

Faculty experience has indicated certain procedures that are important responsibilities of the advisors. These are more in the nature of good commonsense advice than of laws or dictums. The advisor has the responsibility of negotiating with the committee—all of it—

those things that a student cannot negotiate with the committee, such as problems that come up concerning necessary changes in the research during its conduct or personal difficulties of the student. The advisor has to see that the committee is kept informed. Sometimes, the advisor does it; other times, it is appropriate to make sure that the student sees or at least communicates with every committee member. When committee suggestions are sought on a draft, they must be thoroughly discussed by the student and the advisor, and the student should discuss and understand the risks and positive aspects of whatever action is taken. The advisor has responsibility to draw a consensus from the committee so that the student does not suffer from faculty disagreements and so that the individual committee members can continue to serve without feeling that their scholarly reputations are in jeopardy.

The only guiding principle that merits support is for the advisor to relate to all committee members with integrity and academic respect. Good communication by the advisor gives all the committee members the information they need to be helpful and to use their expertise in assisting the candidate to successful completion of the T/D. Technology such as E-mail has made advisor and student written communication easier. The same message can be sent simultaneously to the student and to committee members. Messages can be sent frequently and accurately, with the knowledge that all are getting the same information at the same time.

Administrative Arrangements: The advisor also calls committee meetings for the overview, for the final defense, and for other purposes. Another obligation is to see that the student produces the T/D document in required form and has it in the committee's hands several weeks before the meeting. The chairperson is also responsible for working with the candidate to ensure that all school and university requirements that call for committee action are met in a timely fashion.

Responsibilities to the Institution

Higher education institutions flourish largely because of the integrity of the individuals who make them up—students, faculty, administration, and staff. Not many other major societal units are so free of externally imposed laws and requirements. And few, if any, organizations are so self-governing. Individual integrity of consistently high order on the part of the members of the university community is an essential quality that has fostered that state of affairs and that must be present if university-based academic and professional preparation and research are to continue.

Maintenance of Standards: The first responsibility of the advisor to the institution is the maintenance of high standards of quality in all T/D and related activities. What constitutes quality is a value judgment, of course, but the judgment is not without guidelines. No other single person in the university has that responsibility or could ever discharge it if it were possessed—not the student, not the committee members individually, not the dean, not the program chairperson—no one but the research advisor.

Prevention of Fraud: Deceit, breach of confidence, gain from unfair or dishonest practices or from pretense—all of these fall under the heading of fraud. In the academic and professional community, fraud also includes fabrication, falsification, plagiarism, and other lapses in integrity or trustworthiness. It also means altering data, misrepresentation of results, and publication of another's intellectual property as though it were one's own. It probably is true that fraud in various forms in research reports is as old as the recorded history of discovery and creativity.

There are several guidelines for preventing fraud that should be discussed between advisor and student. We advocate making the same guidelines a part of what every faculty member accepts as a credo in working with students and colleagues in a sincere effort to prevent fraud and the temptation to perpetrate fraud in research.

Faculty are responsible for monitoring and vigorously enforcing standards of scientific integrity, and faculty should help establish procedures for resolving conflicts and professional disagreements promptly. It is the university's responsibility to educate faculty and students about what constitutes scientific misconduct (Mishkin, 1993; Ruark, 2002; Smallwood, 2002).

We make a simple and direct charge to the advisor. Expect the whole T/D committee to exercise keen surveillance on all aspects of the project. To the student, we say, "Never cheat or tolerate cheating." Nothing helps so much as full disclosure every inch of the way.

Relevance of the Student Research: The advisor has the responsibility to ensure the relevance of T/D work. It is not a frivolous document. It should relate clearly to the program or department in which the student is doing graduate work or the question of where the dissertation and the student belong may be raised. If the proposed investigation has an evident and close relation to the expertise of the committee members, one aspect of the question of relevance is well answered. But, perhaps the most important aspect of relevance is the advisor's responsibility to ensure the relevance of the topic to the student. Does the student see the topic as related to his or her own long-term interests? Does the student have the background to work on the chosen topic? Has the student articulated well the reasons for the choicc of topic?

These and other aspects of relevance are detailed in Chapter 3, but two need to be named here: useful contributions to the field and usefulness to the growth of the student. Both are essential criteria in weighing the relevance of a topic. Without a rigorous examination of relevance, T/Ds can descend to the level of trivia. Highly relevant, well-conceived, well-executed, and significant T/Ds indicate top-quality professional and academic programs. The T/D is the one product that represents the best of the student, the advisor, the committee, and the quality of prior preparation. It must be carefully reproduced, bound, microfilmed, or otherwise preserved for posterity as the culminating work of long and demanding training. Whatever the student's subsequent career, the signed, bound copy of a relevant and scholarly T/D stands forever in testimony to the relevance and scholarship of the student, the advisor, and the university.

Academic Interests: Advisor responsibility to the institution includes academic and personal integrity, and integrity finds its severest testing in T/D work, the highest levels of independent study. The predominantly solitary or one-to-one T/D work leaves both the student and faculty member largely to their own resources. Individual student behavior cannot be melded into that of the rest of the class. There is no set course outline and no standard textbook with manual and tests to be interposed between the faculty member and the student. There are no specified number and schedule of class meetings. Colleagues or assistants cannot substitute for the faculty member. The student cannot find help in another student's notes. Instead, independent study leading to the T/D is a type of student-faculty member adventure into the academic unknown. The personal and academic integrity of each becomes a major ingredient in the enterprise.

Perhaps the best way to deal with possible role conflict related to integrity is always to keep in mind the question, "What is the best course to follow in terms of the integrity of the process, the university, and the student?" This question will not necessarily yield easy answers, but keeping the question foremost in one's thoughts is more likely to yield worthwhile answers than bending with whatever wind blows hardest at any given time.

When there are no local institutional guidelines, the matter should not be bypassed. Instead, personal and academic integrity should be discussed in terms of local custom and practice, even though unwritten, and in terms of more general ethical codes of professional associations. We believe personal and academic integrity are not exactly the same, although we discuss them together. For example, keeping or not keeping an appointment by a student or faculty member is a matter of personal integrity, as is either person inventing a falsehood to explain not completing a task agreed on. On the other hand, consciously failing to give credit to someone else for a previously stated concept or idea is a matter of academic integrity, as is failure to acknowledge a quotation or disguising it by reproducing it with minor alterations and without citation.

Differences in Responsibilities at Thesis and Dissertation Levels

The thesis, as indicated, is a work of more limited proportions than a dissertation. While an end in itself for some students, it readies others for more comprehensive and complex investigations.

The thesis advisor works with the honors or graduate student (usually during the fourth or fifth year of university study) to produce a useful, well-written work, supported by evidence. Assessment practices differ, but preferred practice includes the overview of a committee. The work should be circulated in the department and published by the university or at least catalogued in the university library and made available for publication or microfilming for a wide audience.

The principles of advisor-advisee relationships that apply to the thesis process are the same as those applicable to the dissertation as described in the preceding pages.

The responsibilities of the dissertation advisor contrast mainly in quantitative ways with the responsibilities of the thesis advisor. Academic endeavor, the attributes of scholarliness, use of reputable and replicable investigative procedures and methodology, and a clear and readable manuscript are equally applicable. With respect to T/D products other than manuscripts (i.e., musical compositions, works of art, constructions, and the like), applicable similar principles should prevail. There is no reason to sacrifice those attributes because the work level may not be as advanced or the nature of the work may be somewhat different.

SELECTION OF THE RESEARCH ADVISOR

In the search for an advisor, it is best for the student to be armed with some understanding of how advisors operate. In turn, to determine what sort of advisor the student is most likely to need calls for considerable self-knowledge and the inclination to be objective about one's assets and liabilities as a student.

The essential element we encourage the student to look for in the advisor is the special quality of thinking like a teacher. This is a skilled, articulate, rational, abstract thought process that sorts out the academic and professionally relevant facts of the student's situation, ignoring the merely interesting and distracting incidentals. Its aim is to guide the student-advisor relationship toward the most promising topics and toward the most fruitful procedures for attacking the topics.

The student should not be put off because a potential advisor's special way of thinking like a teacher does not manifest itself in a warm and reassuring approach to problems. Sometimes, aspiring T/D students are distressed by what they perceive as detachment from their personal trials. These students may truly need reassurance in that part of their lives. Some advisors may indeed be persons who tend to supply that reassurance to students. But, the student needs to keep in mind the professional objective of the whole process: to obtain the best, most competent, most astute research advice and guidance.

The advisor may turn out to be, incidentally, a good family counselor, financial advisor, and warm friend, but that is not the advisor's job. In making decisions about the selection of an advisor, decisions that involve both immediate and long-range educational and personal objectives, it is helpful to keep that distinction firmly in mind.

Criteria for Selection of the Research Advisor

The single best criterion the student may use in seeking out an advisor for the dissertation is the track record of the faculty member. Traditionally, research advisors do not advertise. Thus, it is necessary for the student to seek these kinds of relevant data about potential advisors:

1. How do other students who are working with this advisor react to the situation?
2. Is the faculty member one who is or has been productive in theory and research of the kind that interests you?
3. Do students who work with this advisor progress with reasonable dispatch in their investigations?
4. Does the faculty member appear to be regarded highly by colleagues and by others you respect?
5. What has happened to the last four or five students who initiated their work under this research advisor?
6. Does there seem to be a strong element of trust between your potential advisor and his or her students?
7. Has the advisor worked well with foreign students on T/D committees?
8. Is the advisor current with respect to modern technology used in research and scholarly production?

University libraries have copies of student dissertations. Read them and look for the names of advisors, committee members, and the academic area of the dissertation. As to faculty academic background and field of expertise, universities usually publish such information, either in print or on line.

These and related inquiries about past performances can supply data on which to base decisions. In all cases, a personal interview with the potential advisor is a good idea once the student has some idea of the area of investigation.

A not uncommon situation is the assigning of advisors to students on their acceptance to the program. The student has nothing to say about the initial assignment. This system may work reasonably well, particularly if it is easy to change advisors without fear of reprisal. However, the choice of a research advisor should be regarded as a decision separate from the academic advisor assignment. That is, the research advisor choice should be regarded by all as a conscious decision that the program expects the student to make, and the student should be completely free to choose to stay with the academic advisor or to go to some other faculty person for research guidance. There ought to be no stigma, difficulty, or discomfort attached to the choice for the skills one looks for in a research advisor may be quite *different* from those possessed by an academic advisor, not better or lesser skills. Every academic advisor has the responsibility of telling students that they should carefully seek a research advisor, even to the point of suggesting one or two names if appropriate, and that they should not feel that they need to stay with their own academic advisor. This point is particularly important for advisors of foreign students for such students may understandably become dependent on the initial advisor or may profit especially from exposure to the methods of more than one scholar in the field. This is a subject that should be brought up by the faculty member for it may be awkward for the student to raise it. In a number of cases, the academic advisor may well prove to be the most suitable research advisor.

Support from the Department Chairperson

What we have already said about the responsibilities of the academic advisor ought to be supported in important ways by the department (or program) chairperson. The chairperson needs to support the freedom of the student in this regard and to protect that important part of academic freedom from the excesses and possessive abuses that occasionally creep into faculty-student relationships. The chairperson should feel free to suggest research advisors for reasons of appropriateness, time availability, and fields of interest. Of course, such suggestions can in themselves become abused if the students and faculty do not feel free to reject them.

The Graduate Faculty's Role

As a collective body, the graduate faculty is responsible for the quality of graduate work, including the quality of advisement and the quality of the student research that emanate from their domain. It is the responsibility of the graduate faculty to regulate the process to ensure high quality. When the graduate faculty fails to do so, there is no other mechanism for quality control, and the quality issue has no appropriate resolution.

Individual honors or graduate faculty members also have something to say about the choice of advisor. An acceptable arrangement is made only when the student and the faculty member agree to enter into it. It is appropriate for the faculty member to decline to be the student's research advisor when, for example, the research area proposed is outside the field of interest or competence of the faculty member or when the faculty member is already burdened to such an extent that careful advisement is not possible.

Changes in Research Advisor

A change in research advisor is often a more sensitive matter than the original choice of one. It sometimes does imply a breakdown of relationships or understanding somewhere along the line, and it can be a sticky matter. Fairness to both faculty and students would indicate that the proposal for a change might come from either and for a variety of legitimate reasons. The faculty member may not have the time that was originally contemplated, or the research may have taken a direction that the faculty member does not welcome. Alternatively, perhaps the new direction involves not so much disagreement as a reevaluation of faculty interest and competence. Either student or faculty may feel that the progress is too slow and come to the understanding that another advisor would be preferable.

In any case, either party should be able to initiate a request for a change, and that request, with reasons, should go to the department chairperson so that an appropriate replacement can be found. In fact, it would be best if a replacement could be found by the student and advisor before they agree to part. This would help to make all persons feel they had discharged their responsibility professionally.

The more informal and low key these procedures can be, the better they are for the student and the faculty, assuming of course that the rights of the individual are respected and that the correct university procedures are followed. It is the primary responsibility of the department chairperson to ensure that the transition goes smoothly, and that the most vulnerable person in the situation—the student—is fairly treated.

SUMMARY

This chapter concentrates on the responsibilities of the research advisor as they are commonly seen in professional schools or academic departments in institutions of higher education. Responsibilities to students, other T/D committee members, and the institution are explored. Some suggestions of particular relevance to foreign students are made. From the student point of view, suggestions are given with regard to the important process of the selection of the research advisor and possible changes in such selection.

3

Developing the Proposal

Between the end of course work and the serious initiation of the thesis or dissertation is a period when most students falter, and many drop out. Immediate attention to establishing a personal time line, to gaining an understanding of the meaning of T/D work, and to locating and agreeing on a research advisor are key steps that very much improve the chances of completion of the requirements of the degree. That is why the first two chapters of this book emphasize those activities. The title of this chapter indicates the next important step: development of the proposal.

The time line (Fig. 1-1), in its first 14 steps, covers the schedule for the development of a T/D proposal. The schematic diagram of the proposal process (Fig. 3-1) can be used to help the student check progress toward proposal completion and approval in a more detailed way. The diagram has been updated and expanded from one presented by

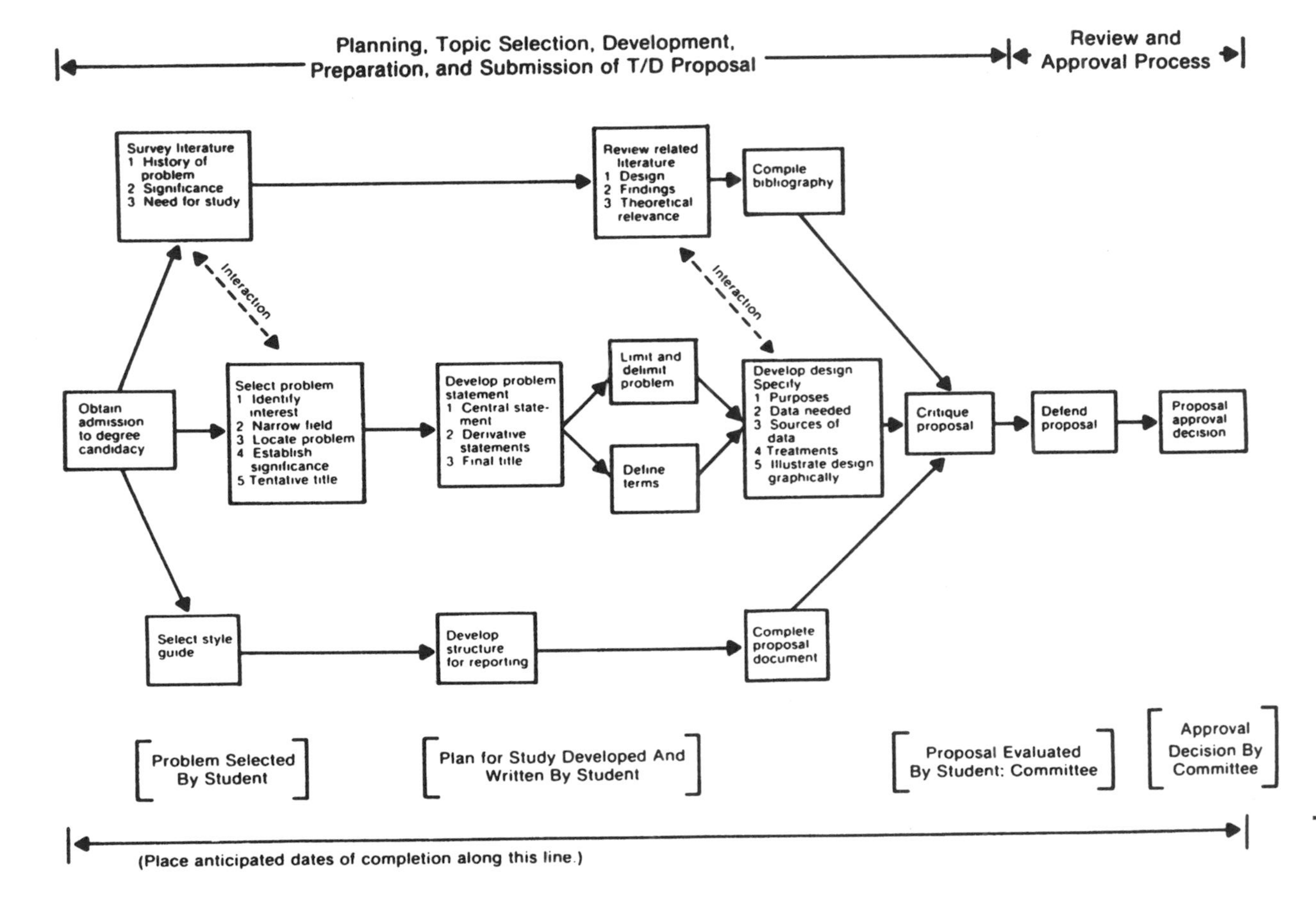

Chapter 3

Figure 3-1 Schematic diagram of the proposal process.

Castetter and Heisler (1988), and we acknowledge the source of the idea with appreciation.

With respect to the schematic diagram, this chapter is concerned mainly with the first major segment at the bottom of Fig. 3-1, namely, selection of the problem by the student. In moving through this and succeeding stages, we again urge students to set target dates realistically and to try hard to meet or exceed them. In this connection, some students report that they make an enlarged photocopy of this diagram and mount it on the wall behind their computer or typewriter keyboard.

The schematic diagram (Fig. 3-1) used terminology applicable to most disciplines, but not all. When the T/D is to be, for instance, a play, a musical composition, or a sculpture, the stages and activities in Fig. 3-1 do not, strictly speaking, fit the project well. With consultation from the research advisor, we most urgently recommend that the student construct a schematic diagram that better fits the proposed project.

INTERACTIONS OF STUDENT AND ACADEMIC ADVISOR

Many students have rewarding T/D experiences because they find their academic advisors genuinely interested, enthusiastic, and ready and able to help in the next step, that of research advisors. If the academic advisor does not fit this description, the student and the advisor can explore together the possibility of selecting another faculty member to serve. Remember the selection of another faculty member to serve as research advisor has no negative connotation. Assuming it is done for the right reasons, it can be a positive step, a demonstration of honesty and maturity.

If the academic advisor suggests that the student work on the T/D topic with another faculty member, the referral should be specific. If the statement is something like "Go work with someone else," a deeper problem may be involved. The advisor who really wants to be helpful will suggest another eligible faculty member who would be more appropriate to the student's topic, will probably talk with the suggested faculty member, and may well offer to continue to be helpful in such ways as, for example, serving on the overview committee.

STUDENTS WITH DISABILITIES

According to the *Digest of Educational Statistics* (NCES, 1999, Table 211), students with disabilities on U.S. campuses made up 5.35% of undergraduate enrollment and 3.20% of graduate and first professional enrollment (the home page of NCES is http://nces.ed.gov/). The percentage may continue to increase.

Section 504 of the Rehabilitation Act of 1973 of the U.S. Congress prohibits discrimination against "otherwise qualified" handicapped individuals. The Section 504 conditions apply to all educational institutions, whether private or public, that receive federal funds.

The courts, including the U.S. Supreme Court, have held that educational institutions, in making the otherwise qualified determination, must provide "reasonable accommodation" to mitigate the handicapping condition.

Determine whether your institution has a distance learning center and how you might use it. Distance learning takes place when a teacher and students occupy separated localities, but interact by some form of technology, such as a satellite or computer telephone network. The practice began more than 75 years ago when public school teachers and classes were linked by telephone or radio with homebound or hospitalized pupils. Now, via the Web and E-mail, distance learning provides opportunities for students at all educational levels, especially those students for whom physical access to the school and its specialized personnel present problems.

Seligman (1992) makes a persuasive case for offering an entire doctoral program through distance learning. While that may not represent reality at your institution, it may prove feasible for some of the T/D work, especially advisement and independent study, when temporary or permanent handicaps present access difficulties.

To avoid problems, misunderstandings, and perhaps costly delays in the T/D process, students with handicaps or disabilities should discuss their special requirements openly and fully with their advisors early, before embarking on a project. Since many faculty members may still be unfamiliar with accommodations to such conditions, the student may have to do some "educating" in the preliminary discussions (C. D. Long, 1997b).

But, just "talking it over" with the advisor is not enough. The student should keep notes of discussions and of oral agreements. Further, in preparing the written proposal for the T/D, the student should include specifications as to how accommodations are to be made, if anticipated, at each stage of the T/D journey, including the final examination. Thus, when the committee signs off on the proposal, the student has, in writing, the commitment that impediments to progress arising from handicapping or disabling conditions will be minimized.

For up-to-date information on relevant laws and regulations, contact the U.S. Access Board in Washington, D.C. (1-800-872-2253) or use their excellent Web site (http://www.access-board.gov), a good source of information about access issues. In addition to its rules governing physical access in general, that board publishes rules regarding telecommunications access and Americans With Disabilities Act Accessibility Guidelines.

The Department of Special Education at the college or university where the student is enrolled is a resource for faculty who are expert in accommodations for all varieties of handicaps. They usually know the local situation well.

CHOOSING THE TOPIC FOR STUDY

Schools and departments differ widely in their acceptance of various substantive content and forms of investigation. For example, one might reject investigative approaches that do not involve controlled experimentation. Another might disqualify studies incorporating extrasensory perception or astrology. Another might welcome controlled experimentation equally with historical and qualitative research and works of biography or fiction. Students, therefore, will save much time in searching for potential topics if they first determine whether they face any restrictions on which types of research or investigative methodology the faculty may approve.

Aids to Thinking About Prospective Topics

Veteran advisors in our interviews seem to agree that students should have little, if any, difficulty in finding suitable topics. The main problem, they contend, is to pick the one best suited to the individual student's interests. New T/D students tend to disagree with veteran advisors on that matter. Many express bewilderment, anxiety, uncertainty, and lack of self-confidence. In short, they do not know how to get under way on a topic search, how to recognize a potentially good topic when they see it, or how to judge the worth of a topic when one is suggested to them (W. G. Bowen and Rudenstine, 1992; Zuber-Skerritt and Knight, 1986).

Use the computer and the Internet to help you think about potential topics. For example, consider reviewing Dissertation Abstracts Online (retrieved August 24, 2002, from http://library.dialog.com/bluesheets/html/bl0035.html). Dissertation Abstracts Online is a definitive subject, title, and author guide to virtually every American dissertation accepted at an accredited institution since 1861. Selected master's theses have been included since 1962. In addition, since 1988, the database has included citations for dissertations from 50 British universities. Beginning with Volume 29, Number 2 (Spring 1988), citations and abstracts from European dissertations have been included in this file.

The index to theses of Great Britain and Ireland (http://www.theses.com/) is a comprehensive listing of theses with abstracts accepted for higher degrees by universities in England and Ireland. This database covers theses accepted from 1970 to 2001.

Award-winning dissertations can be of use in developing a proposal. Typing "award-winning dissertations" in search engines such as Google will provide access to quite good information. To find the dissertations in your own discipline, check with your professional associations or academic societies.

Figure 3-2 is a checklist of sources to help identify potential topics. It can be valuable to use this checklist or to make a personal one as part of your file. The number of "no's" on the checklist can be an index to the thoroughness and seriousness of a student's search for possible T/D topics. One reason why veteran advisors feel that potential topics abound is because, as professors, they are routinely involved in most of the activities tapped by the checklist.

1. Have you ascertained if there is a publication on approved types of topics in your school or department? Yes______ No______
   If there is, have you secured and studied it? Yes______ No______
2. Have you talked with five or more students who are past the overview stage and learned how they found their topics? Yes______ No______
   Did you ask them about other topics related to theirs? Yes______ No______
3. Have you asked for permission to attend T/D defenses at your school for familiarization and topic ideas? Yes______ No______
4. Are there university-affiliated or private research agencies or groups in your region that conduct studies in your field and whose current activities you have explored? Yes______ No______
5. Are you attending local regular meetings or colloquia of professional groups in which you are interested? Yes______ No______
6. Have you examined the T/Ds in your field for the past five years on file at your school? Yes______ No______
   Have you talked directly about T/D ideas with the authors of at least five of them in which you have some interest? Yes______ No______
7. Have you compared and contrasted the scholarly and professional interests of your school's faculty with your own? Yes______ No______
8. Have you discussed T/D work in general with a faculty member with whom you feel comfortable and at ease? Yes______ No______
9. Have you reviewed library sources in print, as well as Web sites, for dissertation abstracts, on-line dissertation services, electronic theses and dissertations, and full-text electronic journals? Yes______ No______
10. Have you browsed through the publications and Web sites of professional and academic organizations that represent your own major and minor fields of study, looking for research needs suggested by authoritative figures or committees? Yes______ No______

Figure 3-2 Checklist of thesis or dissertation topic sources.

Collecting a List of Potential Topics

In the beginning of Chapter 1, suggestions were made about identifying topics that might allow the student to initiate a productive conference with a potential advisor. It was indicated that possible topics would surface from analysis of publications of that faculty member, publications of others writing in the same field, and T/Ds recently directed by that faculty member. Those topics, and any others the student has in mind, should be recorded. It is good to state a possible title for the topic first and then to write a sentence or two about what the study might entail. Examples appropriate to various professions and academic disciplines might be

Title: Emotional and Intellectual Characteristics of Early Readers

Procedure: Children who learn to read before starting kindergarten would be studied to learn their emotional and intellectual similarities and differences from one another and from children who learn to read in the conventional way.

Title: Communication Channels Used in Obtaining Corporate Information

Procedure: People inside and outside corporations need and acquire corporate information. The formal and informal channels they employ in acquiring needed information would be determined, described, and analyzed.

Title: The Emergence of Artificial Intelligence

Procedure: An analysis will be made of devices that simulate human thought processes, beginning with the earliest known ones. It is hypothesized that behaviors like memory and computation were simulated first and only later combined to produce more complex phenomena like problem solving, anticipation, and prediction. Primary data will be records of patents and actual devices in museums and collections.

Title: Shunning as a Social Control Mechanism

Procedure: The origin and usage of shunning in Judeo-Christian religious and secular groups will be found by reference to official and other verifiable documents. The employment and the consequences of shunning will be reported, and shunning will be assessed as to its effectiveness in the control of the social behaviors that prompted its use.

Title: The Behavior of Sound Waves in Earth's Upper Atmosphere

Procedure: Upper atmosphere conditions will be simulated in laboratory chambers. Sound will be emitted and recorded. The recordings will be contrasted with recordings of sound made under like conditions on earth's surface. The laboratory findings will also be compared with the findings predicted by a mathematical model based on theory.

Title: Cause of Pain in Osteoarthritis of the Knee

Procedure: It is hypothesized that the pain of osteoarthritis arises from cartilage wear rather than inflammation, as is now commonly held. The results of administering acetaminophen, a simple painkiller, will be compared with the results of administering the anti-inflammatory drug ibuprofen. The test population will be male and female volunteers aged 65 years and above, randomly assigned to treatment groups.

Title: Estimating Need and Demand for Emergency Transportation

Procedure: Three highly probable conditions of emergency will be simulated. Traffic engineers, police traffic control staff, and public transit management personnel will provide need estimates and their rationales for each simulation. These will be analyzed and a formula developed to maximize accuracy of estimate.

Title: Causes of Runaway Behavior in Children

Procedure: A sample of children who have histories of two or more runaway attempts will be studied to determine the antecedent conditions they connect with the decision to run away. Family, social welfare agency, and police recollections and records will be used as corroborative information

Title: Public Expenditure Patterns in the United States and Canada

Procedure: A comparative analysis will be made of expenditures in the two countries on items that account for major components of national, state and provincial budgets.

Title: The Influence of Awards to Poets on Trends in American Poetry in the 20th Century

Procedure: Determination will be made if and to what extent awards to poets are followed by changes in style or content by other poets.
Title: Cost Containment in Health Care in the United States
Procedure: Inauguration of containment plans will be followed by consequent cost-consequences analyses. Conclusions will be drawn as to trends and gains/losses.

Each of the above 11 examples falls far short of a research proposal. Rather, each notes an idea for possible development. However, a prospective research advisor almost certainly would talk more seriously with a student who presented such notes neatly typed than with one who presented the same material orally. Moreover, to put ideas into succinct written form usually results in one being better prepared to discuss them.

When one has assembled and recorded a group of likely topics, it is time for another major step, a careful examination of each one to determine its relative appropriateness in relation to the others. That will be a matter of judgment, of course, but it is possible to channel that judgment by raising a number of questions that highlight significant factors that deserve consideration. That is the purpose of the next sections.

Social Sensitivity Considerations

Socially sensitive research has an aim, a topic, methods or procedures, subject treatment, conclusions, or reporting considered by one or more groups to be illegal, insulting, indecent, immoral, or unethical. Sieber and Stanley (1988) present a basic and cogent analysis of the concept.

Research qualifying as "socially sensitive" includes, for example, studies that challenge beliefs; expose personal or group-held secrets; invade privacy; question or defy authority; arouse negative emotions; violate religious principles; go against established practices; disregard laws; ignore civil rights; do physical, emotional, or material harm to subjects or to institutions; deceive, ridicule, disparage, or coerce subjects; falsify or hide research objectives or methods; encourage immoral or unlawful behavior; put individuals unknowingly at risk; or distort or falsify data, conclusions, or reports with regard to any of the above. This litany is illustrative only because what may matter little to one person may seem gravely insulting or demeaning to another.

Certainly, social sensitivity should not prevent or even inhibit really necessary and ethically sound research. We do suggest, though, that topics that promise to be socially sensitive be approached most cautiously by T/D students. For one thing, work on such matters often calls for experience and wisdom in research management that students are only beginning to acquire. Moreover, it is difficult enough to conduct a T/D for a topic that is inoffensive without adding the burden of handling the investigation and its defense under a cloud of real or potential social disapproval.

Assessing Topic Feasibility and Practicability

Using the next checklist (Fig. 3-3) can save time and help narrow a group of potential topics to a few that merit more thorough consideration. The list starts with general questions and then breaks into six subsections that are applicable to topics that call for different investigative approaches. It pays to read all of the questions in each subsection because the questions themselves sometimes trigger important ideas.

As a special note, one should not be put off or overwhelmed by these questions. Some of them are tough, and some may seem at first to pose insurmountable obstacles. But, there is help in the rest of the chapter, in following chapters, and from advisors. It is rare that any topic comes through this checklist unscathed entirely at first. It is in the follow-up repair work and polishing that a topic begins to assume acceptable, workable form.)

The most important thing about the checklist's 42 questions is their power to alert one, to force one to think in specific, detailed ways while considering T/D topics.

FOREIGN STUDENTS IN T/D STUDY

According to the Institute of International Education's *Open Doors* (T. Davis, 2001), in 1954–1955 there were 34,000 students from overseas in the United States. They constituted 1.4% of U.S. enrollment. By the 2000–2001 academic year, that number had increased more

A. Questions about the topic in general

1. Is there current interest in this topic in your field? In a closely related field?
2. Is there a gap in knowledge that work on this topic could help to fill? A controversy it might help to resolve?
3. Is it possible to focus on a small enough segment of the topic to make a manageable T/D project?
4. Can you envision a way to study the topic that will allow conclusions to be drawn with substantial objectivity? Is the data collection approach (i.e., test, meta-analysis, archive study, questionnaire, interview) acceptable in your school?
5. Is there a body of literature available relevant to the topic? Is it accessible by computer, and is a search of it manageable?
6. Are there large problems (i.e., logistic, attitudinal) to be surmounted in working on this topic? Do you have the means to handle them?
7. Does the topic relate reasonably well to others done in your school? If not, have you information about its acceptability?
8. Would financial assistance be required? Is it available?
9. Are the needed data easily accessible? Will you have control of the data?
10. Do you have a clear statement of the purpose, scope, objectives, procedures, and limitations of the study? A tentative table of contents for the report? Are any of the skills called on by the study ones that you have yet to acquire?

B. Questions for topics employing a research question or hypothesis

1. Do you have acceptable statements of research questions or hypotheses?
2. Can you specify how you will answer the questions or test the hypotheses?
3. Would the T/D be a contribution if the findings do not support the hypothesis or fail to answer the questions?
4. Have subsidiary questions or hypotheses been identified that deserve study along with the major ones?
5. Are the alternative questions or hypotheses that might explain the findings anticipated?

C. Questions for topics requiring interviews for data collection

1. What style or type of interview is best suited to the objectives of the study?
2. Does an interview protocol exist that fits the purposes of the investigation? Has it been pilot-tested?
3. How will the data be recorded and collated for optimum speed, accuracy, and reliability? Can the computer be used for this?

Figure 3-3 Checklist of topic feasibility and appropriateness.

4. How will matters of confidentiality and permissions be handled?
5. How will bias in the interviewer and the respondent be minimized or measured?

D. *Questions for topics using a questionnaire approach*
1. What forms of questionnaire will be most productive for this kind of study? Has it been pretested?
2. How will questionnaire items relate specifically to the purposes of the investigation?
3. Why is the questionnaire the tool of choice for data collection? Can it be computerized?
4. How will it be assured that the questionnaires will be answered?
5. How will the questionnaire responses be validated? Analyzed?

E. *Questions for topics involving mathematical analysis of data*
1. What quantitative analyses are planned? What will they produce?
2. Are the quantitative analyses appropriate to the kinds of data collected?
3. What level of confidence will be accepted as significant? Why?
4. Are there computer programs that will save time, energy, and money? Are they available?
5. What rational and subjective interpretations will need to be given to the statistical findings to make them meaningful?

F. *Questions for topics making use of existing data from other sources*
1. Are the data relevant? Reliable and valid? Complete?
2. Are there limitations on the present or future availability or utilization of the data? Can data be accessed by computer?
3. Why is it better to use these data than to collect one's own afresh?
4. Will additional data need to be collected? What and why?
5. What obligations to the other sources go along with publication based on these data? Who will own the data?

G. *Questions for topics involving tests and testing in data gathering*
1. Are the tests the most valid and reliable obtainable?
2. Do the tests discriminate against significant groups in the sample?
3. Do the tests provide direct measures of the key variables in the study?
4. How will confidentiality be preserved?
5. What interpretations will be needed to make the test results meaningful in relation to the purpose of the investigation?
6. Are the tests physically or psychologically invasive?
7. Can the tests be administered, scored, and results arrayed, tabled, and analyzed by computer?

Figure 3-3 Continued

than 15-fold to about 547,867 students from overseas. Thus, foreign students make up not only an important segment of higher education in the United States, but also a growing segment as well.

Also, foreign students are critically important to the graduate level, especially some advanced fields such as the physical and natural sciences, business administration, engineering, and computer sciences. Total percentage of doctoral degrees conferred to foreign students was 26.7% in 1994. As the number of U.S. citizens earning science and engineering doctorates has been declining, their places have been taken by foreign students (Atkinson, 1990; NCES, 1997). Foreign students with temporary visas earned 33.5% of all physical science Ph.D.'s and 53.3% of the engineering doctorates in 1994.

In some large research universities, foreign students actually outnumber domestic students in doctoral programs such as business and engineering. If the trend continues, it may be that the majority of faculty members in these areas will be foreign nationals or immigrants since faculty members are prepared in doctoral programs. For example, in 1985, two-thirds of all postdoctorate engineering positions went to non-U.S. citizens (Pool, 1990).

The foreign/domestic ratio of students is not peculiar to the United States. A large proportion of European doctoral degrees go to foreign students (Johnson, 1996). Approximately half of the engineering doctoral degrees awarded in the United Kingdom are earned by foreign nationals. More than a third of doctorates in the natural sciences given in France go to citizens of other countries. In these cases, though, the large segment of foreigners is probably in part attributable to the tradition begun in the days of colonial territories.

Problems Encountered by Foreign Students

Zuber-Skerritt and Ryan (1999) provide important insights into the lives of non-English-speaking graduate students and suggest valuable strategies and practical guidance for individual advisors. Understanding students' lives in the university as well as cultural and academic backgrounds is a prerequisite for successful supervising.

Two difficulties foreign students often encounter are topic relevance and writing. The first arises when students know what problems need solutions in their own countries, but find few professors who understand the problems or think them suitable for investigation. The second, writing, appears as a problem if students have not acquired the specialized composition skills needed to phrase thoughts in the combination of professional and academic prose common to T/Ds in English-speaking countries (CGS, 1991a).

Our best advice about the topic problem is for the student to persist in the search for an advisor who will listen with sympathy and understanding. The student should look for departments and schools that have "International," "Inter-," "Cross-Cultural," "Ethnic," "Pan-American," "Asian," "Middle Eastern," or similar expressions that smack of interests that cross national boundaries in their names. It is appropriate to seek those out, even though they may be outside the school or department in which the student is enrolled. Very often, professors in schools or departments with multinational interests also have appointments in other academic departments or professional schools or know professors there who would be good advisors for foreign students interested in problems that relate to their homelands. Other foreign students and lists of recently completed T/Ds can give clues, too.

With regard to the writing problem, there are three possible solutions. The first is to write in one's native language and to have an advisor and committee members who can read it or employ a professional translator for those who cannot. A second solution is to take instruction in English academic and professional writing. Such courses are offered at a number of universities. A third possibility is to engage the services of an editor. Inquiries among professors and students will sometimes reveal that there are faculty members who provide editorial services for students for a fee. This can be a delicate arrangement, but we have seen it work very effectively. The editor must be someone not otherwise connected with the student's course of study and T/D work. Also, the advisor and committee must know of and sanction the use of editorial help, and the assistance must be carefully provided so that it deals only with organization, style, composition, written expression, and the proper use of language, strictly avoiding any substantive or methodological elements.

If editorial service is to be employed or otherwise provided to the student, it is strongly urged that the arrangement be spelled out in writing, with copies to all relevant parties. At least one copy of the agreed-on arrangement should be initialed or signed by the student, the advisor, the committee members, and the appropriate department chairperson or dean. That copy should be kept on file in the graduate office. Also, it is definitely advisable that the editor employed has a clear knowledge of the terms of the agreement and be acceptable to the advisor and the department chairperson or dean.

PERSONAL CRITERIA FOR STUDENT USE

Without paying attention to the following criteria, the student is likely to make many false starts. Notice that the criteria expand on the ideas in Fig. 3-2.

The Interest of the Researcher

Personal interest is very important, but the completion of a T/D may well involve some very uninteresting work. For example, if a T/D involves statistical analyses, the tables to display the findings may represent hours of tedious work. Moreover, personal interest can engender bias and limit objectivity. On the other hand, some students report that a topic that was "just a topic" at first grew in interest as it moved along the T/D path (Isaac et al., 1989).

The Background of the Researcher

To start with an unfamiliar topic is unwise and disadvantageous. Topics close to one's prior preparation and experience offer better possibilities for success.

Students who propose topics outside the scope of their training or experience must spend a great deal of time becoming familiar with a new field. It is unlikely that such a beginning will ever result in the broad background really needed to do the study well. More likely, lack of a broader understanding of the subject will lead to mistakes in the conduct or in the interpretation of the research.

The Technical Competence of the Researcher

The student should have technical competence related to the topic. For example, the level of competence a student researcher has in research tools should be influential in choosing a topic. Some topics by their nature call for complex statistical analyses. Others may demand sophisticated archival or library search procedures, complex interview techniques, use of advanced computer programs, or facility with foreign languages. Choice of topic and design should be guided by consideration of the skills possessed versus the skills required.

It is not enough simply to follow a recipe without really understanding it. For example, there are computer packages that offer complete, complex statistical analyses, and they can be great time savers. But, the use of such a package does not excuse the researcher from responsibility for understanding fully the techniques employed. A guideline recommended by Gay (1996) is that one should not use the computer to perform an analysis that is not understood, or at least studied extensively. The same writer encourages aspiring researchers to become proficient in using some of the more sophisticated handheld calculators that allow one to enter one or two sets of data and, by using the appropriate keys, to have the results of a desired analysis displayed. Similarly, any other technology essential to the research should be thoroughly understood before use.

Importance of the Topic

Check your perceptions of topic importance with others you respect, such as colleagues, your advisor, other faculty members, administrators, and other investigators. If most others see the topic as important, it probably is. But, also use some other tests. When you are finished with the T/D, will anyone read it? Could it be published? Does it address an issue of topical interest? How will it affect the academic field or profession? Questions like these lead to answers also useful for the written introduction to your proposal for they will help to give readers a background and a context with which to judge the worth of the topic (Association of American Universities [AAU], 1990; W. G. Bowen and Rudenstine, 1992; Isaac et al., 1989).

One element of particular importance is generalizability, that is, whether it is likely that the findings of the investigation can be applied to other situations. A study that would not generalize would be one done on a population and under conditions so unusual that one could not expect the same results in many other situations.

Appropriate Size and Scope

Topics should be limited to those possible and feasible for one person to do within the expected time period. The honors thesis should fit into the last 1 or 2 years of undergraduate study, along with courses and seminars. A master's thesis, if pursued along with the other requirements for the degree, requires 3 to 6 months. Ordinarily, one completes the dissertation in several years if working full time on it. Some do take longer, but universities usually invoke a time limit of 4 to 6 years.

USING LIBRARIES AND OTHER INFORMATION SOURCES

This is a period of information power. From note taking to literature searching and from data collection to data analysis, automation technology now accelerates research while encouraging both more comprehensiveness and more precision in the T/D enterprise.

Central Role of the Librarian and the Library

Because of technological advances, public and campus libraries have more material available than ever before. A library is still a *place*, to be sure, but it now has the capability to provide the user with the resources of many other libraries in addition to its own. Moreover, the user has access to that vastly enlarged store of material with almost incredible ease and speed (King, 2000; Rice, 1989; Sherman, 1999).

For example, UMI's *Digital Dissertation* contains citations and abstracts of 1.5 million dissertations and theses. The database includes theses and dissertations from the first U.S. dissertation (1861) to the most recent. Those published from 1980 include an author-written abstract and are available free to university academic libraries (e.g., the University of Pittsburgh, www.library.pitt.edu). For most dissertations, beginning in 1995, full-text dissertations are available in PDF (portable document format) computer file format. Search screens lead to advanced search strategies. Each record can be searched by author, key word, and title (for example, a title search will examine all dissertations that have a selected word in them, such as *feminism*). Terms can be combined to create a new search using Boolean operators.

Once you find useful information, you can print the abstract, download the complete document in some cases, and in other cases print a 24-page preview of the dissertation. You can also mark the citation list of dissertations for later printing, downloading, or sending an E-mail.

Similarly, there are databases of E-books in academic libraries. Again, using the University of Pittsburgh library system as an example, the system offers Web access to thousands of E-books through *netLibrary*, a virtual lending library accessible through the Internet. These E-books are published references books, textbooks, and monographs that have been converted into digital form. They can be searched as you would search any other materials in the library on-line catalog.

Successful students learn quickly how to use help from librarians and how to use their own computers independently and to operate from distant workstations to make the most of library resources. Here are the most important guidelines:

1. Ask for information and help. Inquire about on-line or compact disk databases related to the topic(s) of interest to you and find out how you can access them, *independently*, if possible. As an example, find out if FirstSearch can be made available to you since it has many databases, is adding to them, is relatively inexpensive, and is considered to be user friendly. There are other good ones, too.
2. Become *fully* acquainted with the library and the roles of the various librarians, many of whom are specialists. If you wish, they will assist you in learning to maximize your skill in using catalogs and periodical indexes; they will advise you on search methodology; they will introduce you to the world of computer-assisted literature searching; and they will guide you to special collections. Also, librarians understand disabled student needs and services. These are but a few of the multifaceted capabilities of professional librarians, but they illustrate that they are powerful allies in the research process.
3. Most modern information technology can be utilized from home or office with a five-component microcomputer workstation: computer, keyboard, monitor, printer, and modem. Such a basic station allows one to capture and store the products of a search

session for personal use by downloading to your own disk. Subsequently, the references can be recast into any of the common bibliographic citation forms using commercially available programs (Rice, 1989). Several programs are available (for example, EndNote, Reference Manager, ProCite) to help you do the citations according to the reference guide you select. They also help with endnotes, reference notes, and the proper way of citing material in text. Trial versions of such programs are available at the ISI Researchsoft home page (http://www.isiresearchsoft.com/).

In summary, recognize each librarian as a highly qualified information specialist as well as a very valuable resource person with respect to the complex and involved operations of academic and professional libraries. Seek the aid of librarians on a one-to-one basis to further your skills. Remember that it is more important that your library affords you *access* to a source than that your library *owns* the source. And, become skilled at accessing your own campus library via computer because that skill can be readily leveraged into access to the other major library holdings of the nation.

Computer Search Services

The university reference librarian is an excellent initial contact. Be ready to say what your purpose is, what field you want to explore, and how you expect to use the information. There are powerful general search engines to help research a topic. Among the most common are AltaVista (http://www.altavista.com/), Lycos (http://www.lycos.com/), Google (http://www.google.com), and Dialog (http://www.dialog.com/). Libraries have access to hundreds of databases, and growth and technical improvement are very fast paced in library information storage and retrieval. Therefore, the student ought to stay in close consultation with reference librarians, the on-campus experts in how best to use the current and emerging tools.

Six Steps for the Student in Database Searches

In the section above on the role of the library and the librarian, we urged students to acquire key library skills and personal computer

(PC) competencies. Now, those capabilities must be extended and put to practical use (York et al., 1988).

1. To search a database efficiently, one must have a topic, or at least a topic area, in mind. To get ready, it is best to examine some current articles bearing on the topic area under consideration. List key words and phrases, as well as their synonyms, to describe each of the concepts in the topic. It might be helpful to consult an index or abstract thesaurus, such as the *Thesaurus of ERIC Descriptors* or the *Thesaurus of Psychological Index Terms*. A printed copy of the index or thesaurus will give you a good idea of the type of citations that will be retrieved using a particular term and the amount of literature available on the topic. If possible, list several citations from the indexes or abstracts to articles that are considered pertinent to the topic.

   Then, try to think of a title for a paper on the subject of your choice. See if you can get all of the main ideas about your topic into the title. An example might be "Government Policy Development and Implementation Respecting Brazilian Universities in the Past Decade." Since databases are queried by the presence of key words, singly or in combination, the words in the title thus concocted will probably include those you will use when specifying the kinds of documents you wish to retrieve. At this point, or earlier, we recommend seeking advice from a librarian trained in search strategies. Since databases can be programmed for retrieval by approaches other than key subject terms, the library specialist may be able to direct you to a more efficient or effective way to call up the information you wish to locate.
2. University research libraries, and thus the university community, have access to many databases. Some are available without cost to students and faculty because the research library paid the annual fee. Even if this is not so, often the vendor offers a free trial for your perusal. The home pages indicated below were retrieved on May 18, 2002.

   For example, the Center for Research Libraries (home page http://www.crl.uchicago.edu/) is a not-for-profit consortium of colleges and universities that make available scholarly research resources to faculty and students of the major research libraries of America. The collection includes over 5 million volumes of research material that is often unavailable in individual libraries.

ISI Web of Science (http://www.wos.isiglobalnet.com) offers citation reports, documents, proceedings, and news in the world of science. ISI Web of Knowledge (http://www.isinet.com/) offers citation products, such as *Social Science Citation Index*, specialized content, evaluation and analytical tools, information management tools, and document delivery. These are available to students for a fee, which may have been paid by the university library.

EBSCO http://www.epnet.com/) offers biographic and full-text databases designed to meet the research needs of academic, biomedical, governmental, and public libraries. It also is a good source for articles from magazines such as *Time* and *Newsweek.*

The Internet Public Library (http://www.ipl.org/) is an initiative of the University of Michigan School of Information. It offers on-line texts, Web searching, references, magazines and serials, and newspapers.

ERIC (http://www.eric.ed.gov), sponsored by the U.S. Department of Education, is a bibliographic database of education literature consisting of two files, *Resources in Education* and *Current Index to Journals in Education. Resources in Education* covers documents, consisting of research reports, curriculum and teaching guides, conference papers, and some books. *Current Index to Journals in Education* covers published journal literature from over 700 publications in the field of education.

LexisNexis (http://www.lexisnexis.com/) provides publications on line in the fields of law, public records, company data, government information, and information from academic and business organizations. It has a searchable directory of on-line sources.

H. W. Wilson (http://www.hwwilson.com/) offers an information retrieval system for the World Wide Web, including search tools to access records in science and technology, art, corporate data, and full-text article-form journals in the general sciences, social sciences, and humanities.

Another source of information is the multitude of mainframe list servers related to various fields. The research librarian is the best source of help in finding what you need. For example, there is a list directly related to higher education, with categories such as *academic*, *administrative*, and *student*. There are many listserv addresses in each category. A related subject listserv (http://www.gseis.ucla.edu/heri/journal.htm) lists journal articles using CIRP (Cooperative Institutional Research Program) data on college students. Such lists are often searched by research librarians and are made available to the university community through the library system's home page.

The home page of other organizations may also offer a great deal of information to the dissertation writer. For example, there is the Library of Congress home page (http://www.loc.gov/homepage/1chp.html), which provides access to legislative information, copyright forms and information, and the library catalog.

The examples above are but a small sample of what is available, and availability changes daily. New sites come on line periodically. The best policy is to ask your research librarian for help and to be specific about the thesis, honors paper, or dissertation topic you wish to research. In addition, it can be productive to search a topic yourself. There is no substitute for spending hours on your computer following leads, opening new searches, and trying new search engines to find information on your research topic.

Database searching often turns up more listings (hits) than you can handle. There is a danger that you will find yourself so interested in the many leads that you get distracted from the main show. It is better to discipline yourself to use that surplus to narrow the search in the most appropriate ways. If you examine carefully the nature of the hits you are getting, you can fine-tune your search strategy to narrow the range and focus on just the information you need for your research. The more you know about your research topic and the more focused you are, the better equipped you will be to narrow your search appropriately.

3. Decide how much of each retrieved document you want to receive and keep, either as a printout or a computer file. For the first trial

of the search, you may wish to look only at the bibliographic citations to judge whether to change your search terms or to combine them in different ways. Once satisfied that the search is retrieving the kinds of documents you need, you may then want to obtain abstracts of the references you have chosen as probably most relevant to your topic. A next step often is to select, from the abstracts, the documents that seem to be most relevant, ones you would consider primary sources. For those, you will need to have the full text.

4. Copies of the full text of books, documents, and articles may be obtained in a variety of ways if they are not shelved and circulated by your own library. Time and ready reference are usually quite important to student researchers, so you may want to own personal copies of the primary source materials you will be studying, quoting, and discussing with your committee members. If a book or monograph is in print, the university bookstore can usually obtain a copy. Before you buy, however, check with the research librarian. Increasingly, libraries are sharing information in hard copy or on the Internet. Often, print materials such as books and journals are available through interlibrary loan or other borrowing processes that will bring you the material on a timely basis. Just one example is the Center for Research Libraries, an international not-for-profit organization of colleges, universities, and libraries that makes available scholarly research to users such as graduate students and faculty. Some database services, such as ERIC, also provide not only bibliographic resource information, but also journal articles, books, conference papers, research reports, and so on in the field of education. Similar databases exist in other academic or professional disciplines. The research librarian is an invaluable help in finding the sources of information you need.
5. Try starting with search strategies that focus on subjects in your academic program area and the research area of interest to you and to potential advisors. The research librarian can be of great help here, of course, but some suggestions for a start, depending on the discipline, might be the *Academic Search Elite*, *MLA International Bibliography*, *Public Affairs International*, *Science Citation Index*, *Social Science Citation Index*, and so forth. These may be accessible through the library system. From this information,

you can get an idea of who are the important authors and researchers, their areas of expertise, and the quality of the work. Another indication of the quality of the work of authors is how often they are cited by peers, and many of the databases, such as those indicated above, will give you that information. All this information is available in your research library and, in many cases, on your home computer through access to the library's home page.

There are specialized search engines for many different categories, such as health and medical information, multimedia information, and legal searches. The work of King (2000) is a helpful source (http://www.onlineinc.com/onlinemag/OL2000/king5.html). There are even a number of sites that can be used to find specialized search engines, a sort of search engine for search engines. One list (http://www.searchenginewatch.com/links/) links the viewer to major search engines including children's search engines; metacrawlers; multimedia, news, and specialty engines; these are divided into subject areas. Another is SearchEngineGuide.Com (http://www.searchengineguide.com/), which lists thousands of search engines, each listed in a subject directory. Each entry provides a brief summary. Finally, there is a Web site devoted to finding information on the invisible Web (http://www.invisableweb.com/). The invisible Web contains searchable information resources with contents that cannot be indexed by traditional search engines. Many search engines fall into the invisible category because their index of links is stored in databases rather than on Web pages. The sites mentioned in this paragraph were retrieved on May 19, 2002.

6. Keep in mind that no computer search will be complete. Many commonly used databases only reach the mid-1960s. Also, there may be a lag from publication to insertion in a database. No matter how well descriptors are selected, significant publications may slip through the net. Moreover, not all journals and other publications are referenced in ways amenable to computer searches.

Despite these drawbacks, this search approach is a major time saver for what it does do. The routine clerical jobs involved are accomplished rapidly and accurately; it is almost incredibly quicker and more efficient than hand-done card index and journal directory work.

When building the reading list, explore the possibility that published bibliographies on the topic may already exist. Ask the librarian about *Bibliographic Index* and other publications used to discover such lists. On-line bibliographic searches will yield useful information. Some are free, but many valuable searches require a fee. Before paying a fee, check with your research librarians at the university; they may already subscribe to the service, which is then available for the use of the whole institution. Examples of excellent services that require a fee are Dialog (http://www.dialog.com/) and LexisNexis (http://www.lexisnexis.com/). If you can afford it, these services may well be worth the money for they provide access to full-text, up-to-date specialized bibliographic databases that may be unavailable on line anywhere else. In evaluating the cost of the service, consider the time and energy, as well as the hidden costs, that the service may save you. A careful cost analysis may lead to the decision that the service is worth it. Research libraries also subscribe to CD-ROMs (compact disks–read-only memory), which may be very helpful in bibliographic searches. Again, the librarian is the person to ask for expert advice.

A fortunate researcher may come upon an author whose work is particularly useful. In that case, one can use bibliographic citations to explore the works on which this author drew as well as works that derive from those of the author. To move backward in time, explore the citations in the author's bibliography. To work forward, ask the librarian about the possibility that your author's work may appear in a citation index. Doing this not only increases the chances of encountering especially relevant studies, but also familiarizes the student with the names of scholars and institutions working in that area of interest.

Book reviews are also useful to researchers. They tell you whether the book is thought to be important enough to review. Often, the reviewer, especially in professional journals, is a respected peer and thus is a person eminently competent to review the book. Even in more general periodicals, the editors try to get authorities to review books. In addition to its importance, the review can tell you whether the book is well regarded, and it can also tell you whether the book is likely to be relevant to your research. Book reviews are an excellent way to bring yourself up to date on the research in your area of interest and to lead you to important names and concepts.

Your research librarian can be a great help in locating book reviews in your research area, and your university research library may subscribe to a number of sources. Some examples are *Book Review Digest*, *Book Review Index*, *Political Science Reviewer*, *Social Science Index*, *Reviews in Anthropology*, *Current Book Review Citations*, *Index to Book Reviews in the Humanities*, and *Humanities Index*. Your library may have its own search system that will lead you to the periodical indexes, then to the subject area, and finally to book reviews. Usually, university research libraries have home page indexes, which will lead to book reviews, and in some cases to full-text reviews.

To summarize, your computer can be a very useful tool in carrying out a literature search, but it will do only what you tell it to do. It will not think for you.

Published Suggestions for Research Topics

A number of academic and professional groups publish annual reviews of research. Recently, also, the interest in *direct publication* of books and periodicals via electronic networks has led to testing the practicality of the idea. For example, the journal *Catalyst* is now available on the net (http://scholar.lib.vt.edu/ejournals/CATALYST/catalyst.html). This journal's emphasis is on continuing education through two-year colleges, so researchers with that interest can read or copy the most recent articles in the journal from their own computer screens. In many cases, sets of electronic journals are made available to research libraries and are made available to users through the libraries' home page. For example, university research libraries may have full-text electronic access to all Wiley Interscience journal titles. Another example is the Cambridge University Press list of journals. *Academic Search Elite*, a multisubject index to over 3000 magazines, may also be available on your university library system home page.

It will pay to inquire of your own library staff about such direct access to books and periodicals relevant to your research topic. These typically contain recommendations about needed studies. Such published suggestions may be of help in selecting research topics. It should be understood, however, that some will be outside the interest and capabilities of the student because they call for special equipment, access to subjects, investigation of competence areas, and special staff and funds beyond those the student researcher can provide. Often, however, the student's professor or department chairperson will be able to suggest portions of those topics that need to be researched and that are within the student's reach. Such suggestions are especially valuable because they imply an interest in the topic by the faculty.

Journals in hard copy or CD-ROM are also excellent sources to search. If you are partial to a particular subject, reading the latest issues of journals in that field can stimulate interesting research possibilities. The problem will be to focus on a few feasible topics from among the interesting things one might do. Many journals can be searched electronically using electronic journal aggregators and services. Such services can usually be found on the home page of the libraries of research universities. For example, the University of Pittsburgh library system home page (http://www.library.pitt.edu/) lists more than 20 aggregators and services. One of them is the Johns Hopkins University library home page (http://www.muse.jhu.edu/), which provides access to hundreds of journals in the social sciences, mathematics, and humanities from a number of distinguished university presses, including Johns Hopkins, the Massachusetts Institute of Technology, and Oxford.

The process you have under way toward selecting a topic can be illustrated in the following sequence of moves:

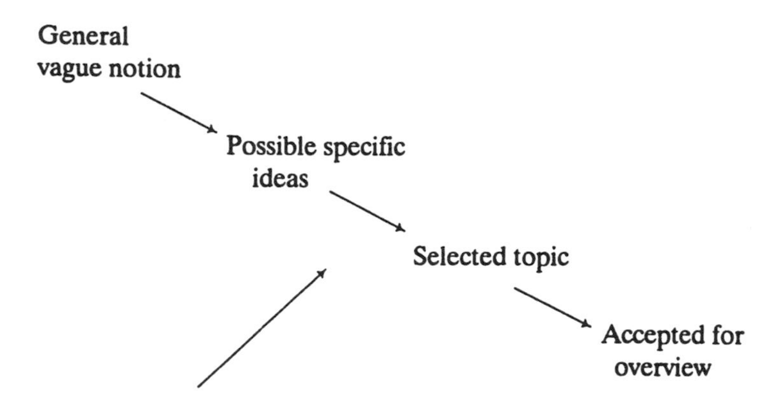

Internet Research Sources

There are many sites that can help your editing task, such as checking references against the text and putting your T/D into American Psychological Association (APA) style. There are even sites that help you more than by providing simple editing. Inputting *dissertation writing* into a search engine (e.g., Overture) or inputting *writing your dissertation* into the Google search will lead to sites that will help in getting started, in organization, in language clarity (if English is your second language), in statistics and data analysis, and in publishing your research. Some sites offer free service, some university sites are available only to registered users, and other sites collect a fee. Examples of some specific sites (retrieved September 25, 2002) are as follows:

1. The doctoral-dissertations.com (http://www.doctoral-dissertations.com) site helps with editing, checking references against the text, putting your study into APA style, and preparing for your oral defense.
2. A site for dissertation writing assistance (http://www.dissertationadvisors.com) provides rewriting, editing, statistical analysis, and other assistance for students in the thesis and dissertation writing process.
3. Advice on research and writing from Carnegie Mellon University, School of Computer Science is provided at http://www-2.cs.cmu.edu/afs/cs.cmu.edu/user/mleone/web/how-to.html. This site is a collection of advice about how to do research and how to communicate effectively (primarily for computer scientists). It has advice on writing and publishing and how to organize your thesis, advice to authors of extended abstracts, hints on good writing, and advice on submitting papers and getting them accepted. There are leads to a number of other very helpful sites.
4. UMI's dissertation services provide a wealth of information to help in preparing the proposal (http://www.il.proquest.com/hp/Support/DServices/prepare/).
5. The Dissertation Doctor (http://www.dissertationdoctor.com/) provides assistance in getting started on your dissertation or thesis, managing advisory relationships, preparing your proposal, boosting productivity, staying focused, troubleshooting, and surviving catastrophes.
6. Dissertation hints from Napier University Business School in-

clude an outline and guide to writing each chapter (http://www.bim.napier.ac.uk/~hazel/diss/diss_write.htm).

7. The doctoralstudents.com (http://www.doctoralstudents.com/) site was created to support research in general and doctoral students specifically. By joining this on-line global community, members are put in contact with other students conducting similar research and have access to useful research links.
8. The Elfin Forest Software Group thesis writer (http://www.elfin.com/home.htm) site provides a package to assist in the writing and preparation of a thesis or dissertation. It includes leads to Thesis Dissertation Writer (version 1.2), which guides you through every step of your thesis, contains a paragraph-by-paragraph content guide, answers all your "What do I write?" questions, gives numerous examples to clarify concepts, and works with stencils that you type over. It has a point-and-click easy-to-use format. This site also leads to APA Reference Writer, with a point-and-click easy-to-use format, and MLA Referencing Software referencing guide, with point-and-click easy-to-use format. Also available is a Point and Click Statistical Package (version 1.0), with easy-to-use point-and-click format, input data from the keyboard or from a data file, and output to a screen, printer, or file.

SUMMARY

Suggestions of research topics are provided, along with checklists to help bring ideas into focus. We offer sample suggestions to illustrate that students will find that each field of study can be reviewed for the research done as well as the research that may need to be done. In some specialized narrow fields, one may not find a source entitled "Needed Research in . . . ," but the needs of the field can be conceptualized by reviewing the research that has been done and then identifying logical next steps. Research is never ending; it usually raises as many questions as it attempts to answer and raises them in the very process of attempting to find answers. That is why almost every report of research contains the seeds of future investigations. Professors who are familiar with the research in their field are, without a doubt, the best sources for ideas about the research that yet needs to be done.

4

Preparation of the Proposal

QUICK REFERENCE TO ANSWERS TO SPECIFIC QUESTIONS

GETTING STARTED

Write Answers to Questions

Moving the proposal* out of your head and into written form can be done in stages. The very first stage can be quite informal (Locke et al., 2000).

One way that works for a lot of students is to write a few short sentences about each of the seven questions below. (Change the order, if you wish, and add other points if you think they are important.) The

*The proposal is sometimes called an overview or a concept paper. Operationally, the terms seem to mean the same.

critical thing is to check your place on your time line and to start to write answers to the following questions no matter how dissatisfying the first draft.

1. What is the tentative title? What do you call what you want to do? What is its name?
2. Why do you want to do it? What will you know or be able to do or say when you are through? (At this stage, an involved theoretical justification is unnecessary.)
3. To accomplish what you want to do, what steps will you have to take? Can you put the steps in sequential order? What facilities will you need? Why?
4. What kinds of help do you think you will need to do what you want to do? When? How might you get that help?
5. Will the project involve people other than yourself? How? To do what? For how long? Will you need any special permissions?
6. What actually goes on if you start to do what you propose? How would it start? What would a typical day be like at the beginning? When you are partway through? At the end?
7. How do you think you could show whether you accomplish what you set out to do? How could you prove it to someone else?

After writing "first draft" answers to these questions, put the document aside for a day or two in your "Proposal Notes" file. Then, come back and reread it. Make whatever amendments you think it needs for increased clarity.

Computer Help in Preparing Proposal

Take the time to enter and save on your computer what you have in mind, even though it may be a rough draft. Be sure spelling and punctuation are correct. Learn to use spelling checks and grammatical helps from computer software. An outline program, such as that of Microsoft Word, helps one to think in orderly and deductive sequence. Double space your work, with wide margins. Set the program to put your name and date on each sheet. Make at least three copies: one for your file, one to hand to your advisor, and one for you to use while talking with your advisor. Save your work in a computer file.

Why so much detailed emphasis on this point? It is essential to set the stage so there is nothing to distract the advisor's attention from the content of what you have written. A businesslike beginning by the student encourages any advisor to try very hard to be helpful. Of course, it is the advisor's obligation to assist the student in any event. But, a clearly prepared and error-free statement, even one that needs much more substantive work, will help the advisor to feel that guidance will be taken seriously by the student.

Moreover, this is often the crucial first step in the student's own filing and record keeping. It should set a model for a continuing pattern of neatness and orderliness. Many students have told us that partway through the T/D process they discovered that sloppy note taking and careless storage made information retrieval an all but impossible task. Early attention to details will sharply reduce the chances of losses and misplacements. Thus, the first stage in writing the proposal is one that can be quite informal as to style, but it is one that should be very deliberately organized to introduce a businesslike tone into both the initial conference with the advisor and the records of the student. Develop a regular system to save and file all work on the word processor or computer in a T/D directory, always properly cited in the form to be used eventually in the final document (e.g., APA, MLA). Endnotes, footnotes, and citation systems can immeasurably help store and later find notes and their citations.

There are Web sites that will help you in thinking about selecting your topic. One is filamentality (www.kn.pacbell.com). Filamentality helps you in selecting a topic by providing Web searching tips. It lets you "fill in the blanks" to gather good Web sites and guides you with interactive pages that help you shape your ideas around your goals.

Dissertations Abstracts (http://www.dissertation-abstracts.com/) is a guide to abstracts on all dissertation topics on line; it includes thesis help and free consultation. This guide was prepared to help graduate students in preparing theses and dissertations.

Use University Guidelines and Regulations

Even though we encourage informality in first drafts, we also suggest that familiarity with formal guides and requirements for the T/D will pay dividends for the student. Problems are less likely to occur if guidelines on procedural and editorial matters are studied at the outset by the student and the advisor together. Such joint study ought to be done in a spirit of understanding. Clarifying the rationale for each of the guidelines and determining how they can be most helpful to the student, while they also serve the broader purposes of improving communication among the professions and other scholarly groups, is the goal.

Figure 4-1 contains an alphabetized list of topics about which universities often have specific regulations pertaining to T/D procedures and format. We urge students to use Fig. 4-1 as a checklist while developing the T/D first draft and, as needed, later. If, for instance, you think you may need to include a drawing in your manuscript, if you may need to preserve the confidentiality of certain data, or if you have questions about any other of the 87 items in the figure, it is best to ascertain the facts early. Your advisor, your department chairperson or executive officer, your dean's office, and the graduate office of your university are the places to go for details about any of the checklist items.

Many professors believe a useful approach is for the student to become familiar with the contents of the university procedural guide at the same time that the T/D problem is being conceptualized. Following that, frequent reference to the university manual can help the student organize notes and rough drafts so that minimal time is lost in moving toward an acceptable final manuscript.

Use of Style Manuals

Faculty members and students need style manuals. The former use them to quickly refresh their memories about questions, to look up recommendations about new problems in writing as they arise, and to monitor, generally, the consistency of their own writing. Frequently, faculty members write for more than one colleague audience; the accepted styles of the two may vary. For instance, the American Educational Research Association, the American Institute of Physics, the American Psychological Association, and the Social Work Yearbook all have somewhat different styles prescribed.

Some style guides associated with academic disciplines are available on line. For example, the home page of the American Institute of Physics (www.aip.org) leads you to their *Style Manual*, avail-

Abbreviations, symbols, and nomenclature
Abstract
Acknowledgments
Ann Arbor, Michigan, services and depository
Appeal procedure for variation from regulations
Appendices
Artwork mounting

Binding

Changes and corrections
Checklist of final clearance requirements
Citation systems
Citing Internet information
Classified materials
Committee size and composition
Computer searches
Computer programs appropriate to the T/D
Confidential documents and other material
Copies required
Copyright
Copyrighted material; quotations and other uses

Database searches
Dean's responsibility
Definitions of terms
Department chairperson's responsibility
Differentiation of university, school, and department requirements

Editorial consultation or assistance
Endnotes
Enrollment at time of T/D defense
Exceptions to the written T/D

Faculty responsibility
Final copy (deposit copy)
Footnotes
Foreign language use
Format consistency
Forms requiring signatures

Figure 4-1 Administrative and technical matters included in thesis and dissertation regulations.

Grades for T/D

Illustration captions
Illustrations (including foldouts)
Instructions for nonfilmable material and color

Line drawings
Local style regulations

Major divisions of T/D
Manuscript reproduction or duplication
Margins
Microfiche
Microfilming
Model overviews (proposals, prospectuses)
Multiple authorship
Music scores

Optional forms of T/D report to university
Order of contents
Overview, submission and approval of
Ownership of T/D (literary rights)

Paper specifications
Personal copies
Photographs
Placement of nontext materials
Previously circulated, published, or publishable material
Proofreading responsibilities
Publication rights

References and bibliographies
Residency requirements

Sample committee approval form
Sample title pages
Selecting a title
Separate volumes (long papers; multivolume)
Software programs
Spacing
Special fees and dates for payment
Statistical packages
Student responsibility

Figure 4-1 Continued

Style manuals suggested
Style manual troubleshooter's checklist and supplements
Subdivisions of major divisions
Survey of earned doctorate's report

Table of contents (sample)
Tables and figures
Time limits and schedules for submission
Typewriters
Typing contracts
Typing services

University copies
Use of reprints of student or major professor
Using the work of others

Vita (biographical sketch)

Word processor formats and programs
Working with the committee

Figure 4-1 Continued

able on line. Graduate students should become familiar with the accepted style manual in their discipline and use it from the day of admission to the day of graduation. Knowing the style system for citations in scholarly papers will save a great deal of time in graduate school as well as later in professional life. The APA style manual, commonly used in the social and behavioral sciences, is another example of a style system for which there is on-line information and help. The home page (http://www.apa.org) will lead writers to help in understanding and using APA style in writing papers and articles. There is also help (APA, 1999, 2001) on how to format references, citations, headings, statistics, tables, and Internet document citations. An excellent text to help new writers is *Mastering APA Style: Student's Workbook and Training Guide* (Gelfand and Walker, 2001).

The most commonly used style manuals are listed in this book's reference list. Each faculty member and student should inquire about the school's style requirements and abide by them. Foreign students, still developing skill in scientific and professional English writing, often need to be attentive to the characteristics of T/D prose (Gibaldi and Achtert, 1999; Land, 2001, Turabian, 1996).

Style manuals do not necessarily help improve writing skills or be logical and clear in thinking and writing. There are books published to do this, and some are quite readable and useful (Evans and Evans, 1957; Fowler, 1965; Gelfand and Walker, 2001; Newman, 1980; Strunk and White, 1979; Zinsser, 2001). Once adequate general writing skill is attained, however, the style manual, if used thoughtfully, can be a material aid to producing high-quality prose in a form acceptable for professional publications.

OUTLINING THE PROPOSAL

In developing the proposal, you can use the Internet to find examples of outlines that may help you think through in an orderly fashion the contents of a dissertation or thesis proposal. A simple way to find outline help is to enter terms such as *outline* (*outlining*) or *outlining skills* into search engines (e.g., www.google.com) and find a site like ActionOutline (www.greenparrots.com). This is software that lets you organize your bits of information in a tree outline form. This software is for sale, but there is a free trial download that may help you construct a useful outline.

Many universities and colleges maintain Web sites that have outline samples and assist in imparting outlining skills and guides to grammar and writing. For example, Capital Community College has a site that helps (webster.commnet.edu), as does the Purdue University Online Writing Lab (http://owl.english.purdue.edu). This site has sample outlines; information about writing research papers; search engines; search helps; help with grammar, spelling, and punctuation; reference materials and resources; and professional writing aid.

Format of the Presentation

Some advisors recommend that the student prepare only a two- or three-page prospectus to take to the committee for approval. Others go much further, requiring not only a detailed research plan, but also a summary of preliminary research results. Many schools and departments have, in recent years, printed information on proposal requirements in a *Bulletin on Master's and Doctoral Study* or something similar. Also, ask your advisor to let you read two or three recent proposals that were considered of good quality to help you plan yours.

At this stage, writing must become more formal. It will save time if drafts approximate the form and style of an actual proposal as it will appear when completed. Then, each draft will be a closer approximation of the end goal. You will find this step-by-step development helps you to reach closure on what, at the beginning, might appear as an overwhelming task. Use of a word-processing program can greatly facilitate the preparation of each approximation and reduce the task to more manageable proportions.

In T/Ds, often a substantial amount of first-hand, observable data are gathered and analyzed. Yet, many other T/Ds take the form of a policy conceptualization analysis and interpretation or of a theory-based, critical examination and synthesis of a specific body of knowledge on a particular issue or topic.

Every T/D, of course, relies on the assembling of systematic evidence to focus on the problem at hand. The sources of evidence and the nature of data vary, though, and so do the methods of acquiring and analyzing material. *Theoretical syntheses* ordinarily depend heavily on both primary and secondary sources. Much of the material studied will be more qualitative than quantitative. It is in the uniformity, the consistency, and the systematic approach to such data that the theoretical synthesis displays its objectivity and its openness to replication. *Policy analyses* tend to rely largely on library sources such as articles, books, documents, essays, informants, official transcriptions, special surveys, and reports. The arraying and ordering of pertinent information from such sources for analytical assessment is a major challenge to the investigator, and the skill, clarity, and sophistication with which that is done is a prime consideration in judging the merits of the work. *Empirical studies* emphasize control, in the sense that the investigator sets up the conditions of the investigation and specifies detailed questions that will be answered or hypotheses that will be tested. The identification, application, or observation of a treatment effect is a common part of such studies, as is the analysis of data.

Each of these T/D forms is probably best presented by following a somewhat different structure or outline. In this chapter, the Table of Contents of the most frequent form of proposal, the empirical study, is highlighted (Fig. 4-2). Appendix B offers expanded outlines that might be helpful for other T/D types. They are suggested guides; prescriptions cannot be written because no two projects will be exactly alike.

Adapt the Format to the Problem

The goals and methods of a study shape the proposal; different studies will emphasize different things. Some may fit the standard format, but others may require adaptation (Krathwohl, 1988).

The same point about using the objectives and the procedures of the intended study to determine the format of the proposal is made by Meloy (2002). She devotes a large portion of her book on qualitative research to elaborating that principle, using correspondence from dissertation students for illustrative examples.

The most recent statement of the Council of Graduate Schools (199lb, p. 13) on options for the form of the dissertation points out the following:

> Whether the form of the dissertation is a monograph, a series of articles, or a set of essays is determined by the research expectations and accepted forms of publication in the discipline, as well as by custom in the discipline and the student's program. In the humanities and some of the social sciences, the dissertation . . . reflects the individual scholar's approach to research and can ultimately form the basis for a monograph published by a university press. Several article length essays . . . may be the heart of the dissertation in economics at a number of universities. In engineering and the physical and biological sciences, which are increasingly team disciplines with large groups of investigators working on common problems, dissertations often present, in varied formats, the results of several independent but related experiments.

The council goes on (p. 14) to make a very important point: "How a discipline normally conducts its work is distinctly related to that discipline's expectations for the Ph.D. dissertation."

Table of Contents

I. Introduction

II. The problem
- A. Rationale, significance, or need for the study
- B. Theoretical framework for the proposed study
- C. Statement of the problem
- D. Elements, hypotheses, theories, or research questions to be investigated
- E. Delimitations and limitations of the study
- F. Definition of terms
- G. Summary

III. Review of the literature
- A. Historical overview of the theory and research literature
- B. The theory and research literature specific to the T/D topic
- C. Research in cognate areas relevant to the T/D topic
- D. Critique of the validity of appropriate theory and research literature
- E. Summary of what is known and unknown about the T/D topic
- F. The contribution this study will make to the literature

IV. Research procedures
- A. Research methodology
- B. Specific procedures
- C. Research population or sample
- D. Instrumentation
- E. Pilot study
- F. Data collection
- G. Treatment of the data
- H. Summary

Appendices
- Appendix A, B, . . . (as needed)

Bibliography

Figure 4-2 Table of contents for a proposal.

Thus, it is vital that the student knows, or ascertains, the norms and expectations for dissertations (and theses as well) in the student's program and discipline. If in doubt, ask the advisor. Also, review several dissertations or theses recently completed in the department; note the name of the research advisor and the format, content, theoretical basis, and the methodology employed in the examples reviewed (Hawley, 1993).

Although no format is common to all institutions of higher education, Fig. 4-2 encompasses the topics ordinarily included. View this outline as a general guide rather than a prescription. Adapt it as necessary or as required by the advisor or the university. The material that follows is keyed in sequence to the items in the Table of Contents shown in Fig. 4-2.

FILLING IN THE OUTLINE

Introduction

Acquaint the reader with the topic. Make it short—only a page or two—but make it useful. First, tell the reader what the study will be about and why it is important and timely. Arouse the reader's interest; build a desire to read on and find out more. Set the stage for what comes after, putting important parts of the topic area in their proper perspective.

Second, be direct, not tedious. Make the Introduction a tasty tidbit, a sample of the good things to come. Aim it at an intelligent, well-informed person, but *one who is not deeply involved* in the particular problem addressed.

Writers rely on diagrams to explain ideas or concepts too difficult to put into simple sentences. Most languages are unidimensional and sequential, so it is impossible to verbalize several things at the same time. But a diagram, like a picture, can readily accomplish what mere words cannot. The same is true of graphs and charts. Therefore, we urge that the capabilities of the computer be used to create and insert illustrations in the body of the T/D. This helps the reader, as well as the researcher, to visualize complex relationships or interactive processes. It can be especially important in making this and other sections of the proposal both concise and clear. Tufte (1990, 1997, 2001) supplies superior examples of illustrations made by computer.

After reading the Introduction, one should be able to guess accurately what the problem is. Everything in the Introduction culminates in the statement of the problem as the next logical step.

The Problem

Rationale, Significance, or Need for the Study: Since the heading "The Problem" begins a new chapter of the T/D proposal, it is appropriate to link it to the prior chapter by first summarizing what appeared in the Introduction, which ought to take no more than two or three sentences. What appears in this section in addition should serve to sharpen and make more precise the purpose of the study. Remember, the committee rightfully expects the student to be able to state, convincingly, the chief reason(s) for doing the study, the potential value(s) that could flow from doing the study, and the urgency to do this particular study at this time. This section needs usually only three or four short sentences. Point out that what is presented here will be elaborated later in the T/D document, if that is necessary. This *is* the place to present, succinctly, the rationale, significance, or need for the investigation.

Theoretical Framework for the Proposed Study: Many important research topics do not have a clear relationship to a theory. One example is a study that established the most appropriate type size for reading materials to be used by persons with severe vision impairments. It was an important study, but one that was essentially pragmatic, meaning that it pertained to or primarily was concerned with practical results or outcomes. In the case of the type-size study, the problem was to ascertain a size of print that would allow as many visually impaired persons as possible to have access to reading materials while at the same time keeping the size and the bulk and the cost of the printed materials within reason.

On the other hand, some T/D proposals are eclectic in their frames of reference, meaning that they select from a variety of theories or systems of thinking rather than building on or testing some part of one theory. Examples can be found in the literature on methods of rehabilitating criminals, for which a variety of parts of theories of criminal justice, social learning, punishment, and morality may be interactive.

Finally, there are many studies that aim specifically at challenging or attempting to validate individual theories or at testing the accuracy of predictions made from specific theories. Individual theories are numerous, ranging across all academic and professional disciplines.

Two essential points ought to be included in this section of every proposal. First, it should be made clear whether the framework of the investigation is pragmatic, eclectic, or focused on a single theory, with a brief explanation of why and how. Second, the framework, whichever it is (or in whatever combination), should be stated, with appropriate references to the primary sources where full information on the applicable theories or systems of thought may be found.

Statement of the Problem

The Statement of the Problem is a short section, but perhaps the most important in the proposal. It lays down a guide to follow in all that comes after. At the same time, it is a serious agreement between the proposer and the faculty. Some institutions even refer to it as having contractlike characteristics. In any case, the statement of the problem will be carefully scrutinized by the faculty and, once accepted, will not be changed without faculty permission and agreement. Once accepted, the student researcher will live with the statement until the mission is completed or aborted.

State your concept of the problem in clear prose. Make it the initial paragraph of the statement of the problem. Be brief. Build on the introduction to provide information concerning the reasons why the study is proposed, what it would accomplish, and the anticipated outcomes.

After the purpose is given, a paragraph or two ought to suffice for the remaining statement of the problem. Choose words carefully. Do not promise more than is necessary to do the study in a reasonable time. The problem statement has to follow logically the purpose statement. It may be expressed as a question or a statement, preference depending on the individual researcher, the faculty member guiding the research, and the nature of the topic. The statement gives direction to the study, gives essential information about the scope of the study, and suggests, without giving details, how the study will be carried out. The statement must be clear, concise, and unambiguous.

Elements of the Problem

Elements are stated in studies that do not require hypotheses.* Sometimes, elements in T/D proposals are called research questions or components. By whatever name, they are the specific parts of the problem studied as opposed to other parts, usually unnamed, not studied. Thus, the elements help define and make more specific the problem statement.

Hypotheses, Theories, and Research Questions

The hypothesis is stated as a suggested solution to a problem or as the relationship of specified variables. It retains the character of a guess until facts are found to confirm or discredit it.

As one might expect from the spelling, the word comes from the Greek *hypothesis*, meaning groundwork, foundation, supposition. The plural is hypotheses. It has come to have a meaning similar to one of the Greek meanings—supposition. It could be called a supposition, proposition, or unproved explanation tentatively advanced to account for observed facts or phenomena.

One or more hypotheses may be generated by a thorough analysis of the theoretical and factual background of the research problem. Without formulating hypotheses, a researcher wastes time in directionless investigation.

People sometimes go beyond giving tentative explanations for what they seem to see. They often use these explanations as a base for further investigation to determine, if possible, whether the tentative explanations seem accurate as a description of what is happening and even whether the explanation predicts what will happen under certain conditions. There we find the relationship between hypotheses and research. Researchers usually want to find an explanation for a phenomenon (i.e., Why is there so much more divorce than ever before

---

*Some complex investigations may contain both elements and hypotheses.

in the United States?). First, they review the research and the speculation of others. They then develop likely hypotheses (alienation from earlier mores, breakdown in family life, increased mobility, societal changes, loss of influence of religious groups, and so on). Finally, they formulate a problem (study) that may more accurately ascertain what is contributing to the rise of the divorce rate.

Investigators develop hypotheses to help give direction to their work. The engineer who scans mountain terrain before directing a mining operation or laying out a roadway makes inferences based on facts and observed conditions in coming to a decision. The engineer *hypothesizes*, that is, expresses an informed opinion as to the correct approach to the problem. The child development specialist notices that boys seem to take to science and mathematics more readily than do girls. The specialist guesses, that is, *hypothesizes*, that the difference arises because young boys and girls are differentially exposed to science and mathematics and differentially rewarded for showing interest in them.

Hypotheses are not confined to the experimental research mode. In fact, it is the rare study in any research mode that does not involve hypotheses, either explicitly or implicitly. A hypothesis is a shrewd guess, an assumption, an opinion, a hunch, an informed judgment, or an inference that is provisionally put forward to explain facts or conditions or to guide how one starts to attack a problem. A hypothesis helps in determining the information (data) to be gathered and the investigative methods to be used.

Most students have working hypotheses when they start to consider investigations. These are conjectures formed to guide the initial stages of any inquiry.

A student can hypothesize (state a hypothesis) about almost anything because the term simply refers, as we have said, to a more or less educated guess. It is a little more difficult, though, to make a testable hypothesis, which means phrasing the educated guess in such a way that you can determine how correct the guess is. Sometimes, one can state the hypothesis in a way that makes it absolutely testable. But, most of the time, it is possible only to obtain a qualified test, not an absolute one.

If hypotheses are to be used, they should be well chosen. Keep each one simple, straightforward in language, and ascertain that it meets recognized criteria, such as the following:

1. Are there good reasons, practical experiences, theories, or previous research findings that tend to support it? If so, it can be said to have *construct validity*.
2. Is it possible to collect and analyze data in such a way as to show whether the hypothesis stands up? If so, it is *testable*.
3. Does the hypothesis focus on the problem being studied? To be *relevant*, a hypothesis must answer part or all of the matter being investigated.

Another important and conceptually related, Greek-derived word is *theory*. Perhaps the most misleading notion is that a theory is an impractical explanation, something that sounds great but will not work or, even if it does work in some sense, it is so far above the common person that it is not useful. In sharp contrast is the comment by Gardner, who said a theory is one of the most practical tools of the modern world. He gave the example of the plumber who daily uses theory to practice the trade in an expert manner. The plumber who uses inflammable plastic pipes in the walls of a new house or expects water to drain uphill does not know much about either theory or plumbing (Gardner, 1978).

Webster's Ninth New Collegiate Dictionary (1985, p. 1223) defines theory, for our purposes, as "a plausible or scientifically acceptable general principle or body of principles offered to explain phenomena." In comparing hypothesis with theory and scientific law, the same dictionary (p. 594) makes a useful distinction in that

> Law means a formula derived by inference from scientific data that explains a principle operating in nature. Law implies a statement of order and relation in nature that has been found to be invariable under the same conditions. Hypothesis implies insufficient evidence to provide more than a tentative explanation. Theory implies a greater range of evidence and greater likelihood of truth than hypothesis [but much less certainty than law].

Theory explains the relations among events or facts, although not completely. For example, theory attempts to explain the relationship between economic conditions and buyer preferences or between home conditions and child-abuse behavior. Theory can provide a framework to generate hypotheses or questions or problem element statements. In turn, they guide research procedures, objectives, and data collection. For example, to propose and study the effects of a new prison discipline code, we should be able to say why (in theory) we think it will be better. In this general sense, every T/D proposal should be based on theory.

If the investigator is seeking direct answers to certain questions, it is not necessary to state hypotheses formally and design the study to test them. If it is believed, however, that coincidental relationships may exist and should be revealed, or if it appears that one factor may be the cause or the result of another, a hypothesis may be the best way to state what the investigator is setting out to uncover. We encourage students to take the initiative with their advisors to discuss whether a given topic might better be approached through setting up hypotheses, by posing questions, by enumerating the problem elements, or by some combination of the three. Significant parts of the study design will be influenced by that decision, notably the data collection, data analysis, and presentation and interpretation of the results.

Delimitations and Limitations of the Study

The two words delimitations and limitations are often confused. A *limitation* is a factor that may or will affect the study, but *is not under control* of the researcher; a *delimitation* differs, principally, in that it *is controlled* by the researcher.

In psychology, it is common to use a questionnaire to ascertain the status of something, for example, the job specifications of clinical, school, or counseling psychologists who are employed by public agencies. In such studies, a very common *limitation* is the willingness of individuals to respond at all, to respond in a timely fashion, and to respond accurately. These are limitations on the study; that is, they are important possible effects on the outcomes of the study, and they are not controlled by the researcher.

In such studies, also, it is common to have a *delimitation* as to size or nature of the group questioned, for some appropriate reason. In the example used, the size might be limited to those in one state, those working in urban regions, or those in certain types of agencies. Also, the size might be limited to 10% or 20% of known psychologists in such employment to keep it to a manageable number.

Limitations and delimitations should appear only when they are imposed by the nature of the problem being studied. Limitations typically surface as variables that cannot be controlled by the researcher but may limit or affect the outcome of the study. Research honesty demands that every important limitation be spelled out for the reader and the committee. In our experience, limitations become problems to students when they are not specified. Every study has its limitations; it is best to call the committee's attention to them. If the limitations are critically damaging to the study, the best time to find that out is when the proposal is in the thinking-and-planning stage, not later.

In a similar way, plainly stated delimitations help everyone involved to think through the design of the study. Delimitations are integral parts of the design because they set parameters; they tell the reader what will be included, what will be left out, and why. A good statement of the problem will itself be somewhat limiting and delimiting, of course. However, in this section, one should find detailed strictures recognized by the researcher, but not apparent in the brief problem statement.

Definition of Terms

There are two major reasons for defining one's terms in doing research. *First*, define each expression that is used in a special, very precise sense in the proposal. Unfortunately, unless it is defined, there is not always agreement on the meaning you intend for a word or group of words. If a common word is used in a specific way in the student's field of study, that needs to be stated.

Second, the proposed research may depend on an operational definition of a term. *Operational* means that the expression used must be definable in terms of observable, identifiable, and repeatable operations. For example, the expression *functional literacy* is, in itself, open to many interpretations. But, if it is specified as a 5.0 or higher-grade equivalent score in reading speed and comprehension on a particular nationally standardized test, then functional literacy becomes defined by those operations used to identify it, and its meaning is unambiguous because of the operational definition. For another example, two common terms in education are *school quality* and *achievement*. Neither of these concepts means very much unless the user defines the meaning operationally. For example, achievement may be defined as the level of test scores from *x* test, *y* form, given at *z* time throughout the school system. School quality may be defined operationally by a number of variables, such as expenditure per child, educational level of teachers, years of teaching experience, and pupil test scores on specific tests. Thus, an operational definition is one that specifies the operations that will define the word. Operational definitions not only allow one to say precisely what is meant by terms used, but these definitions also establish a basis for objective tests for the outcomes of the proposed study.

Four general dictionaries we have found useful in defining terms are the *Oxford English Dictionary* (13 vol.) by J. A. H. Murray; the *Random House Dictionary of the English Language*, *Unabridged*, the *Webster's New World Dictionary of the American Language*, *College Edition*; and the *Webster's Ninth New Collegiate Dictionary*. Many professional fields (e.g., education, medicine, psychology) have well-recognized specialized dictionaries. Librarians are excellent consultants on this and related matters.

Terms that are current or changing in concept may be best defined by their usage in professional and scholarly writing. Eminent persons in the field of inquiry you have chosen will define precisely the difficult terms in their work in order to be clearly understood. The student researcher is on safe ground to cite and use those definitions if they are needed in the proposed research.

Another variation is to review the definitions used by the top scholars in the field and critique them in terms of their appropriateness to the proposed research. There is nothing wrong with ending up with your own new definition based on a review of definitions found in the literature provided your definition is demonstrably more useful and appropriate for the study.

Review of the Literature: Sources

At least five sources of literature should be searched: journals, major books on the subject, monographs, relevant collections of images or objects, and dissertations. Today, much of the identification of relevant material in these five classes of publication can be done via computer access to bibliographic databases.

By this time, you should also have ascertained the bibliographic citation form required for your T/D. You should take pains to record, from every reference you use, the exact information you will need if you decide to cite it in the future. It is much better to err on the side of recording too many references now than to have to return a few weeks or months hence and spend hours trying to relocate some document.

If you are using a computer, we recommend strongly that you store the data for bibliographic citations. Much drudgery can be avoided, too, by using a computer program to structure your bibliography as you build it. Such a data file stores all types of references and can generate citations in more than 200 publishing styles, plus write footnotes in a variety of styles.

The term *literature* is employed to include anything appropriate to the topic, such as theories, letters, documents, historical records, photos and other images or objects, government reports, newspaper accounts, empirical studies, and so forth. Some of these, like letters or reports, are called "fugitive materials" because, while such items may actually be of key importance to your topic, the originals may be quite difficult to locate. This is another point at which a professional librarian can prove to be a great help.

Searches by computer for images (photos, sounds, drawings, settings, maps, paintings) that do not have text captions pose challenges because current software may not recover such material directly. With conventional databases, computers look only for exact matches of key words.

Software now in development may use artificial intelligence processes that allow the search engines to be sensitive to enough nuances about English (or another language) syntax to broaden or deepen a search and find more matches. Thus "sunny day at the beach" and "warm sand and sparkling surf" could produce a "match" instead of a "no match" response. Examples of Web sites potentially helpful with the above problem search areas are those for Cycorp, Inc. (http://www.cyc.com/), Virage, Inc. (http://www.virage.com/), and IBM (http://

www.ibm.com/). These sites were retrieved on May 19, 2002. See Chapter 3 for home pages of general and specific search engines.

Figure 4-2 contains six subheadings under Review of the Literature. In all six subheadings, if theory and research are each treated in chronological order in the writing, usually a coherent picture of the topic's background emerges. The key is appropriateness.

Extent and Depth of Literature Review

A review of the literature is necessary for every T/D, but there is disagreement about the detail and depth of the review at the proposal stage as compared with the final stage. Some advisors recommend a short review, hitting the high spots of the literature and anticipating the complete review in the final document. Others insist on a complete review in the proposal. Those who take the former position feel that the whole proposal, as a matter of principle, ought to be brief (up to 10 to 15 pages) and ought to concentrate on a statement of what the researcher wants to do, why, and how, plus how it will add to what has already been done. This, it is argued, permits a maximum of student independence and freedom from committee constraints and reviews during the study.

Those who take the complete review position feel that the student researcher will have a better proposal, clearer procedure, and better final product if the review is thoroughly done before embarking on the study. Further, they say, the review has to be done anyway, so it is not lost effort. A full analysis of the literature beforehand provides opportunities to educate both the student and the committee to some of the pitfalls ahead.

We lean toward the complete review view, but we prefer to focus on what the student researcher should try to get out of the review at the proposal stage. Whatever the depth and detail of the written requirement of this section of the proposal, we encourage students to read widely in the literature, take careful notes, and maintain an organized file and record.

For more ideas on literature review, use your search engine for on-line information. Also, the work of Clark and Oxman (2000) is a source for guidelines and format for systematic review of the literature in the health care field. The works Gash (2000), Hart (1998), and

Cooper (1988) are all good sources of information. C. W. Bowen (2000) describes a meta-analysis approach to conducting literature reviews. He illustrates the power of this approach by reporting the effects of cooperative learning on chemistry achievement in high school and college classes. Finding samples of literature reviews in your field would be very helpful to your progress.

Benefits from the Literature Review

The *most important benefit* to be gained from a review of the literature at the proposal stage is good knowledge of the field of inquiry—what the facts are, who the eminent scholars are, where the parameters of the field are, and which ideas, theories, questions, and hypotheses seem most important. The reviewer at this stage ought to be able to carry on an informed, intelligent discussion about the field with an expert, using references and citing authors and concepts important or critical to the field.

Another benefit from the review at this stage is knowledge of the methodologies common to the field and a feeling for their usefulness and appropriateness in various settings. The reviewer can get ideas of which methodologies are most often used, methodologies appropriate for the proposed research, and when and how these ideas have been successfully used in the field. A careful look at the prevalent methodologies may also convince a student either to alter the topic of inquiry because skills are lacking to do that kind of research or to keep the topic and acquire the needed skills.

A *third potential benefit* is reinforcement for an earlier hope that the proposed research is really needed. Even if similar research has been published, the literature review often turns up statements such as "It would be interesting to know if Clark's work could be replicated in other places or with different groups." Or, "It would be very useful to know if Clark's pioneering work is still relevant today." These are clues that an important study needs to be replicated, essential information to know before the proposal is drafted (Lindvall, 1959).

One vexing problem researchers have faced for years is how best to maintain objectivity when reviewing prior research to assess whether further research on the topic is needed. This is especially difficult when there are many published studies reporting conflicting results. Some researchers have attempted to build tables or charts of the various study results to aid in "eyeballing" the prior reports and to estimate which might be considered more credible.

An impressive breakthrough in weighing the evidence from earlier research (Asher, 1990; Bangert-Drowns and Rudner, 1992; Glass, 1977; Hodges, 1986; Hunter and Schmidt, 1990) is now available. Called meta-analysis, the procedure allows one to add substantial objectivity to research reviews. Meta-analysis applies well to reviewing empirical studies with treatment means and control group means compared. Such studies constitute a population with results that are quantified by the literature searcher and put together into a database. The researcher then analyzes the database statistically, much like any other set of quantitative findings. We recommend its use not only to minimize reviewer bias, but also to help determine the nature of the hypotheses or questions and the directions they might take. Moreover, meta-analysis can be classed as a research methodology in its own right, and it is a widely useful one.

There are Web sites that permit free downloads. The University of Kentucky Computing Center (n.d.) citation is an excellent source. The work of Kenny (1999) is another good source, designed to assist the user in computation of statistics during meta-analysis. Another strategy is to enter *meta-analysis* in your search engine to see how much will be useful information. Finally, always consult your reference librarian for advice and for the names of download sites that are free to the university community.

Fourth, a literature review at this stage often helps to narrow a problem. Some get so overwhelmed with the flood of literature that severe frustration sets in. Where and how does one narrow a topic to make it feasible, yet not cut out the important details that impinge on it and make it more understandable and researchable? This is a common problem, shared by almost all beginning researchers. We recommend parsimony based on criteria agreed to with the advisor.

Try narrowing the scope of the review by employing a three-step sequence. Initially, read widely in the proposed field of interest. Then, think and analyze, attempting always to narrow down and weed out. After that, arrange to spend some review time with an experienced researcher in the proposed field of study and carefully talk through the problems encountered. If your advisor fits all the requirements of a good listener in this case, you are fortunate; use the advisor.

If you still have trouble getting the ideas to add up to a literature review for your proposal, go back to the first step. Each time the sequence is repeated, it will go more quickly. Vary the use of persons as sounding boards. At some point, a light will flash in the mind, and a good review for the proposal will come into focus.

A *fifth value* we urge students to wring out of the review is the generation of hypotheses or questions for further studies. The more one knows about a subject, the more questions come to mind. To a researcher, there is always a reason why something (person, group, organization, body, material) operates (behaves, works, acts) the way it does, but that reason (or complex of reasons) is simply not known. It may not have been researched enough, the data may be inadequate, or the theoretical constructs may not yet be available to guide and direct further research. From the literature analysis will come a multitude of ideas for further research based on the work that has already been done.

Keep a list of the questions and hypotheses that come to your mind or that are mentioned in what you read. (In the latter case, be sure that you also record *where* you found them so that you can properly cite their sources later, if you wish.) In particular, that list will prove useful when you are writing the section of the final chapter of your T/D in which you discuss the implications of your own findings and the additional research directions your work supports or suggests.

Sixth, the topic being researched now could start a long-term interest, particularly if it is frequently updated and maintained with a consistent citation system in a computer file. Obviously, that makes it easily available for further articles and follow-up investigations.

In searching the literature, it is good also to develop a list of subject headings that relate to themes of interest. We recommend working back from the new to the old and from the general to the specific. Thus, a researcher might start with current reference sources and recent texts and research reviews concerning, for example, nuclear energy applications, dental hygiene in old age, public policy on the rights of victims of crime, adoption practices, or the education of gifted handicapped children. Then, working back through the earlier research will provide a depth context and understanding of current problems. Starting with the general topic will provide leads to specific areas of interest and help develop an understanding for the interrelationships of research. For example, the relationship between education of gifted children, handicapped children, mental tests, public policy, equal educational opportunity, inclusion, separation, and mainstreaming would be cases of interrelationships currently topical in psychology and in the public affairs, legal, social work, and education professions.

Currency of Literature Review Data

For those in the stage of reviewing literature, recent journal issues often provide leads to content that should be in the review. The parameters of academic or professional areas, the current thinking in the field, the investigators who are writing in the field, the ideas being discussed, and the references that are most cited and respected in the field are all displayed in recent issues of important journals. At an early stage of preparing thc review, hours spent with journals identified as central to the topic may be very cost-effective.

One word of advice about journals: There is wide variation in quality. Some journals are very careful about what they publish; others are not. Some are refereed by top experts; others are hungry for any manuscript that turns up in the mail. Some are read by outstanding scholars; others would have difficulty finding their way into a scholar's wastebasket. How does one tell the difference? Ask professors, colleagues who know the field, and librarians who specialize in the field and look through journals. Read a copy of the journal; look at its format, its publisher, its board of editors; examine the qualifications of writers; and review the procedures for determining what gets published in the journal. You can also visit the Web of Knowledge home page (http://www.isinet.com), which will provide access to the major citation indexes (e.g., *Social Sciences Citation Index*, *Science Citation Index*, and *Humanities Citation Index*).

A similar comment could be made about the library's book collection and the library's databases that give access to the collections of other libraries. As a researcher putting together a review of the literature, you do not have to agree with the major contributors to the field, but you do have to know their work and cite it. Often, this work exists in books. The seminal work in almost any field is likely to be in the university library book collection, and that is an appropriate place to spend a good deal of time doing a review of the literature or research. There is no substitute for the hours one must spend browsing the bookshelves and computerized databases of the library and reviewing the major works in the selected field of inquiry.

In short, this part of the proposal should present information about the evolution and present state of theory and speculation and research on the topic proposed for investigation. The review should conclude by showing how the proposed study will add to the subject's knowledge base. The review should make unmistakably clear to the reader that there are some missing pieces to the body of research and what those pieces are and that the proposed study is directly aimed at filling in one or more of those missing pieces.

RESEARCH DESIGN

As we use the term, research design is a total plan for carrying out an investigation. Research methodology, research type, or general method are considered synonyms for research design. A completed research design shows the step-by-step sequence of actions in carrying out an investigation essential to obtaining objective, reliable, and valid information. The completed design also indicates how the resultant objective information is to be used to determine conclusions about the accuracy of a hypothesis, a theory, or the correct answer to a question (Dillman, 2000; Eisner and Peskkin, 1990; Leedy and Ormrod, 2001; Miller and Salkind, 2002).

Advanced study in the United States is tremendous in scope and complexity. Also, it is growing and changing. Probably no other sector of higher education generates so many exciting and difficult questions. The varied nature of the questions calls, in turn, for the application of many different forms of research.

To assist students from a variety of academic and professional disciplines envision the overall concept of research design, we include Fig. 4-3 as a general model. The model, it is hoped, will supply an

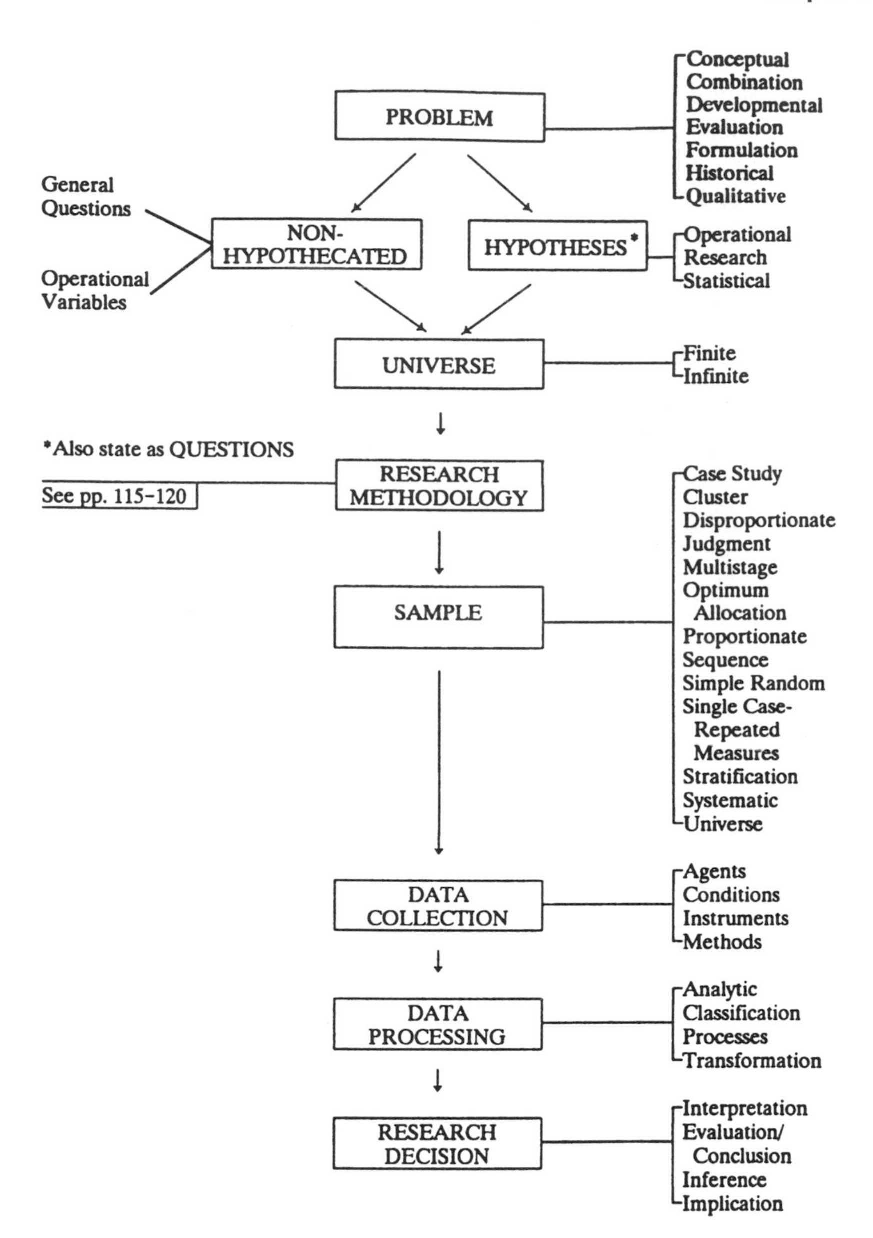

Figure 4-3 General model for research designs.

additional conceptual structure for students to supplement the outlines in Appendix B. The general model does not parallel exactly the chapter or the topic development of this book, but all the items in the boxes in the figure are treated. If referred to in discussions with an advisor and other committee members or consultants, the model can be useful in maintaining the focus of a conference on specific problem areas and in working out solutions to them.

RESEARCH METHODOLOGY

The research methodology part of the proposal should identify for the reader the one or more research methods the student plans to use (i.e., opinion polling, case study, experimental, or other). The student's objective should be to give the reader a capsule statement about the contemplated research methodology, while indicating that details are to be found in succeeding portions of the proposal.

After the research questions and/or hypotheses have been decided, the single most important choice to be made by the investigator is the research methodology to employ. Once selected, the research methodology tends to govern, or at least limit, the range of choices as to how the data will be collected, how it will be analyzed, how results will be reported, and even the nature of the conclusions that may reasonably be drawn from the results.

We found no generally accepted classification of types of research. For example, two texts (Gay, 1996; Slavin, 1992) each list five research types, but they agreed on only three of them. Moreover, one text considers qualitative or ethnographic research a distinct and major classification, while the other subsumes qualitative investigations under another general category of research. Yet, they both agree that qualitative research developed primarily in anthropology and was borrowed as a methodology by other fields. They also agree in defining qualitative research as describing a situation as it exists, without involving formal hypotheses, but focusing on explaining social processes in great detail.

Because there does not seem to be anything comparable to a taxonomy in the classification of research types, we chose instead to simply list and briefly illustrate a variety of frequently utilized approaches to research.

Types of Methodology

For more specific aid to the student, we interrupt our orderly development of the outline in Fig. 4-2 to insert the section below. Types (or methods) are named and illustrated. A review of the types may prove useful in helping the student decide what will be written under the Research Methodology heading in the T/D proposal.

Accepted research methodology legitimately embraces a wide variety of forms:

> In fact, there are many actions that can assist in discovering knowledge, and humanity learned much about human nature long before there was [formal recognition of] science and scientific method. Any actions that lead to accurate statements about nature must be considered as having some methodological legitimacy; the characterizations of contrasting methods are simply arguments that some scientific actions are more effective than others at producing statements of good generality. (Johnston and Pennypacker, 1980, pp. 412–413)

The methods chosen for a study certainly have profound effects on the outcomes. The same holds for how subjects are selected and for how data are collected and analyzed. *Most important*, though, is the match between methods and the theoretical or hypothetical propositions under scrutiny in the investigation. It is the statement of the problem that properly serves as a launchpad for all the subsequent steps. The correct research methodology should fit smoothly into its place in the research plan sequence to move from what one seeks by doing research to how one goes about seeking it.

These inquiries should govern selection of a research methodology: "What is (a) the most practical, (b) the most efficient, (c) the most promising, and (d) the most readily available way to solve the research problem or answer the research question?" Rarely will one method provide a "Yes" answer on all four points. More often, a compromise proves necessary.

Inevitably, the methodology choice influences the outcomes of the research. What matters most is that the student knows and acknowledges the influence and does not ignore or try to hide it.

In preparing the several editions of this work, the authors found no standardization in research methodology terminology across academic and professional fields. To reconfirm this, we examined five research methodology texts published from 1993 to 1997. Altogether, they listed 15 types of research. All five books agreed on only 2 of the 15 classifications. Every book included at least 1 classification of research not found in any of the other four books.

The terminology we decided to use includes all the types of research we could identify and illustrate. Even so, the name of the research type you choose should be reviewed with the advisor before being included in a proposal. The same methodology may be known by a different name in another field.

1. Type: *Analytical*: Classes of data are collected, and studies are conducted to discern and explicate principles that might guide action. Special subtypes under this heading include micro-, macro-, and policy analysis.

   Examples: State court interpretations of permissive legislation on nonschool use of school property

   Criteria for accepting applicants in housing cooperatives

   Management of extremes of human behavior in hospital emergency rooms

   Employment of handicapped high school graduates in an economically depressed region
2. Type: *Case study*: The background, development, current conditions, and environmental interactions of one or more individuals, groups, communities, businesses, or institutions are observed, recorded, and analyzed for stages or patterns in relation to internal and external influences.

   Examples: A case study of open admissions in an American junior college

   The development of cognitive functions in three autistic children: case records analyses

   Establishment and growth of the National Association of Retired Persons

   The National Association of Manufacturers' labor policy; a case study of development
3. Type: *Comparative*: Two or more existing situations are studied to determine and explicate their likenesses and differences.

Examples: Concepts taught in secondary school chemistry in Canada, Great Britain, New Zealand, and the United States

Self-control of children and adults during cardiac diagnostic procedures

Bid specification procedures for public playground and recreation supply and equipment purchases in New York, Pennsylvania, Illinois, and California

4. Type: *Correlational-predictive*: Statistically significant correlation coefficients between and among relevant phenomena are sought and interpreted; this type includes the determination of the extent to which variations in one or more factors correspond with variations in one or more other factors and the use of such findings in making predictions.

   Examples: Interaction of gasoline prices and automobile travel for business and vacation purposes

   Relationships between nature of crime and amount of recidivism

   Relationships among size of family, age, and use of home health agencies

   Relationships between teacher backgrounds and their attitudes toward international cooperation

5. Type: *Design and demonstration*: New operationally related business systems, personnel training curricula, professional education programs, instructional materials, disease control plans, and the like are constructed and described; this type is often called action research and includes, at least, formative evaluation.

   Examples: A literacy program for the Sudan

   Feasibility of a lighter-than-air freight transport system for Africa

   A curriculum in motor development for the period birth to 3 years of age

   A cytotoxicity test for insoluble dusts

   Design and establishment of a comprehensive health information system for western Australia

6. Type: *Evaluation*: A program or a project is expected to be carried out in a certain way and expected to produce a certain result; research is intended to determine whether the anticipated procedure and the outcome are realized. Evaluation research that

focuses on the procedure is called formative, and that which attends particularly to the outcome is called summative.

Examples: Effectiveness of mental health programs that serve hearing-impaired children

Evaluation of a regional family planning program

Impact of county drug and alcohol programs

Evaluation of a rural marketing plan for fire insurance

Effectiveness of rehabilitation counseling: an evaluation

7. Type: *Developmental*: The changes over time in one or more observable factors, patterns, or sequences of growth or decline may be traced or charted and reported.

   Examples: Growth of child care centers in American business and industry

   Emergence and spread of credit card utilization

   The written language development of children

   The computer and the knowledge explosion: a developmental study

8. Type: *Experimental*: One or more variables may be deliberately manipulated and the results analyzed and rationalized—"true" experiments requiring tight controls and subject randomization.

   Examples: Reduction of separation anxiety through use of mental imagery

   Use of programmed instruction to correct errors in the written language of deaf adolescents

   The effects of listening training on salesperson effectiveness

   Effects of a parental intervention strategy on reading skill development

   Effects of different options for continued employment on retirement decisions

9. Type: *Exploratory*: Investigations into new or relatively unknown territory for the purpose of searching out or closely scrutinizing objects or phenomena to lead to a better understanding of them.

   Examples: Telescopic and satellite observations of the composition of the surface of the moons of Jupiter

   The parasitic life in the feces of wild horse herds of the Rocky Mountain region

The behavior of molten metals under conditions of virtually zero gravity

The characteristics of "private" languages used by twins and triplets in communication between and among themselves

The study of extraterrestrial objects for evidences of life forms

10. Type: *Historical*: Individuals or activities are studied to reconstruct the past accurately and without bias to ascertain, document, and interpret their influences or to check the tenability of an hypothesis.

    Examples: The relevance of the thought of Albert Camus for education

    Sources of individual differences in solutions to management problems

    Historical landmarks in the management of environmental noise

    The search for the perpetual motion machine: its contribution to engineering

    Origins and status of the Montessori movement in the United States

11. Type: *Meta-analysis*: A procedure for combining results of research across areas in which measurement systems are not precise by adding together sources of variance to get a population value of the standard deviation as the basis for establishing effect sizes. Used both in assembling meaningful literature reviews and in testing hypotheses.

    Examples: How "real" is the gender gap in aptitude test results?

    What is the evidence that air pollution is associated with human illnesses?

    Are large automobiles safer?

    The effectiveness of hypnosis in curing addiction

12. Type: *Methodological*: These studies examine new approaches (methods) with potential advantages over present approaches (methods). The study content includes, but is not limited to, building, measuring, observing, organizing, displaying, and communicating. Such studies frequently make use of both developmental and evaluative procedures.

    Examples: The relative advantages and disadvantages of digital and analog television

Longitudinal versus cross-sectional age cohort approaches in studying personality development

Advantages and disadvantages of meta-analysis in gauging the import of past research

Prestructured or self-designed majors in collegiate education: pros and cons

13. Type: *Opinion polling*: The behavior, beliefs, or intentions of specified groups of persons are determined, reported, and interpreted.

    Examples: Food preferences of hospitalized individuals by age and geographical region in Canada

    Opinions of students and alumni regarding the graduate program in counseling psychology

    Political and social beliefs of experienced engineers

    Citizen views on a volunteer system of armed forces

    Attitudes of Sunday school teachers toward religious and secular educational objectives

14. Type: *Status*: A representative or selected sample of one or more phenomena may be isolated and examined to ascertain the characteristics of the object(s) of study.

    Examples: Freemasonry in New Zealand: contemporary status

    The mail order catalog business in America

    The training, background, duties, activities, and job perceptions of public health officers

    Employment among minorities in large U.S. cities

    The yearbook in public high schools

15. Type: *Theoretical*: Inclusive and parsimonious explanatory principles for phenomena or data are developed, proposed, and described.

    Examples: A conceptual analysis of creativity

    A theory of compensatory education

    An explanatory model for mass appraisal: extension of Rosen's theory of implicit markets to urban housing

    A psychological theory to explain faith healing

    A theory of intellectual evolution

16. Type: *Trend analysis*: Phenomena that are or have been in the process of change are examined to identify and report the directions of trends and to make interpretations and forecasts.

Examples: Trends in the teaching of parenting in American secondary schools
The use of public transportation in Mexico: a trend analysis
Dow-Jones average changes during selected periods of federal monetary policy
Trends in availability and cost of dental health insurance
Trends in public tax support for private colleges and universities

17. Type: *Twenty-twenty (20/20) analytic*: Extremes of populations are studied by comparative techniques and measures to determine whether and to what extent actions intended to impact evenly or proportionately across a population actually do so (Reynolds et al., 1996). The analysis focuses on accountability for success or failure to reach explicit or implicit goals.
    Examples: Police calls, responses, and follow-up in high- and low-income neighborhoods
    Health status of Canadian citizens at extreme income levels
    School effectiveness in serving exceptional children at mobility extremes
    Achievement in school districts with high and low per-pupil expenditure levels
18. Type: *Qualitative*: This is a general form or style of research rather than a specific methodology. In fact, qualitative research encompasses several methodologies and quantitative approaches that might well be used with many of the examples of studies listed above (see p. 17 for a fuller discussion of the nature of qualitative research).
19. Type: *Quasi-experimental*: Experimental rigor so far as manipulation, control, or randomization is not feasible, but the comparison of treatment versus nontreatment conditions is approximated, and the compromises and limitations are stated, understood, and taken into account in all conclusions and interpretations.
    Examples: All of the examples under Item 8 (Experimental) would be applicable here if they were carried out under conditions in which only partial control was possible of variables, treatments, populations, or other important conditions—the

case in many real-life situations for which field and operational studies are the only feasible kinds of professional and ethical codes are to be properly upheld.

These forms of research do not exhaust all that could be listed. Also, as noted, our category names may differ from those that others would use. Evaluation (Item 6, above), for example, may have many subgroups. Some are called outcome based, objective based, and consumer oriented, to name a few (Schalock, 2001). The most significant point is to recognize and employ the method most appropriate for the problem whatever the approach may be called.

Two other points should be noted. First, so far as can be determined, each of the several listed research approaches has resulted in significant new contributions to knowledge. No one deserves higher regard than another. Second, all students should learn about all of the research approaches. Naturally, a student will tend to become much more familiar with the approaches used in that student's T/D. However, all students should become familiar enough with the listed approaches to know how to use them and to know when an approach is not appropriate.

The proposal should clearly name and briefly describe the research method. Citations from authorities may clarify and support the choice of methodology, although the methodology selected is a responsibility of the researcher. The criterion measure of appropriateness is whether the methodology will yield useful evidence with regard to the statement of the problem. Thus, the choice is always directly related to the problem statement. Ask yourself, Will the method yield the data needed to make an intelligent and useful response to the problem statement? Raise that question with yourself, your advisor, and others who critique the proposal.

Specific Procedures

In the Specific Procedures section, tell the reader, step by step, what will be done in the conduct of the study. This may include correspondence, the design of questionnaires, pilot studies to be mounted before the complete study, the application of some treatment, the conduct of interviews, the distribution of inquiry forms or other instruments designed to gather appropriate data, obtaining permissions, the use of consultation, or other actions. Leave out matters to be dealt with under other headings.

Start with a chronologically ordered list of the procedures to be used. Elaborate each item in only enough detail to let the committee know what will be done. In a proposal, "enough detail" may vary from a paragraph on one item to a full page on another. If you go beyond a page, ask yourself if the writing is as parsimonious and succinct as it should be. Surplus words obfuscate the problem, annoy the committee, and raise the question of how sure you are about what you intend to do.

Research Population or Sample

In the Research Population or Sample section, a few essential points must be covered. What is the population to be studied? Is it a type of flora? Is it a group of research reports on which you will conduct a meta-analysis? Is it a form of virus? Is it a group of people? What are its characteristics? Will the universe (everyone or everything in the population group) be studied, or will there be a sample? If a sample, how will it be selected from the whole? What is the justification for selecting the sample? Is it possible to determine the representativeness of the sample? If not, does that fact constitute a prohibition or just a limitation? How does one gain access to the sample population, and how difficult a problem is that expected to be?

One reminder here—the research population and the sample, if any, should tie in very clearly with the statement of the problem. If the problem indicates a dependence on perceptions of urban residents or workers, for example, one might expect such individuals to be in any research population designated. Similarly, if one wants to be able to generalize to nursery-grown trees in the United States, the sample must be constructed with that goal in mind.

Instrumentation

In the Instrumentation section, detail the relevant data about instrumentation (tests, apparatus, interview protocols, questionnaires, and the like) proposed for the study. The purpose of any instrument should be to help produce or gather data to answer questions raised in the problem statement.

Review the potentialities in contemporary technology for ways to enhance the speed, the accuracy, and the reliability of instrumentation. For example, there are computer programs for administering questionnaires, for displaying stimulus material of a variety of kinds, for administering tests, and for a number of other uses requiring an interface with a subject. Such material comes onto the market in a steady stream as researchers recognize its value in minimizing human error factors.

Choosing the right package, for a particular set of data, among all the alternatives is a difficult task. Some Web pages that perform statistical calculations have links that will help in this task. For example, several university library Web sites will lead to bibliographies, journal searches, links to statistical packages, and on-line help (University of Kentucky Computing Center, n.d.; University of Miami Libraries, 2001; University of Minnesota Libraries, 2002). Several contain an integrated collection of statistical tests combined with a system that helps you to select, and then perform, the most appropriate analysis. Trochim (2002) at Cornell provides an interactive set of Web pages to help in the selection of appropriate analysis for data. It asks a simple series of questions about the data, then makes recommendations about the best tests to use. The work of Kenny (1999) is another good source, designed to assist the user in computation of statistics during meta-analysis. Another strategy is to enter meta-analysis in your search engine to see how much will be useful information. Finally, always consult your reference librarian for advice and for the names of download sites that are free to the university community.

Technological instrumentation employed must be cited, giving its name and where to locate it. As with any other reference or citation, the purpose is to allow a reader to access the material directly to verify that it was represented accurately by the author.

Careful advisors tend to want to see any instrument before it is applied to a research population. At least the specifications for any instrument should accompany the proposal, and it is much better if the entire instrument does.

Pilot Study

If you plan a pilot study, the proposal should describe when, where, and how it will be carried out. A pilot study, by definition, takes place before the actual study to determine feasibility of the study and to work out bugs. It is important, then, that the pilot have a provision for soliciting and gathering formative evaluation from the pilot study population. This pilot population, in other words, ought to have built into it a systematically designed opportunity for the student to learn the points of view of respondents, including any problems or suggestions the respondents may have.

Tell the reader if and how the pilot population differs from the proposed study population and how that difference may affect the study. Be completely honest. A difference may not threaten the validity of the study if recognized and accounted for beforehand.

After the pilot study, the researcher decides whether the proposed procedures need to be revised. The proposal must tell the reader what the researcher intends to do after the pilot study is completed and how it is to be done.

Data Collection

In the Data Collection section, one describes the nature of the data and how the data will be collected, including, for example, the mailing of questionnaires, the gathering of specimens, the scheduling of interviews, the search for documents in libraries in specified locations, or the recording of differences between two groups of subjects. A statement of provisions for follow-up is expected. Whichever type of research is proposed, the committee will want evidence that the researcher has thought about the possibility that data may not come easily and has made plans for the eventuality. Also, if animal or human subjects are involved, the protection of their rights must be indicated (see Index).

The process of collecting data must be appropriate to the research problem and the specific nature of the data. For example, interviews are very inefficient ways to collect large-scale survey information, although they may be used to supplement or to ascertain validity and reliability of such data. Other examples of inappropriate data collection procedures—which may spoil otherwise excellent research studies—are those that unacceptably invade the privacy of respondents or put subjects at risk.

Advances in computer technology now make feasible the first-hand collection and analysis of many kinds of data involving events and behavior. A laptop computer may be used to collect and store data and then to generate a variety of tables and reports, including answering many different questions about probability relationships between and among events. (More about computer utilization is discussed below.)

Treatment of the Data

After the proposed data are collected, what will be done? Will tables and charts be constructed, and if so, what will they display? If the data demand analysis, describe that analysis. Will the analysis be done in concert with some theoretical construct? If so, provide a description. The committee expects to find such content in the Treatment of the Data section.

Usually, the theory, the hypotheses, or the research questions guide the researcher in sifting through a mass of data. They focus the search and provide implicit criteria for the evidence search. A simple analogy might be made to archaeologists at a dig. There is a mountain of stuff to sift through, and perhaps all of it is interesting, but without theory, questions, or hypotheses guiding the search, it is possible that some important artifacts will be glossed over, and some critical relationships missed.

Here, too, computer software can make substantial contributions to the research process. Many colleges and universities maintain centers that furnish consultation to students and faculty on the selection and use of the most appropriate statistical procedures for answering questions or testing hypotheses from a given set of data. Such centers are much like the libraries in the way they operate, being there for use as needed. In some instances, they will store data for the researcher and run analyses as requested.

Doing such work on one's own is made easier, too, by statistical software packages on the market. SPSS and SA are popular sources for a large variety of statistical and graphic analysis packages. In addition, there are others. *Statistical and Statistical Graphic Resources* (retrieved May 20, 2002, from http://www.math.yorku.ca/SCS/Stat Resources.html) provides resources for statistics, statistical graphics, computations related to research, data analysis, and teaching. It contains over 580 links.

The T/D student must remember, though, that use of a statistical procedure carries with it the responsibility of understanding and being able to explain the reasons that the procedure is appropriate. An American Psychological Association Task Force on Statistical Inference (1997, p. 10) recently reemphasized the need for *understanding*: "Computer programs have placed a much greater demand on researchers to understand and control their analysis and design choices." This is part of the prevailing ethics of research in academic and professional circles. If you are the author, you accept responsibility for everything in the manuscript.

Appendices

An appendix may be needed to present drafts of letters to be sent, briefs of related research, as well as drafts of questionnaires and/or interview schedules, tests, or rating forms. This is also an appropriate place to put an appendix that shows a time line or flowchart of how the research will proceed. This could be adapted from Figs. 1-1 and 3-1. In general, an appendix contains documentation or evidence of important points made in the body of the proposal and referred to in the proposal. An appendix is the place for important tables, displays, or other items too long and detailed to be in the proposal's main body. For the proposal itself and its appendices, we recommend parsimony. If in doubt, leave it out. After all, items can always be added if that is the wish of the committee or the advisor.

Bibliography

A thorough, focused, succinct bibliography is mandatory. List only the materials cited in the proposal. This is not the place to list everything you can find on the subject in the library. Remember that the bibliography helps to indicate the authority of the work by the quality of sources cited, not the quantity.

A major purpose of the bibliography is to enable the reader to use the works cited. Therefore, each entry must be complete so the work cited can be found. If you must use documents that others cannot obtain, tell the reader in a footnote what the documents are and why they are important to your study. It will not help the reader if you simply cite such works in the bibliography.

Scholarship requires precision in citing, too. Lalumière (1993) distinguishes two kinds of citations. One refers the reader simply to a source of information, and the other kind gives support to a claim. He breaks the latter kind into four types (p. 913) that refer

> (a) to an opinion of an author, (b) to conclusions derived from a narrative review of empirical studies, (c) to the method and results of an empirical study, and (d) to the method and results of a quantitative review of empirical studies (meta-analysis).

We join Lalumière (1993) in encouraging writers to be specific about the basis for a citation so as to avoid misleading the reader as to the weight attached to a cited report.

When specifying a reference, always seek to cite the *actual* source. If an article you are reading contains a pertinent quotation from another source, there is a temptation sometimes to use the quotation in your own manuscript as though you had found it yourself in the original source. First, that would be dishonest. It would not give due credit to the author of the article in which you really found it, and it would give the impression, falsely, that you had read the original source and discovered the pertinent quotation yourself. Second, to appropriate material in that way exposes one to dangers of two kinds. Some studies have shown (Adler, 1991) that citations are likely, often, to have been referenced incorrectly in even otherwise well-edited books and journals. Further, if you pretend to have quoted from an original source, you risk embarrassment if one of your committee members knows the original source well and begins to quiz you about what else it contains. Moreover, even if you have been motivated to locate and study the original source of the pertinent quote, it is a professional and academic point of courtesy to acknowledge the author who led you to do so.

MAKE SOFTWARE YOUR SERVANT

Almost every aspect of T/D work can be enhanced in appearance, done more efficiently, completed more quickly, or made more accurate using readily available software. This applies from the moment one begins to think about possible topics until the T/D is completed and being readied for journal or book publication.

Where can you find the software you need? First, ask the research librarian. Also, search the Web. For example, the Association for Survey Computing home page (http://www.asc.org.uk/) leads to more than 170 software packages with attributes and suppliers, with a built-in search facility. Information includes statistical design, design analysis, sample size in survey research, multilevel statistical models, and survey sampling routines. Also, follow other sites listed in the references (Clarke and Oxman, 2000; Florida Community College, 2001; King, 2000; Stempner, 2001; Trochim, 2002; University of Miami Libraries, 2001). To search for appropriate software, one can also use search engines such as Yahoo, AltaVista, or Google. Type *buyer's guide* and choose *computer Internet software* to find sources of information. There are also meta-analysis programs (Kenny, 1999; King, 2000) that may allow a free download. These sites often assist the user in the statistical computation and provide an array of computational options. Some have links to other sites for data analysis.

Consider *keeping records* for a fine illustration of how truly helpful software can be. Make a habit of entering, daily, one's thoughts, musings, ideas, questions, and discoveries in a computer's memory, in the form of one or more *files*. Such files then become your stockpiles of raw material to which you will probably return again and again as you find new uses for what was originally stored there. Moreover, you will find yourself elaborating on the items already in storage and adding new items.

A key point about filing notes is the value—even the necessity—of keeping track of the sources of your notes, especially those that came from reading books or journals, listening to lectures, or participating in discussions. This need emphasizes the importance of being able, later, to *cite* precisely the source of the information. The need for complete and accurate knowledge about where one got an idea or a quotation points to the urgency of starting immediately to construct and maintain a *bibliography*.

A number of students have found it valuable to put the headings in this chapter into outline form right in their own computers so they can then insert relevant material as they learn about it or conceptualize it. Appropriate software not only will allow this, but also will make it possible to rearrange and edit to help clarify your vision of what you want to do and could lead you to make your writing more grammatically correct and compelling.

SUMMARY

This chapter helps the reader prepare the proposal by discussing the most relevant criteria for the process. A suggested format for the overview is presented, with recommendations about how to deal with each section of the proposal. An outline in the form of a Table of Contents is presented as illustrative material. Sections explaining, for example, the problem statement, the review of the literature, and the research design are major parts of the chapter. A list of different kinds of research methodology, with a brief explanation and some examples of each, is included, as are suggestions about maximizing the help available from contemporary technology.

5

The Thesis or Dissertation Committee

QUICK REFERENCE TO ANSWERS TO SPECIFIC QUESTIONS

Normally, reputable institutions of higher education require that graduate and honors student research be guided and monitored by a committee. The committee typically consists of the chairperson (usually the student's advisor) and an additional number of faculty. Commonly, the thesis committee has three members and the dissertation committee between three and five, depending on the institution regulations. Sometimes, there is a requirement that one committee member be from another department or even from another institution.

The committee serves through the proposal stage until the satisfactory completion of the project. Occasional exceptions require two quite separate committees, with separate functions appropriate to the differences between an overview and a final defense.

FUNCTIONS OF THE COMMITTEE

The committee provides both guidance and evaluation. It is the most important guardian of the quality of honors and graduate study since completion of the T/D culminates in an advanced or honors degree. The process challenges the student to operate effectively at a high level of independence in investigating concepts of considerable sophistication. The committee must ascertain that the student has in fact reached the high level indicated by the awarding of advanced or honors degree. Evidence of this expectation is that the final oral examination may include questions not only on the investigation, but also in the substantive area of academic study or the profession. Thus, the committee functions to ensure the quality of the T/D as well as of the student's knowledge and understanding in the appropriate discipline. The list that follows includes the main functions.

1. The committee provides advice and consultation to the candidate throughout the process of the research.
2. It approves or in some other way acts on the proposal of the candidate.
3. It makes qualitative judgments about the candidate's written work, including substance, format, style, grammar, design, methodology, procedures, and conclusions.
4. It sets the direction of the study by approving the proposal and assists the chairperson in providing direction for the study.
5. It approves the style manual to be used by the candidate, with particular attention to any proposed deviation from a standard style manual.
6. It approves, when constituted as a final defense committee, the final draft.
7. It ensures that the rights of human subjects are protected.

Figure 5-1 displays an evaluation form used by a number of experienced advisors. We recommend it for students and faculty members because it shows what committees look for in proposals and final documents.

STUDENT/COMMITTEE NEGOTIATIONS

Sternberg (1981) correctly points out that candidates face two sets of negotiations: those with the committee as a whole and those with individual members of the committee. He recommends that the candi-

Name of evaluator and date:______________________________

Title of dissertation or thesis:______________________________

Name of student:______________________________

Characteristics being evaluated	Poor	Mediocre	Good	Excellent	Not applicable	Evaluator's notes on items rated
1. Title is clear and concise						
2. Problem is significant and clearly stated						
3. Limitations and delimitations of the study are stated						
4. Delimitations are well defined and appropriate to solutions of the problem						
5. Assumptions are clearly stated						
6. Assumptions are tenable						
7. The research projected by the proposal does not violate human rights or animal care obligations						
8. Important terms are well defined						
9. Specific questions to be studied are clearly stated						
10. Hypotheses, elements, or research questions are clearly stated						
11. Hypotheses, elements, or research questions are testable, discoverable, or answerable						

Figure 5-1 Thesis/dissertation evaluation form. It may be used for either the proposal or the final document. When used for the proposal, omit asterisked (*) items.

Characteristics being evaluated	Poor	Mediocre	Good	Excellent	Not applicable	Evaluator's notes on items rated
12. Hypotheses, elements, or research questions derive from the review of the literature						
13. Relationship of study to previous research is clear						
14. Review of literature is efficiently summarized						
15. Procedures are described in detail						
16. Procedures are appropriate for the solution of problem						
17. Population and sample are clearly described						
18. Method of sampling is appropriate						
19. Variables have been controlled						
20. Data-gathering methods are described						
21. Data-gathering methods are appropriate to solution of the problem						
22. Validity and reliability of data gathered are explained						
23. Appropriate methods are used to analyze data						
24. Sentence structure and punctuation are correct						
25. Minimum of typographical errors						
26. Spelling and grammar are correct						

Figure 5-1 Continued

Characteristics being evaluated	Poor	Mediocre	Good	Excellent	Not applicable	Evaluator's notes on items rated
27. Material is clearly written						
28. Tone is unbiased and impartial						
29. Overall rating of creativity and significance of the problem						
*30. Tables and figures are used effectively						
*31. Results of analysis are presented clearly						
*32. Major findings are discussed clearly and related to previous research						
*33. Importance of the findings is explained						
*34. The relationship between the research and the findings is demonstrated with tight, logical reasoning						
*35. Conclusions are clearly stated						
*36. Conclusions are based on the results						
*37. Generalizations are confirmed						
*38. Limitations and weaknesses of study are discussed						
*39. Implications of findings for the field are discussed						
*40. Suggestions for further research are cited						
*41. Overall rating of the conduct of the study and the final document						

General comments:____________________

____

____

____

Figure 5-1 Continued

date show each chapter, as it is written, to each committee member for approval. We consider that to be a matter to be determined in consultation with the advisor, but we agree fully when he also points out that lines of communication can be sustained by notes or phone calls. Many advisors we interviewed felt the same way and suggested using E-mail.

In our judgment, the regular progress report, in memorandum form, is the single most effective way to stay in touch in a constructive way with each committee member. We suggest that memos be sent *on a regular schedule* every two or three weeks and that a computer file or file folder be used to save copies. Such reports are common practice in major research institutes, so it is good to learn to use them. The memo should be written, reviewed with the advisor, and with advisor approval, duplicated and sent to all committee members. The key to good communication is to keep the memo short and factual. A useful format for the progress report memorandum is shown in Fig. 5-2.

The Activities, Problems, and Other headings cover the substance of the progress report. They are linked in terms of time to the calendar Period covered, that is, from some date to some later date.

Activities completed might, for instance, be a series of interviews started during the period of the prior report. Activities continued might be a literature search or certain data processing. Activities initiated might be the start of a pilot study. The kind of material reported obviously depends on the nature of the project and what actually occurred during the two or three weeks of time covered. If something is both started and finished during that period, report it under Activities completed.

The Problems section should be used for unresolved problems only. State the problem briefly and tell what you are doing to try to solve it. Indicate if you are working with a particular committee member or another consultant on the problem, or if you intend to do so. The Other section covers situations like delays because of illness, unanticipated developments in the investigation that are significant but are not problems, and similar matters. If there is something (i.e., a reprint) you wish all committee members to have, mention it under this heading and attach it.

Project title: ______________________________

From: ______________________ To: __________

Date: ______________________ __________

Period covered: ______________________ __________

Investigator's telephone: ______________________

Activities completed: ______________________

Activities continued: ______________________

Activities initiated: ______________________

Problems: ______________________

Other: ______________________

____

Figure 5-2 Progress report memorandum.

Committee members who receive periodic, short, factual progress reports written in clear English with complete sentences know that the student is taking the research work seriously. In that case, the committee members are inclined to be more serious in their interactions with the student. Also, the student who makes regular reports is unlikely to face confrontations later with faculty who felt left out or not consulted. The fact that your E-mail address and telephone number are on every report makes it easy for a committee member to contact you if there is reason to do so.

In addition to the written progress report, which can be mailed, faxed, or sent by E-mail, we recommend that telephone contact be made with each committee member at least every month or six weeks. Even if there is no pressing reason, use an approach like checking to see that the progress reports have been arriving and that they are clear. Ask if there is any particular part of the investigation on which the committee member wishes more information. In this and other ways, keep communication channels open.

As to whether to provide members with chapters or other segments of the document as it is being written, we are less adamant about that than Sternberg (1981). Some dissertations do almost require that approach. A critique or a theory development about social policy or monetary policy might profit very much from step-by-step committee input. A poll, a case study, or an experiment, though, might more usefully be reviewed by committee members in a first draft of a full report. We recommend discussing this matter fully with the advisor and then, if appropriate, with individual committee members. Try to accommodate the advice of the advisor and the individual style preferences of committee members. It is appropriate to ask the advisor to clear the arrangement with the other members of the committee if it appears you might be caught in a conflict of views in which you have responsibility but no authority.

MAINTAINING COMMUNICATION

The best way to guard against unpleasant surprises in any aspect of the T/D study is to keep in constant contact with the advisor. This does not mean to be a pest, but it does mean to make an effort to keep the advisor informed of the progress and problems. The regular progress report is basic to serve that purpose. However, there are needs for added personal contact, too. Often, this can be done informally by E-mail. The student should keep a log, including date, time, and subjects discussed. It may also involve writing the advisor from time to time summarizing the decisions and reports made in the written communications and requesting further clarification, if needed. When visits are necessary to the advisor's office, schedule them in advance with the advisor or the secretary. Advisors, like students, are busy people with many roles. Determine whether your advisor is usually available for a drop-in visit or whether appointments are preferred.

Normally, the committee does not expect to see the student researcher as often as the advisor. Much of the nature and quantity of the student-committee interaction is a result of the particular style of the advisor. The advisor often serves as a communications medium with respect to the committee expectations. Within that framework, it is wise to let the committee know of progress through the progress report and to offer to meet and share additional information with any committee member.

SELECTING THE COMMITTEE MEMBERS

Preferred practice calls for committee members to be named with care. Competence, interest, and current workload should be the chief criteria. Deans, chairpersons, or graduate study directors who act arbitrarily in naming committee members and who do not involve students in that determination deny them a potentially rich experience in decision making. Also, anyone who assigns faculty to committees without prior consultation with them comes dangerously close to infringing on academic freedom.

Elsewhere in this book, a number of suggestions were made to help students exercise intelligently their share in the choice of a chairperson. The same considerations can be reviewed while thinking about other committee members. Some added ones are as follows:

Can you identify faculty members who, when put together as a committee, provide good resource coverage for all the proposed project's parts?

Do you have a particular weakness in one aspect of the projected work? If so, have you located a committee member who has recognized strength in that area?

Are you going to propose the use of a procedure or of a tool that is very specialized or so new that many faculty members would be unfamiliar with it? If so, have you found at least one prospective committee member who is acknowledged by the rest of the faculty to be a responsible authority or specialist with that procedure or tool?

Do you know enough about the possible committee members to feel confident that there are no personal or professional animosities among those you are planning to propose? Are you reasonably compatible with each?

Selection Criteria

Universities have formal criteria for the selection of committee members, but the criteria tend to be concerned with bureaucratic rules rather than with the more value-laden qualitative judgments significant for students. For example, a common requirement is that the majority of the committee be members of the graduate faculty. Another example is that usually at least one member of the committee must be a member of a department or school other than that of the candidate.

For the student and the advisor, qualitative criteria ought to determine the membership of a committee. They should look for faculty known for integrity, scholarship, expertise in the candidate's field of study, high standards in writing, and both T/D guidance and personal research experience. The bureaucratic criteria are important for they generally guard the institution from abuses and improprieties, but the more qualitative criteria are essential to a high standard of scholarship.

Procedure

Students should find and follow the published or unwritten local rules that govern the selection process. Usually, the rules involve both the advisor and the student. The school or department faculty ordinarily reserves the right to approve the selection of the advisor and the committee members. This right may be latent, it may be clearly authorized but unused, or it may be used in a pro forma way, but it is usually there to be exercised. This approval process may extend to chairpersons and deans in addition to faculty recommendation or approval. The advisor is responsible for whatever needs to be done to satisfy this matter.

Student Role: The extraordinary importance of the committee strongly suggests that students take special care about their part in the selection. How does one use good judgment in this matter? Review the criteria recommended previously for committee members. Are they reasonable for the selection of your committee members? Try to assess prospective committee members in some of the ways described in previous chapters; consult your advisor, fellow students, graduates of the department's program; talk to a number of faculty members about your proposed statement of problem to see if they are interested in or knowledgeable about it. Ask for advice and suggestions from those with whom you talk. Carefully weigh the reception, the consultation, the expressions of interest, and the quality and direction of advice you receive. Work carefully, but try to move quickly, too. The early selection of appropriate committee members can save a great deal of time, effort, and frustration later and will certainly enhance the quality of the final product.

Advisor Role: The advisor has the most important faculty role in the committee selection process. The research advisor is normally the person who, with the student's help and concurrence, makes the selection of faculty members to serve on the committee—such persons meeting both the formal rules of the university and the qualitative criteria applicable to the proposed research topic.

It is common, as noted, for the advisor to submit the proposed committee to some superior person or body. Approval is usually expected. It is difficult to disapprove a proposed committee unless the committee does not meet the formally stated requirements of the university.

The most certain way to continue to ensure high quality in committee selection (and, indeed, committee action) is by ensuring that the process is open to peer checks and review. Such review should include the posting of defense times well in advance, distribution of notices of receipt of proposals and final drafts far enough in advance to permit faculty review, and announcing and scheduling final defense meetings in such a way as to encourage the attendance and participation of any faculty or students having an interest. The advisor's role in committee selection includes taking leadership in ensuring that student rights and welfare are respected and safeguarded, too.

Departmental Chairperson Role: The role of the departmental chairperson is one of ensuring quality and equity. The interests of the student, the faculty, and the institution have to be protected. This is expected of the chairperson by all who take part in the process.

The chairperson should have formal authority and the power of appointing or approving the advisor or the committee. Also, chairpersons work in less formal ways by suggesting, encouraging, and rewarding.

The effectiveness and integrity the chairperson can maintain is directly related to the strength and academic vigor of the administrative leadership of the school or university. All faculty and students need to be vigilant to ensure proper emphasis on the two essential attributes—high quality and equity for everyone.

A Committee Selection Model

We found much variation in committee selection and assignment practices. Of all the practices, the ones with the features in the list that follows seem to have most to recommend them.*

1. The dean or department chairperson's office distributes annually to all honors and graduate students a list of faculty members that contains three items.
   a. The titles of *completed* T/Ds the faculty member chaired in the previous three academic years.
   b. The titles of *completed* T/Ds on which the faculty member served as committee member in the previous three academic years.
   c. A list of the one, two, or three special-interest and competency areas of each faculty member, as prepared by themselves, such as law, social psychology, anthropology, welfare policy, transportation, rehabilitation, early childhood, finance, microbiology, astrophysics, computer science, research methodology, human stress, supervision, counseling, speech pathology, program evaluation, instructional theory, or others.
2. Students are advised in writing by the dean that they are encouraged to discuss prospective T/D topics with *any* faculty members.
3. Faculty members refer students to one another with the primary objective of helping the students learn for themselves what others think of their ideas in the early formative stages.
4. Each advisor maintains gentle but steady pressure on advisees to formulate proposals in writing and to discuss them.
5. There is a published departmental deadline by which time the

---

*We urge students to find this information on their own if it is not supplied by their school or department.

student must have a proposal approved by a committee, or the student will not be permitted to enroll for more courses.
6. The advisor offers assistance to the student in identifying a research advisor and committee members.
7. Students are made aware from the outset that it is their responsibility to take the nominations of chairperson and committee members to the department chairperson.
8. Once nominations are received, the department chairperson is obliged to first check two items.
   a. Do the student's nominees already have full loads with respect to these tasks?
   b. If not, are they willing to work with this student?
9. If conditions 8(a) and 8(b) above are acceptable, the department chairperson notifies the student, the student's advisor, and the nominated committee members of the appointments.

This model for committee selection and assignment has the virtues of openness and orderliness. Misunderstandings are minimized. The interests and the workloads of faculty members are taken into account; the student is supplied with useful leads and clear guidelines. Within the school and departmental contexts, the process and its outcomes are public and can be maintained on a professional plane. The model does presume that the matter of faculty workload, as it relates to advisorship and committee membership (discussed below), has been settled. There are quite interesting case studies and articles that relate to the way dissertation committees work. Some of this information is disturbing but informative, indicating how things can go wrong even in the best of institutions in ways not expected by the student or the advisor (Hernandez, 1996; Ruark, 2002; Smallwood, 1992). These sources provide ideas for practical questions the student might raise while seeking committee members and trying to understand the process.

Size of Committee

We recommend committees of four and five for the thesis and dissertation, respectively, which is larger, by one, than the usual requirement. Usually, there is no prohibition against having a committee larger than that specified in regulations. Often, the final defense committee is encouraged to add members for the purpose of enlarging its scope as an examining group.

Large committees take large amounts of time; that may be one reason for the prevalence of very small ones. While a small committee—some schools require only three faculty members for the dissertation committee—may be reasonable, a larger number can enhance quality and equity. Five is not too many in light of the variety of expertise usually needed. In case of emergency, the committee can be authorized to operate with one less than the required number, that is, with three and four for the thesis and the dissertation, respectively. Thus, if one member retires, moves, becomes ill, or goes on a sabbatical leave, as is not unlikely in a committee constituted over a number of years, it is less likely to hold up the progress of the student. Finally, a very subjective comment: Our experience suggests that larger committees tend to be run in a more open and aboveboard fashion and that they tend to focus more on the quality and relevance of the work than on the worker.

COMMITTEE MEMBER ROLES

The role of a committee member is similar to the research advisor's role, but there are important differences. A committee member's role does not carry as much responsibility. Also, the depth of the role is greater for the chairperson. Such differences allow committee members to exercise more flexibility and creativity in role definition and to make the relationship one of positive growth and maturation for the student.

Foster Creativity

The T/D committee membership is not well defined in higher education literature or by easily observed modeling of role incumbents. The lack of overt, consistent definition means the job is open to a good deal of professional judgment, independence, and self-direction. It also means that there are opportunities for both the student and faculty to be creative in determining how a committee member works on a given study. For the faculty member, much of the joy of working with students on creative projects is present without all the responsibility of the chairperson.

Seeman (1973) offered a theory-based point of view on supervising student research. He emphasized the creative aspect of what the student is to produce, namely, a contribution to knowledge, defined as a novel product. Then, he drew heavily on published research on creative persons, leading to the conclusion that "an optimum learning climate [in which to foster creativity] would involve considerable latitude for the student to go off into unconventional cognitive byways, along with a support system that provides them with occasions for doing so."

In a pamphlet called *Research Student and Supervisor* (LaPidus, 1990), the Council of Graduate Schools offers its viewpoints on that relationship and suggests ideas relevant to disciplines that prepare students for the Ph.D. Some key observations from that publication are as follows:

> A peculiarly close relationship exists between the research student and supervisor. They start as master and pupil and ideally end up as colleagues. Obviously, under the circumstances, it is desirable that the student and supervisor should be carefully matched.
>
> There are two aspects to supervision. The first and most important has to do with creativity and involves the ability to select problems, to stimulate and enthuse students, and to provide a steady stream of ideas. The second aspect is concerned with the mechanics of ensuring that the student makes good progress. (p. 1)

Note the similar emphasis on creativity by Seeman (1973) and LaPidus (1990), almost 20 years later. The Council of Graduate Schools (1990b) also urges that originality on the part of the student should be fostered as a central concern in the T/D process. And originality is another word for creativity.

However, Seeman (1973) argues that what really happens is almost the opposite: A climate of conformity prevails, produced and sustained by the research guidance given the student. He blames this, in psychology, on the discipline's homage to the conventions and procedures of "science." He says:

> For students, the phenomena of scientific ritual and scientific respectability appear in the form of rapid and insistent preoccupation with questions about sample size, controls, instrumentation, statistical procedures, and other formal questions about the structure of their inquiry. I am saying that a too-early concern for these structures puts the accent on formal rather than substantive issues, deflects the students' energies from their original questions, and, most crucially, emphasizes an external locus-of-control attitude that may dilute the sense of ownership and responsibility which the students feel for their problems. (p. 901)

Going on to suggest a connection between student behavior and the perceptions conveyed to students by the learning atmosphere in which they start to think about research, Seeman says:

> It is small wonder that many students experience the development of a research problem in terms of finding some preexisting question "out there." They search the literature, read other student's theses, seek ideas from professors, and in general disregard the possibility that a research problem might come from some question of their own. (p. 901)

As to the role of the system in generating that kind of student behavior, and as to the function of the faculty in keeping the focus of the student's attention narrowly on the formal aspects of T/D work, Seeman (1973) reasons that a restrictive, limiting learning climate is the inevitable result, not an optimum learning climate. He puts it this way:

> What I am suggesting here is that science has become a quasilegal system, and that deviance is just as much punished in this domain as in any other domain where people make laws. Seen thus, the task as experienced by the student is to go about his/her proper business while at the same time making sure to obey the law. In this context, professors are part helpers and part social control agents of a very powerful kind. They become advisers—policemen who assist the student, but who also make sure

> that the student obeys the law with respect to scientific procedures.
>
> In short, the psychological climate for the student is one in which the helping process and the evaluative process become thoroughly entangled. The most likely consequence is interference with learning. (p. 901)

If Seeman's 1973 analysis is correct, it raises serious questions that seem applicable to many of the conventional forms and processes in graduate and honors student investigations. Research procedures and designs used in a number of professions have been drawn from psychology, long recognized as an undergirding discipline with major applications in professional human services work.

Seeman (1973) does not report data drawn systematically from students or from faculty members to verify his analysis or his conclusions about the climate of learning and about the behavior of students and advisors. Neither do LaPidus (1990) or CGS (1990b). Seeman finds analogs in studies of other situations, mainly those that involve counseling and psychotherapy, and argues from those presumed parallel instances. It would certainly be valuable if his provocative and insightful ideas were put to a more direct test.

We have drawn a number of implications for the professor-student relationship from the Seeman analysis (1973) and our own observations. They are potentially helpful guides to action for students and faculty.

1. Foster a secure relationship in which the student has confidence in the support of the professor. (The professor says, honestly, "I believe in you and in your ability and integrity. You can count on my guidance, and I will give it freely and in a helping spirit.")
2. Recognize and encourage independence in the student. (The professor praises students for taking actions on their own. The professor says, "You can expect me to encourage you to make decisions for yourself whether or not I agree with them. This will be, all the way, *your* project. I will enjoy helping you to make it that. At the same time, I will try to teach you how to judge the adequacy of what you do.")

3. Teach the student to understand how the professor views personal and professional accountability. (The professor lets the student know that both their professional reputations are on the line, afresh, with each decision they make about the investigation. The professor says, and means it: "It will be important to me to help both of us to avoid conflict with each other and with our associates. At the same time, if either of us believes in the rightness of what we propose to do, even though it appears to be leading to a confrontation, we should not hesitate to initiate a discussion about it. We should speak our minds, try to work out the differences, and if that fails, separate with full respect and regard for each other.")

Seeman (1973) believes that the experience of autonomy can be used to make explicit the nature and kinds of responsibilities the student and the faculty member each will accept. He says:

> I have started to take this route by making explicit contracts with my students. For my part, I accept two kinds of responsibility . . . I take responsibility for certification of a student's performance; that is, I accept as a social responsibility the evaluation of professional competency. My second responsibility is to make available to the student the professional resources and skills that I have. On the students' part, their enrollment in a program signifies that they have committed themselves to developing competence. . . .
>
> I see the concept of a contract as a powerful tool for developing responsible interpersonal relationships. (p. 905)

Aside from anecdotal pieces (Krathwohl, 1988; Mecklenburger, 1972; Meloy, 2002; Merrill, 1992; Pulling, 1992; Sternberg, 1981), there seems to be little established information about the student as such in the T/D process. Yet, a discipline's most able students, as they do graduate and honors research and afterward, would seem to be most logically and most appropriately the best sources of information and insights about how to make the most of the major commitment colleges and universities have to that advanced work. MacKinnon (1962) remarks that

> Creative students will not always be to our liking. This will be due not only to their independence in situations in which nonconformity may be seriously disruptive of the work of others, but because . . . they will be experiencing large quantities of tension produced in them by the richness of their experience and the strong opposites of their nature.

He was describing the behavior of creative architects when they were students. He went on to report that

> Clearly, many of them were not easy to take. One of the most rebellious, but, as it turned out, one of the most creative, was advised by the Dean of his School to quit because he had no talent; and another, having been failed in his design dissertation which attacked the stylism of the faculty, took his degree in the art department. (p. 495)

Other professions, too, attract individuals who combine the ingredients that make up creativity. The academic and professional nurture of such men and women can be a stormy experience. The long-range outcomes, however, enrich the student, the advisor and committee members, the institution, and the professions. Data about how to best encourage such positive outcomes are needed.

One of the opportunities to foster creativity is to brainstorm to explore problems, hypotheses, and conjectures without being too evaluative at the early stages. It is important in this context for students to be encouraged to *see* and to *understand* side issues, offshoots, parallels, and branches of their topics and to acquire the discipline to stay on the main track. It is a chance to explore with the student the relationship of the emerging T/D to the development of personal effectiveness and personal goals such as autonomy and professional and academic maturity. Faculty-student interaction around the graduate or honors research project provides many opportunities to help the student grow as an autonomous, self-directed person at a time in life when that help is perhaps needed most. The honors or graduate student experience up to that stage has often been directed by others; the T/D stage is a transition from dependence to autonomy.

Committee members also have excellent opportunities to enhance both the student's and their own research competence. Committee members can help the student-writer on a one-to-one basis to examine the associative relationships that are projected in the study. It is a time to help the candidate to look for possible cause-and-effect relationships in variables identified or phenomena to be observed. It is a time to examine theory and engage in some preliminary efforts at building new theoretical constructs. Opportunities to teach the value of suspending early judgment, to teach by example some aspects of critical thinking and deductive or inductive reasoning are available to the committee member throughout the advisement process. These opportunities are especially valuable because they come at a time, with respect to an interest in a commonly shared subject, when the openness to learn and to share ideas is strongest.

Encourage Clear Writing

Not all committee members have the same interests or expertness, but everyone should care deeply about the student's ability to express ideas about complex matters in clear and direct prose. Many investigations deal with complicated subjects; students often feel that their writing has to be equally complicated. Committee members can help students see that there is an artificiality about complex and overly complicated sentences and paragraphs full of long words that obfuscate rather than foster understanding. Further, such writing all too often is a facade hiding a student's lack of clear comprehension. There is no subject that cannot be made clear in simple words to the average intelligent adult if the writer knows the subject well enough and has good facility with language. Committee members who help students express themselves in clear, concise, and direct language perform an invaluable service. The student gains not only with respect to the immediate task, but also in future writing and publishing (Henson, 1993; O'Connor, 1997).

Foster Growth Through Writing

Committee members can set examples for students by participating in professional meetings and engaging in scholarship. Also, committee members often have the contacts and information that permit them to encourage student participation in professional and scholarly meetings. Some of the most valuable experiences have come to students who were encouraged to write, publish, and read papers at such meetings during their advanced study years. Often, these activities were related to T/D work—perhaps literature reviews, descriptions of pilot studies, or the findings of the T/D research itself. Numerous examples, from our own experience, can be cited regarding the encouragement of students to write, to publish, and to prepare papers for professional and academic meetings. There are, for example, citations in this work that refer to important contributions made by students on whose committees the authors served or who worked with the authors in some similar way. Papers can be written and presented jointly. Panels and reactors can be chosen to include a student researcher.

If money is a problem, often ways can be worked out to help the student researcher attend meetings and present papers through the use of awards, travel with faculty colleagues who may drive, and the payment of modest honoraria for services performed at the meeting. We have seen examples of colleagues helping to pay expenses of students. None of this is a part of the formal responsibility of the committee members perhaps, but it all could be a part of the mentoring role that faculty members define for themselves. Sometimes, just words of encouragement and the offer to help are enough to set the student off in the proper direction, with self-motivation taking over the progress toward final autonomy and participation.

The role of the committee member must always be seen as fostering the autonomy and academic maturity of the student researcher. This does not assume that the student is immature or dependent, but the behavior typically encouraged or enforced all too often turns out to be toward dependence and following directions. For that very reason, the obligation is there, in the research stages of study especially, to encourage the emergence or reassertion of autonomy and self-direction.

Serve as a Model

Advisors and committee members themselves acquire role behavior through observing models. New faculty members watch committee members and chairpersons in action while in the process of doing honors, master's, or doctoral work and later imitate them. Committee members' behavior also impresses the student and tends to be remembered and copied if, later, the student assumes the committee role. Therefore, the behavior of senior committee persons is of great significance. It becomes the model for others.

Modeling is also one very good way students learn to become advanced researchers. This has implications for the role of the committee member who works closely with the candidate on a research problem or who thinks through the formulation of a research problem with the student researcher.

Students and colleagues respect the committee members who insist on excellence and fairness. It is the responsibility of each committee member to provide serious and consistent help to the student, with the aim of ensuring the high-quality work of which most students are capable, and to work toward making the whole process as rigorous and fair as humanly possible. Every vote counts on the committee, and every vote cast, in some instances, could be the vote that makes the difference between outstanding scholarship and just sliding through.

Sternberg (1981), Krathwohl (1988), and Meloy (2002) all picture the student as walking a tightrope. The choice may sometimes seem to be between alienating the committee, on the one hand, by sticking to a point of view of what should be in the T/D and becoming completely confused and prey to every shift in committee thinking on the other. We believe, as they do, that the advisor and the student should figuratively link arms in such a case, and together they should stand for what they believe. When that happens, committees tend to work around to accepting the candidate's way of dealing with the matter as long as there is confidence in the integrity of the individual and confidence that the knowledge base is sound.

SUMMARY

Universities normally require a research project supervised by a faculty committee as the culminating work of honors or graduate study for a degree. Committees of faculty are appointed to work with the candidate on the project from the proposal stage to the final defense.

The committee functions as a guide and help to the student through the process, and it also evaluates the work as it progresses to the final defense. A form for use in T/D evaluation is included. The committee is so important at most institutions that great care is taken in the selection of members, and there are various roles played in the selection process. The obligations of committee members to one another, the student, the advisor, and the institution are specified and discussed.

6

Approval of the Overview

The overview document takes its form from the nature of the problem to be investigated. In the first part of this book, we suggested a format that covers essential proposal elements. The time line (Fig. 1-1) adapts readily to any qualitative or quantitative study plan. Terminology differs from place to place, but the most common names given to this document are the *study plan*, *proposal*, or *overview*.

The *goal of the student* at this point is to gain the approval of the committee to embark on the conduct of the proposed project. This approval, if given, is certified by an actual vote of the committee. The committee members affix their signatures to a form that specifies salient information about the meeting.

The committee's collective judgment is reached by the end of the overview meeting. Each member has earlier read the proposal itself. During the overview meeting, members raise questions, engage in discussions with the student and each other, and offer suggestions about the proposal.

Each committee member should have assisted with the proposal idea earlier in conference with the student, and each committee member should have seen earlier drafts of the proposal. However, the overview meeting may be the first group discussion regarding a document that the student now believes is ready for the entire committee's stamp of approval.

The *committee's goal* at this point is to determine whether both the student and the written plan are ready to move into the operational stage of the T/D activity. The overriding questions are, "Has a state of adequate preparedness been reached by the student, and has satisfactory preparation been demonstrated in the written project proposal?" A crucial part of the proposal is the section that sets forth how the investigation is to be conducted. That section, sometimes called Procedure, includes the steps the student expects to take from the moment the plan is approved to the time the analysis of findings is completed.

The proposal should be a coherent document in that each part is linked meaningfully to each other part, but while other parts of the document may be in less than final form (i.e., the literature review), that cannot be true of the procedure section. If the overview committee is to approve the study plan without imperiling the future of both the project and the student, procedures should be complete and detailed.

Many colleges and universities have detailed published policies on the dissertation process. A good example is the J. Mack Robinson College of Business at Georgia State University (home page http://www.cba.gsu.edu/). The process and written policies are described in detail for students and faculty, with a discussion that focuses on presentations, committees, format, procedures, and forms. Check to see if your university has such a detailed home page or printed presentation describing the process.

CHARACTERISTICS OF A SOUND OVERVIEW

Advisors and committee members vary in their views as to the necessary components for an appropriate overview. Our recommendation is to try to satisfy three criteria.* *First*, include consideration of at least these elements:

A brief title that describes the investigation.
A face sheet with appropriate identifying information.
A table of contents.
An introductory statement of the problem to be studied.
A specific problem statement couched in terms of questions to be answered by the study's results; hypotheses to be tested; definitive information to be supplied; a theory, an explanation, or a product to be developed; or some combination of these. This is a good place to define terms, if necessary. Here the investigation types given in Chapter 4 and the general model for investigations (Fig. 4-3) may be helpful. They may also stimulate thinking about the next elements in this list.
A list of classes of literature (i.e., theoretical, research, philosophical, and so on) germane to the problem with a critical and analytical review of that literature that supports the need to conduct the proposed study.
A step-by-step procedure section that includes specific information about which data will be collected, from which sources data will be obtained, how the validity and reliability of the information will be assessed, and how the data will be analyzed to respond to specific problem statements.
A brief summary of the proposed investigation as previously outlined plus any other matters that should be part of the record (i.e., human subject concerns, threats to the study).
A sample of each data collection form, test, or similar material to be used in the study.
A bibliography of the references in the overview document.

Second, try to ensure that the ambiguities and anticipated problems are openly discussed. For example, suppose some of the data to be collected depend on responses to inquiries mailed to parents. Sup-

*For more details about organization and structure of the proposal, review Chapter 3 and pay particular attention to the T/D evaluation.

pose, also, that there has been a history of very low response rate to similar inquiries to parents in similar circumstances. This should be brought out in the overview document with a clear statement of which measures are to be taken to encourage a satisfactory return and with a contingency plan should the return be insufficient for analysis.

Third, we recommend the inclusion in the proposal document of a systematic planning procedure that spells out the anticipated time line of the investigation. This may well be an appendix. Help in setting forth the entire procedure and time sequence may be found by studying Fig. 3-1.

Even though there is variation among advisors' and committee members' views regarding what constitutes an approvable overview, the elements suggested include what many professors expect. The three key elements are a full and detailed proposal, clarification of potential ambiguities, and a rational time sequence.

PURPOSES OF THE PROPOSAL OVERVIEW MEETING

University in-house publications tend to specify administrative details, such as that a proposal be in typed form, how many committee votes are required to approve it, and where the approved document must be filed. In some cases, certain of the purposes for an overview meeting can be inferred from university publications. In addition, we list purposes drawn from an analysis of interviews with experienced faculty members. The committee should, according to them, ascertain that

1. The topic of the investigation is suitable.
2. The student is competent to undertake the study.
3. The program (or department) in which the study is undertaken is appropriate for the topic.
4. The study would constitute a valuable contribution to the literature.
5. The topic is manageable in relation to the student's time.
6. The study would be a relevant learning experience for the student.
7. The student has access to the needed human and material resources.
8. The student is able to be objective about the study.

9. The student and committee members understand the agreements resulting from overview approval.
10. Ownership of the T/D and related material as intellectual property is understood and specified.
11. The student understands any alterations needed in the proposal.

The student, the chairperson, and each committee member might well use the 11 items as a checklist to make sure that the items are adequately covered in the course of the overview examination or before it. Each item is amplified in sequence below.

SUITABILITY OF THE TOPIC

This first item means that the topic is suitable in terms of the scholarly and research interests of the academic discipline, profession, or field of study. Demonstration of the relevance and suitability of the topic to the discipline is the proposer's responsibility.

Another aspect of suitability might have to do with the utilization of human subjects. Some investigations could require that human subjects be deprived for a time of food, educational stimulation, affection, compensation, or rights that other subjects receive. Such studies would be unsuitable unless acceptable compensatory arrangements could be made and higher-level approvals received. In like manner, animal subjects require humane consideration.

Suitability ought not be taken for granted. The student should deliberately ask each committee member for confirmation of suitability, so by the time the overview meeting is convened the student's log and notes will show that suitability is not in question.

Student Competency to Undertake the Study

Three main factors to scrutinize regarding student competency to undertake the study are the student's substantive academic and professional background, the student's investigative skills, and the complexity and difficulty of the proposed study in relation to the first two factors.

For the first factor, let us suppose that the proposed topic is "*Design* of a *Graduate Curriculum* Model for Training *Community Plan-*

ners in *Brazil*." The operative expressions in the title are in italics. The student proposer needs knowledge of design procedures and principles, knowledge of graduate professional curricula, appreciation of the personal and professional characteristics and job requirements associated with community planning, a sound conceptual base regarding Brazilian higher education, and in-depth understanding of the history, present status, and goals of community development in Brazil. Certainly, it would not be necessary that the student have *all* of the background at the outset, but it would be questionable if the committee should allow the study to begin without ascertaining that it was feasible for the student to fill in any gaps quickly and thoroughly.

As to the investigative skills, the student should know how to unearth already existing information about the operative expressions in the title. This would call for knowing sources and how to search international literature. Reading knowledge of Portuguese seems essential. Also, it might be necessary to plan and to conduct interviews.

The judgment of expert faculty members or other consultants would be essential to assess the complexity and difficulty of this study. They could determine whether the country's educational and political climates would be supportive. They could judge how much time, if any, would need to be spent in Brazil. They could help judge whether substantial ground preparation would need to be done or if the foundations were ready and waiting for such a study. And, they could ascertain whether the proposed study might be overambitious and suggest how to reduce its scope to match the investigator's capabilities.

Appropriateness of the Topic for the Department

In this instance, let us assume that the student proposes a study called "Career Preparation of the Private Black College Graduate Relative to National Manpower Needs and Trends." If the student is enrolled in a department of elementary education and is specializing in early childhood education, it would probably be far-fetched to consider the topic appropriate to the department. It would be unusual to find faculty members in elementary education who have and maintain sophistication about the broad field of college career preparation.

Occasionally, students do put forward ideas that appear, on the surface, quite out of harmony with the departments in which they are matriculated. It is good to discuss them rather than to dismiss them out of hand. Sometimes, such apparently divergent proposals are signs that students' interests or goals are changing, and those possibilities deserve thoughtful attention from the advisor. Actually, at the time of the overview meeting, it should be very unusual to see topics proposed that are patently outside the scope of the particular department in which the major part of the study is to be done. More often, the questions are subtler.

For example, if a study is to deal with interactions among school of business faculty members, business education faculty members, and the local business community, should its home base be in the school of business, the school of education, the department of sociology, or elsewhere? If there is any question at all about such a matter, and if the question does not surface until the actual time of the overview meeting, the guiding principles for resolution ought to include the following:

The student should not be delayed or otherwise inhibited from pursuing the study simply because of interdepartmental or interschool disagreement.

The department or school in which the student is enrolled should continue to have responsibility for administering the T/D process of the student.

Members of other departments and schools should be added to the committee to the extent necessary to ensure that the necessary faculty competencies are represented.

Contribution to the Literature

Most discussions of the essential requirements of the T/D include the statement that the product be a "contribution to the literature." Yet, few phrases have been so ill defined. In the absence of helpful guidelines, students may conclude that, to make a contribution, one must discover a hoard of new information, demonstrate a new truth, devise a new instrument, or at least construct and validate an original theory. Actually, graduate research studies that did any of those things would certainly be welcome, and they would be hailed as contributions. But, they would be extraordinary T/Ds. There can be quite valuable contributions of lesser magnitude. Most are in the last class.

Students often worry about getting negative results or about "finding nothing" at the end of a heavy investment of time and effort in an investigation. Rumors abound regarding the flat rejection of theses or dissertations that wind up with either equivocal findings or with no solid basis for supporting the hoped-for outcome.

Krathwohl (1988, p. 234) has this to say about the absence of positive results:

> Must the dissertation have positive results to be acceptable? A proposal ought to have a reasonable chance of showing positive results. But if it doesn't work out as expected, must you start over? . . . I know of no instance where this has been required. Instead, students are asked to explain as best they can why negative results appeared and what can be learned from the apparent blind alley.

Earlier, Sternberg (1981) made much the same observation about negative outcomes. A Council of Graduate Schools publication (LaPidus, 1990) offers an additional cogent comment: "One must, however, remember that we are talking about original research where, by definition, things do not necessarily go as intended" (p. 6). In short, it is certainly a helpful contribution to identify and demonstrate that a research approach that appeared to have promise is actually not fruitful and to delineate the reasons why.

The committee, at the overview meeting and before it, will keep in mind that the *process* of T/D work needs to be given somewhat more attention than the *product*. *The student's knowledge and application of investigatory processes, including intelligent reporting of what transpired and what was found, is what is being demonstrated.* The topic certainly must be shown by the student to be both relevant and significant to the literature. But, it is enough to ask simply that the potential results of the study be judged capable of adding to or helping to clarify a matter that needs investigation, and that the findings will probably have some generalizability.

In thinking about these criteria, both student and faculty should note that one of the most obvious needs in many fields is to redo studies that have already been reported. Exact replication is seldom needed; we mean repetition with new or enhanced populations and with strengthened design and improved controls. Frequently, also, creative reanalysis of previously reported data opens the way to clearer interpretations. Studies that help us to understand better an already reported phenomenon or principle, studies that make our knowledge more reliable or more generalizable, as well as studies with findings that are suggestive of further exploration or that tell us that a given course of investigation is probably not profitable can all be contributions to the literature in the sense that the term should be applied by the overview committee.

Manageability of the Topic in Relation to Time

T/D work has specified time constraints. A six-year time span, for instance, is usually allowed between permission to begin the doctoral dissertation and its completion. The period is less for the master's thesis. The honors thesis is ordinarily done during the last two years of undergraduate study. In some cases, students are admitted to study for the doctorate after achieving the baccalaureate, but are required to complete a master's thesis along the way. In that instance, the student may not be permitted to take courses after a certain number of credits have been earned or after a certain elapsed time unless the thesis is finished and approved. There are temporal factors, too, such as sabbatical leaves, the period the data or the study populations will be available, and the decay of data relevance over time. All things considered, the overview committee needs to help the student reach a rational decision about which anticipated completion date to place on the overview approval document.

The Study as a Learning Experience

Many doctoral students already have a substantial amount of academic or professional experience. Some of the experience may have included involvement in or responsibility for research. The advisor and committee members should be familiar enough with the student's background to ensure that a proposed study is not simply a rerun of competencies that had been demonstrated at an earlier time. Naturally, the use of already confirmed capabilities is appropriate if the T/D tasks build on them and exert them significantly beyond any prior work.

From another direction, too, the committee has to satisfy itself that the student will be assured fruitful learning opportunities. Sometimes, a chairperson is so caught up in the T/D itself that the student has little or no opportunity to work out problems or procedures independently. At such times, the student may be led by the advisor so closely and meticulously that questions are answered before they are fully asked, and there are no opportunities to make mistakes and acquire understanding by working out how to recover from them. Finally, on this point, the atmosphere of the overview meeting itself may be viewed quite differently by each advisor and committee member. Some of the variations in the tone and attitude of faculty toward a student during the meeting are shown in Fig. 6-1. They are arrayed from desirable to undesirable.

As in a class or seminar, individual research students are entitled

Undesirable *Desirable*

- Collegial
- Instructional
- Consultative

- Advocate
- Maternal/paternalistic
- Nondirective
- Laissez-faire

- Adversarial
- Dictatorial
- Punitive

Figure 6-1 Faculty tone and attitude during overview committee meetings.

to the best instructional efforts their faculty advisors can muster. To be sure, the instructional style is different. It is closer to the one-to-one tutorial sometimes; at other times, it takes on the interactive fashion that characterizes peer consultation or the approach of partners in seeking the solution to a problem of mutual interest. Student entitlement to top-flight instruction holds, too, not only for the overview meeting, but also for the entire length of T/D activity. It is particularly important, though, to highlight it for the overview meeting, for if that standard is not upheld, the overview meeting can degenerate into something it should not be, an examination,* or even worse, an inquisition.

Access to Needed Resources

Which needed resources come immediately to mind if one is to attack the topic "A History of Changes in U.S. Public Policy Toward Migrants and Their Children"? Choose from the following: "Predicting Reading Achievement of High-School Students with Measures of Intelligence, Listening, and Informative Writing Ability," "Reactions of Married Persons to a Geographic Move Resulting from Spouse's Job Transfer," "The Influence of Unionization on Equal Employment Opportunity Practices," or "Organizational Behavior in Time of Crisis."

The student's advisor would ordinarily encourage the adoption of some orderly method for keeping track of resource needs as they appear in the process of developing the proposal and would assist the student, if necessary, in gaining access to them. The culmination of that aspect of planning should be exemplified in the proposal document. If there is any question about whether the needed resources (a) have been identified and (b) access to them is ensured, the question should be satisfied before approval of the study plan.

---

*In a certain sense, the overview meeting is an examination, and the proposal is or is not accepted as presented. The focus is less on the student's achievements in doing research, however, and much more on helping the student to produce a proposal that will get a whole-hearted positive response from the faculty. It is an examination much in the sense that a diagnosis is an examination; the purpose is to find the difficulties and improve the prognosis.

Student Objectivity About the Study

A student designed a portable floor mat on which was imprinted a hopscotchlike game of numbered spaces. It was expected that children with number-related learning disabilities could be helped to overcome them by individualized exercises that employed the mat. A well-controlled, carefully planned study was proposed for a dissertation by the student to determine whether the expectation could be substantiated.

In the meantime, the student's device was manufactured and widely marketed commercially. The student received substantial royalties. Anecdotal information, based on uncontrolled observations and individual case records, suggested that children did improve their number skills as a result of prescribed exercises. That information was also distributed to prospective buyers.

The dissertation study proposal was approved. The investigation was conducted. The results indicated that individualized exercises on the floor mat had no appreciably different effect on the number skills of children with learning disabilities than did ordinary number instruction.

The student, after completing the dissertation, could not accept the results. An entire additional year was taken up in fruitless tinkering with the data, attempting to find a way to make the findings say something else. In all, more than a year of that student's life was spent in a turmoil before the matter was resolved. In the end, the student did complete an approvable dissertation, but the personal and professional costs are still being paid by student and faculty members alike.

Wise instructors caution to practice objectivity from the beginning of professional study. Yet, a number of students each year take the hazardous course of proposing topics about which they have strong personal beliefs rather than strong scientific curiosity. If the proposal itself needs improvement, a very subjective attitude on the student's part might well deter the committee from suggesting ways to make it approvable. Even if the student's proposal is sound, the committee should move cautiously if the student's anticipation of confirming conclusions prejudices the proper conduct of the investigation or threatens the student's own welfare.

First, it is advisable to make the student aware of the committee's concern. This can be done directly in the meeting, and it can be confirmed by attaching a memorandum to the approval document and mentioning it in the letter that informs the student of the official approval.

Second, the committee can insist that data collection and analysis procedures be made explicit in the overview proposal, including the provision that the collection and analysis be done or closely observed by a disinterested third party. This is not to be thought of as suggesting that the committee distrusts the student. Rather, it is an example of how any professional person should behave when faced with the task of investigating a matter in which there is known to be a strong enough personal involvement to be potentially biasing.

Third, the committee should give more than ordinarily close attention to the student's literature review. Particular committee attention may focus on ensuring that the review does not overlook publications inimical to the student's viewpoint, and that all publications are given evenhanded treatment.

None of this should suggest that T/D work ought to be completely unemotional. There is a noticeable excitement and an evident spirit of zestful probing in students and in faculty during much of the enterprise. This should be encouraged. Rather, it is the possible limiting and even destructive effects of overcommitment on a highly personalized level that the committee is enjoined to help students avoid.

The Quasi-Contractual Relationship

Some speak of the approved proposal document as a contract between the higher education institution and the student. Lawyer-sociologist Sternberg (1981) found that both Washington University (St. Louis, MO) and Columbia University had, within the previous 20 years, been in court over charges that explicit or implicit conditions of dissertation preparation had been violated. As far as the proposal itself is concerned, he concludes "that a contemporary candidate is warranted in proceeding *as if* a dissertation proposal contract is in force once his committee approves his proposal" (p. 75). If the proposal and the circumstances around it fall inside the purview of American contract law—even in a limited and qualified way—the fact gives some welcome reassurance to the student. As Sternberg comments, "In the generally zero-sum model of power and authority in which he [the student] finds himself in relation to dissertation-supervising professors, the contract element is perhaps the only 'guarantee' of some substance upon which he can rely" (p. 75).

Certainly, the approval of the proposal does signal an agreement by the committee on behalf of the faculty that an acceptable plan has been submitted and that the student is judged ready to move ahead with the study. In addition, the approval sets certain limits, directly or by implication. For example:

The anticipated time of completion is indicated.

The voting members of the final oral committee are specified since they are the same as the voting overview committee members, unless otherwise provided in university regulations publicly available to students.

The work to be required of the student is that which is projected in the proposal as approved.

These limitations have a protective effect for the student. No one can justifiably press for earlier completion than the anticipated date specified on the approval form. While other faculty members may take part in the final oral examination, they have no votes. Capricious changes in expectations about what will be included in the T/D study are obviated.

The limitations previously enumerated tend to be more binding on the faculty than on the student. If more time seems to be needed, for instance, the student is free to open discussions with the committee about it. Negotiations about other matters also are usually started on the student's initiative. Tradition has it that the committee does all it can to adapt, support, and encourage the student. All things considered, it may be overstating the case to refer to the approved proposal as a contract. It is, however, evidence of a legitimate set of professional and academic understandings and agreements that students have every reason to expect to be honored. It carries with it also all of the same responsibilities that are present between a faculty member and students in a course, seminar, and guided or independent study.

Ownership of Intellectual Property

For student or faculty purposes, in this discussion one's thesis or dissertation is considered a piece of intellectual property. So too are notes, drawings, computations, or other items or materials used in preparing the final T/D draft.

As used here, *property* refers to something owned, particularly the exclusive right to possess, employ, and dispose of something by virtue of having legal title to it. *Intellectual* specifies that the property results from mental labor, rational thought, and exercise of the intellect. Examples may include tangible objects or recorded notes. Also included are materials developed by theorists, artists, researchers, authors, performers, or other creative persons in the academic or professional disciplines.

Ownership can be established through such means as patent, copyright, contract, registration, affidavit, or court decision. Ordinarily, the person to first exercise one of these in connection with an item of intellectual property is deemed the owner.

Naturally, ownership has greater priority in one's mind if the property is or can be expected to be of financial value. Yet, it is not always apparent at first if, for example, a new process, test, methodology, or finding will have future worth. Wisdom dictates that ownership should be decided on and established legally as early as possible.

The home pages of research universities usually have a section on dissertation copyright policies, often linking to the government home page (http://www.loc.gov/copyright/). Some examples of university home pages that inform about copyrights are the University of California at Berkeley (http://www.grad.berkeley.edu) and the University of Pittsburgh (http://www.pitt.edu). General search engines, such as Google, will turn up a great deal of information if you search using the term *copyright*. In any case, the above home sites will lead you to copyright policies, forms, and procedures on line. Although the thesis or dissertation is normally assumed to be the student's work, in some cases faculty members may assert some copyright, patent, or other interest in allegedly jointly developed work, including an interest in the research and resulting document (Smallwood, 2002). You are advised to resolve any issues about ownership of data or other joint work in the thesis or dissertation when there is a possibility that a faculty member may assert some right or interest. Copyright registration is important to the protection of your rights as author and researcher.

Serious problems can arise in the absence of clear understandings about the ownership of intellectual property. Grand theft or felony charges, heavy fines, and prison sentences can result (C. D. Long, 1997a). We urge students and advisors to ascertain that specifications about the following appear in all T/D approval documents:

Ownership of the T/D and related materials
Rights and conditions regarding publication
University or outside contractor limits or privileges

If the student research is done as part of a contract for research with the university or the advisor, the student should be supplied with a copy of the contract (or its relevant parts) before the student embarks on any research under it.

Advisement About Final Alterations

An overview meeting that results in approval is not completed until all required changes in the proposal are communicated to the student. It is common practice that, when the signed approval document is forwarded to the school or university office that houses such records, it is to be accompanied by a copy of the proposal as approved by the committee. The student is expected to amend it so it will in fact reflect what the committee did approve. The actual procedures that can be employed in assembling and monitoring the proper inclusion of amendments are discussed below.

In addition to the items already discussed, an overview session may have other, longer range impacts. For one, the meeting is an example of group consultation. It may very well be a precursor of similar meetings in which the student will take part after graduation in employment as a university faculty member or as a staff member or consultant for a company, a government, a school system, or another agency. For inexperienced faculty members on the committee, the overview meeting and the behavior displayed by the chairperson and other experienced members may become models to emulate. These effects should be recognized and their potential importance acknowledged.

CONSULTATION WITH COMMITTEE MEMBERS

Students who complete T/Ds satisfactorily agree that they remember three peaks of progress along the way. Faculty members experienced in research advisement tend to name the same three:

The actual selection of the problem to be attacked
The approval of the proposal document
The completion of the final oral examination

All concur that effective consultation with committee members is of fundamental importance in reaching those peaks. Consultation is more than a casual conversation; it is a complex set of interactions. Also, it is work. Like most complicated and strenuous undertakings, planning makes it go better.

T/D problem selection, in its early stages, is usually a consequence of informal consultation with a faculty member. Often, something referred to in a class triggers student interest. At other times, it is a follow-up of a paper or seminar presentation by the student. Increasingly, students are required to take seminars that survey the significant research in their discipline for the dual purposes of learning about the state of the art and of stimulating their interest in contemporary problems that need investigation. Also, departments or prestigious individual professors engage in programmatic study that provides a multitude of possible research topics. In addition, some universities house research and development institutes that, while independent of the "teaching" schools, have overlapping faculty who carry on investigations and other creative activities that include an abundance of opportunities for students in search of suitable topics. Contact with any of these can spark initial interest. The next move, though, is up to the student. For best results, it should be a planned move toward faculty consultation.

Consultation Regarding Problem Selection

A sensible first move is to confer with the advisor. But what to talk about? How to talk about it? What expectations to hold about the results? Actually, those questions and others like them are quite legitimate ones to start; we addressed them briefly in a previous chapter. Now, we go into more detail.

It is reasonable for the advisor to expect that the student will have made at least a minimum level of preparation for the initial consultation regarding problem selection. If the preparation includes these elements, the probability of a successful consultation will be enhanced.

Make an appointment with the advisor. Clear the meeting for at least 45 minutes of the advisor's time.

Clear personal time for about 30 minutes before the appointment and for an hour afterward, if at all possible. The time prior to the consultation is to ensure being on time and to allow opportunity to review notes and other preparations for the session. The time following has the function of allowing the interview to go on longer if the advisor wishes it and has time. Second, it gives the student a period for collecting thoughts, to make notes and summaries of the items discussed.

Some students send a copy of each conference summary to the advisor and to anyone else being used as a consultant. This helps to reduce or correct misunderstandings at the same time that it guarantees a record of thc meeting in the student's log and in the consultant's folder. As noted, information technology makes such communication and record keeping convenient and practical.

The choice of a faculty member to direct the study: If the student knows that a topic is well within the range of the advisor's professional specialization, it is appropriate that the student ask the advisor to chair the committee. If that seems inappropriate because of existing commitments or other reasons, the advisor should recommend other faculty members who might be appropriate chairpersons.

The choice of members to serve on the committee: The advisor leads the student to identify the kinds of special help that might be needed in planning and conducting the study being discussed. Then, the advisor helps the student match those identified problem areas with faculty members who have particular potential to help.

Students who plan carefully, as we have said, will already have in mind persons who would be suitable committee members. Students will often pick persons they have had as teachers and with whom they have established cordial relationships. The advisor often knows about the strengths of colleagues with whom the student has had little contact. Between them, they can build a tentative list. As one result, the student broadens an already existing base of acquaintanceship with faculty personages.

The T/D problem selection process has no clear beginning and no definite time limits. Students usually make one or more false starts before a firm choice emerges. During this period, it is essential to employ advisor and faculty consultations, as already suggested. It is also essential during this exploratory period to avoid final commitments to a chairperson or to committee members. However, once the student and an advisor reach agreement that a certain topic is feasible and is to be pursued, the committee should be formalized.

Consultation Regarding Preparation of the Proposal

This is a period of intensive consultation. It is very demanding of time and energy for student and faculty members alike. From the student's point of view, the most serious potential hazard arises from failure to keep all committee members up to date through periodic contacts. Use of our recommendation about regular written or computer-mediated reports can ward off that danger.

Advisors should inform themselves about the frequency and the manner in which their students are in contact with other committee members. While it is not essential in all cases, a number of advisors make direct and frequent contacts with other committee members. Some call brief, informal meetings so committee members can update each other. In highly complex projects and in those that run over a long period of time, the last is certainly preferred practice.

COORDINATION ROLE OF THE ADVISOR

When a student gets input from individual committee members, what should be done with it? Particularly, what should be done when the recommendations of some committee members conflict with or diverge from the recommendations of others? Resolution of those problems makes up a major part of the advisor's coordination role. This necessitates, of course, that both advisor and student keep close track of the views of all committee members and understand the reasons for their views.

A number of advisors are quite directive to their students in this connection. They say, in effect, "Listen carefully to each committee member's criticism and suggestions. Probe, if necessary, to be sure you understand. But *do not argue*. Also, *do not agree* immediately to make the changes that compliance with the criticisms or suggestions implies. Respect the consultation you are receiving. Indicate, politely, that you will give it serious thought. Ask about any matters that you want to be clarified. Then bring the matter to me for discussion."

Whether the research director's style is as forthright as that or not, the essence of that message must be conveyed to the student. Otherwise, chaos is probable. Unless the director defines and takes on the coordinator role, neither members nor students have anywhere else to turn for the ajudication and reconciliation called for by strong, disparate viewpoints. Thus, students ought to be able to look to the chairperson for assistance in making optimum use of consultation from other committee members. Like the fabled course of true love, the course of proposal preparation may not run smooth. The skill and diplomacy of the advisor should then serve as a shock absorber, all the while maintaining high professional and academic standards. This exemplifies the preferred approach to meeting the responsibilities of coordination.

From time to time, advisors take quite another course. Like steamrollers, they attempt to smooth the way for their students by crushing and overriding any viewpoints but their own. This action defeats one of the purposes of research consultation for it prevents the student from experiencing the thrust and parry of ideas in a setting in which the best ideas should survive. Also, it sets a poor example, displaying a model of undesirable, irresponsible behavior in the delicate role of chairperson and teacher.

Setting the Stage for the Overview Meeting

Scheduling the time for the meeting about the proposal is simple enough once there is agreement that the student and the document are ready. The best criteria for the latter are these:

The characteristics of a sound proposal document given in earlier chapters have been achieved.

The comments and suggestions of other committee members have been analyzed and, if feasible and appropriate, worked into the study plan.

The student understands the purposes of the meeting and expresses readiness to take part in it.

It is the advisor's responsibility to set a date acceptable to the committee and the student. School regulations sometimes require more lead time than this, but the proposal should be in the committee's hands at least two weeks before the meeting. (The document should be a clean, fresh copy and complete.)

Helping to set the date by contacting the other committee members is a worthwhile organizing experience for the student. Also, it supplies another occasion to talk with committee members to obtain any last-minute suggestions they might volunteer. A quiet, uncluttered room should be scheduled. It is advantageous to seat the committee and the student around a table since there may be considerable paper shuffling and note taking. Usually, two to three hours is sufficient time for an overview. To be on the safe side, it is best to schedule at least two and one-half hours.

The date, time, location, and subject of the overview meeting are best circulated from the chairperson's office by a memorandum to committee members, the student, and other interested persons or offices. The official notice ought to reach its recipient at least two weeks prior to the meeting date, and it should request a confirmation of attendance. If it has not been distributed earlier, the proposal can accompany the notice of the meeting. Thus, the confirmation of attendance can be taken as assurance that the document came to the committee member in time for careful study.

The advisor and the student researcher should ascertain that all materials necessary for the meeting will be on hand. Some presentations may call for slides or charts for certain parts. Others require the use of a chalkboard, models, or drawings. Whatever is essential for an effective presentation should be on hand in the room where the meeting will be held. The student should have an opportunity to rehearse the presentation there if that seems advisable.

Importance of Organizational Arrangements

Students and faculty members both deserve, as a *first* priority, setting and conditions conducive to excellent work. This includes matters of space, noise level, accessibility, and well-managed procedures.

Second, student research work on the university campus ought to be, in all of its aspects, a realistic introduction to participation in scientific investigation as a career expectation. To help accomplish this, the mechanical and administrative procedures ought to parallel the best operational principles and details found in highly respected public and private enterprise, in state or local governmental agencies, on university campuses, and elsewhere.

Third, the student engaged in faculty-guided investigative activities ought to find it stimulating and intellectually worthy. The experience should encourage a lifetime commitment to respect and to use research and development findings. The likelihood of that outcome is enhanced when the student observes evidence that the university administration and faculty attend meticulously to the physical and administrative conditions in which proposed research work is reviewed and its conduct approved. In short, the way T/D work arrangements are staged by the school tells, bluntly and vividly, how the significance of that work is evaluated by the faculty and the administration.

The Conduct of the Overview Meeting

If students know anything about overviews, it is usually what they pick up from other students. Some of that is useful; much, though, may be unrepresentative anecdotal material. Students are grateful when advisors explain ahead of time the general scenario of an overview meeting. The appreciation grows when the explanation is accompanied with tips on survival skills. We recommend that the following role descriptions be discussed in detail with the student well before the meeting.

Chairperson's Role: As *presiding officer*, the chairperson conducts the meeting. An agenda like the following represents preferred practice:

1. The chairperson and the student arrive at the meeting room in enough time to check whether it is adequately prepared.

2. The chairperson arranges for the student to wait in a comfortable place near the meeting room.
3. When a majority of the committee is present and the appointed time is reached, the meeting is officially convened.
4. The chairperson ascertains that the committee is ready to meet the student if there are no valid objections on the part of any member.
5. The student is asked to join the meeting. The chairperson requests a brief summary of (a) the student's education and professional experience and (b) the proposal being offered for the committee's approval.
6. Questioning and commenting about the proposal begins; the chairperson makes sure each committee member has a chance to participate.
7. The questions and the related discussion and suggestions continue until the chairperson senses that the committee members may be ready to conclude the meeting. The chairperson then asks if anyone wishes to continue the session. If so, it goes on until all members finally signal willingness to stop.
8. Then, the chairperson asks the student to return to the waiting area while the committee deliberates.
9. The chairperson puts the main question to the committee: Is the student's proposal to be (a) rejected, (b) approved with conditions, or (c) approved unconditionally?
10. The committee reaches its decision and signs the form provided by the chairperson to make the decision a matter of official record.
11. The chairperson recalls the student and, in the presence of the committee, reports the decision. The student may be asked to summarize the decisions and conditions as an affirmation of the mutual understanding of the student and the committee and to make sure that the results of the meeting are clear to all.
12. The chairperson and the student have a conference in which the decision of the committee is interpreted and in which any conditions placed by the committee on its decisions are discussed with the student.

This 12-point outline is a summation of the role of the chairperson as presiding officer. Some may feel that it appears too formal, not suited to the easy relationship that should characterize student-faculty and faculty-faculty interactions. To that objection, it should be said that the process outlined (or, for that matter, any other procedure recommended in this book) can be carried out with whatever degree of formality or informality is most comfortable to the participants.

Our concern here is not so much personal style as it is obligation and orderliness. It is imperative that all parties acknowledge and carry out their responsibilities. For instance, it is not a matter of style when a committee member lounges into a meeting one-half hour late and announces, while flipping through the pages of the proposal, "This is too long! I haven't had time to read it." This shows plain disrespect for colleagues who did their homework, and it shows disregard for the worth and dignity of the student and of the review process itself. The outline presented and other procedures recommended in this book are intended to support an orderly approach to the task at hand. This outline provides a framework for the grand strategy of the overview meeting. The tactics ought to be as individualized as the topic, the student, and the individual faculty members require. The chairperson's role, though, is multifaceted, not confined to directing the course of a meeting. Several other sides of that individual's responsibility are indicated next.

A *record-keeping function* falls to the chairperson. Most keep a personal folder on each doctoral advisee in their own offices, in addition to the student's official departmental file. The personal file has copies of official records plus the transient and incidental notes necessitated by day-to-day advisor-student interactions. In connection with the overview meeting, the advisor needs copies of the official document (the proposal, the signed decision of the committee) plus notes taken at the meeting. If both the advisor and the student take notes, they can compare them after the meeting to produce a more complete and reliable picture of what transpired. This is particularly important if the overview proposal is approved subject to conditions. The chairperson, during Steps 9, 10, and 11, reaffirms the conditions the committee has agreed to with the student. Some are substantive, requiring that specific parts of the proposal be altered. Others may be procedural. For instance, final approval of some changes may be left to the chairperson, while others may need to be seen by one or more other committee members. Records of these conditions are obviously highly important; it is up to the advisor to ensure that they are part of the written history of the meeting, and that they are conveyed fully and accurately to the student.

Support of the student also ranks high as a role of the chairperson in the overview meeting. One advisor reports a premeeting conference with each student during which these things are said.

1. "I am going into this session as a strong supporter. I would not have agreed to hold it now if I did not think you are ready and that the proposal is a good one. I, and all of your committee, have confidence in your ability and want you to succeed."
2. "Do not be surprised if changes are suggested in your proposal. Even though you obtained reactions earlier from all these individuals and adapted to their reactions, almost every proposal review meeting produces some new ideas that call for amendments in the document."
3. "Answer questions as directly and simply as you can. If you don't know, say so. In any event, keep your responses straightforward, short, and to the point."
4. "This is not an examination. Rather, it is a review of your proposal, a proposal that these faculty members helped you prepare. They want it to be a good plan for a good study, and their questions are aimed at making the proposal more solid, both conceptually and procedurally."
5. "As your advisor, feel free to look to me particularly for assistance in the meeting if you have questions or if there seem to be misunderstandings. I will try to clarify questions and to explain their reasons, if you ask me."

Sometimes, an advisor agrees to an overview meeting while still unsatisfied about the readiness of either the student or the proposal. Some students insist, and some apparently cannot be convinced of the weakness of their work other than by committee rejection. In such cases, a comment like that in Item 1 would be unsuitable, although Items 3, 4, and 5 would still be appropriate sentiments to voice. Each advisor's way of transmitting a supportive feeling to students is unique. Students, too, differ in the amount and kind of support they need. The essential point, though, is that the student be made aware that the advisor is an ally in the overview meeting.

It is sometimes difficult to accomplish one job of the chairperson, namely, to *ensure balanced participation* by those present. This does not mean equal time for all. There are some occasions when a committee member is so carried away by an idea that no others can get the floor without aggressively interrupting. The chairperson can note when others want to participate, when an idea has been discussed sufficiently, and can then transfer attention to other speakers or topics. Occasionally, it is necessary to invoke the prerogative of the chair arbitrarily to shift the topic to one waiting to be discussed by another person. In this connection, the chairperson, too, must beware of being the offender by monopolizing the floor.

The behavior of the chairperson *establishes the tone of the session.* A quiet, thoughtful manner that is respectful and considerate of others sets a good example. Good humor and receptiveness, too, are fine attributes to bring to the situation. It is definitely out of place, however, to harass the student, to take advantage of position, or to make the student the butt of dubious pleasantries. The way the chairperson sets the tone of the meeting has a great deal to do with how everyone will respond.

Probably no one else at the meeting knows the background and the style of thinking of the student as well as the chairperson. It is especially necessary, then, that the chairperson be alert to how questions are asked, to be sure that the student perceives their true import. From time to time, the chairperson may clarify questions by asking that they be rephrased or by doing the rephrasing. The same is true for responses by the student. This can be a very delicate matter, for few people tolerate well the feeling of being corrected. Also, the chairperson should not intrude in ways that actually change either questions or answers.

Overriding all other roles for the chairperson is that of *maintaining the focus* of the meeting. Few people other than university faculty members are so easily stimulated to divergent thinking. A meeting that reviews a proposal for an investigation is an enticing invitation to a brainstorm bout that moves farther and farther away from the main purpose of the gathering. So, the chairperson must hold a firm enough rein to minimize irrelevant discussion and at the same time encourage creative consideration of the matter at hand. These items do not exhaust the functions of the chairperson. They are, however, some of the salient ones.

(Special note: In some universities, the chairperson is appointed administratively as a nonvoting committee member simply to convene and conduct the meeting. In such cases, most of the preceding information would apply, although the role functions would be divided between the chairperson and the T/D advisor.)

Committee Members' Roles: Individual committee members have fewer of the overview meeting management tasks to occupy them. Collectively, though, they carry more weight in the approval of the study plan than does the chairperson, for approval takes their majority vote (sometimes unanimous vote, depending on local regulations). Each committee member is, of course, chosen for particular competencies. In the end, however, each must voice an opinion on the overall merits of the proposal that is up for review. Thus, each committee member is expected to be familiar with all parts of the potential study.

Committee members can help the process to get under way smoothly by being on time for the meeting, by bringing with them all materials they need, and by falling in with the style of the meeting that the chairperson conducts. It is a reasonable consideration to the chairperson to spring no surprises. If a last-minute question or problem about the proposal surfaces, collegial and procedural courtesy demands that the chairperson be made aware of it prior to the meeting or during the preliminary stages. If the student is involved, as might often be the case, the committee member and the chairperson should bring that individual into the matter in a way they decide between them. The guiding principle is that the student is entitled to a thorough, helpful, professional review of the study proposal, and all efforts should be made to ensure that.

Criticism of either the study plan or of new ideas advanced at the meeting should be dispassionate and constructive. Animosities occur among university faculty just as they do elsewhere, and sometimes those personal differences are fed by conflict over ideas. Committee members, when they take on the role, accept with it the obligation to abjure emotionalism. Further, part of the committee member's role is to aid and assist rather than to ridicule or denigrate.

Direct physical or technical assistance from committee members is sometimes needed by the student in the course of the overview session. It can range from something as simple as help with a projector in a slide display to something as involved as the demonstration of a complex piece of testing or instructional equipment with which one of the committee is expert. Committee members can put students at ease and help them to ensure that their proposals are well understood by offering such assistance. It is best, of course, if that kind of physical or technical assistance is planned before the meeting, but impromptu participation is appropriate and appreciated if the need arises.

Perhaps equal in value to every other part committee members can play is that of the encouraging consultant. Students often doubt their own abilities. When a committee member openly expresses confidence in a proposal's worth and feasibility, even while suggesting some changes in it, the student's self-confidence is maintained or elevated. Evidence of another's confidence can strengthen the student's resolve to carry T/D work on to completion rather than become one of the all too many who do stop at the all-but-thesis (ABT) or all-but-dissertation (ABD) level.

Finally, any committee member who accepts the role does so with the understanding that it might be necessary to take over the chairpersonship. Things can happen that take the chairperson out of the picture: health problems, changes in jobs, family considerations, and the like. In such cases, it is usually in the student's best interests that someone familiar with the proposal from the beginning act as chairperson.

Student Participation in the Overview Meeting: This section deals with two forms of student participation in the overview meeting. The first is that of the student whose proposed study plan is being reviewed. The second is attendance at the meeting by student observers. Much of what has gone before is relevant for students and for faculty members alike. Only a few items need to be addressed solely to students who are preparing for the approval of the proposals:

Pay attention to little things. Faulty spelling and punctuation, grammatical errors, and incorrect sentence structure can interfere seriously with transmitting the ideas in the overview document, as can improper collation of pages or tables. Blaming such things on the typist or the computer does not provide absolution in the committee's eyes; it compounds the matter.

Prepare for the meeting. Rehearse the introductory statements to be made. Ask friends to listen and critique them. Plan what to wear. Make a checklist of all the material needed at the session. Look at the room where the committee will meet.

Be rested. Organize the day before and the day of the meeting to avoid excessively tiring activities.

Share any concerns with the advisor. Schedule a premeeting visit or phone call to ascertain that all details are in order or can be arranged.

These four items become second nature to experienced investigators prior to important conferences at which they will make proposals. For a student who is just acquiring proposal presentation experience, they must be attended to consciously.

There seems to be a tendency to open overview meetings to students. When this is done, ground rules protect the participants while giving advanced students the benefit of learning by watching actual sessions in progress. Reasonable regulations may include

Only the portion in which the student is introduced and the consultation and discussion takes place is open to observers.

Observation must be with prior consent of the student and the committee.

No participation or potentially distracting behavior is allowed. Ample space is provided so the observers are clearly physically separated from the meeting participants.

The chairperson (and committee members, if they wish) is available after the session to interpret what occurred and to respond to questions and comments by the observers.

In a number of schools, individual faculty members employ simulations to prepare students for overview sessions and for final oral examinations. These, of course, can be designed to bring out specific problems for which students should be prepared.

Whether in real life, in observation of real life, or in simulation, the quality and completeness of the student's study plan and the student's own academic and professional readiness to conduct the study are the key matters at issue. These will be revealed in how the student states the problem at the outset, how the student responds to committee members during the meeting, and by the nature and degree of the conditions the committee imposes on approval at the close of the session.

AFTER THE OVERVIEW MEETING

Above, it was pointed out that the overview session concludes in one of three ways: rejection of the proposal, approval with conditions, or unconditional approval. In any of these eventualities, follow-up by the chairperson and the student is necessary.

Rejection: Rejection is rare. When it does happen, the chairperson ordinarily makes the reasons a matter of record in a letter that summarizes the committee's decision. A copy is filed in the student's record with the statement in the school's file. Another copy goes to the student. Rejection does not *necessarily* mean that T/D work must be abandoned. It may mean that this proposal is not acceptable, but that another proposal might be. The intent of the committee in this regard should be explicated in the letter that notifies the student of the rejection.

Approval with Conditions: By far the most frequent outcome, the decision of approval with conditions should be discussed in detail between the advisor and the student. It is most important to establish the conditions precisely and to make clear what will constitute satisfaction of the conditions. Often, the student is asked to circulate a brief memorandum to committee members specifying the significant changes to be made. In most cases, it is advisable to agree on a time schedule, too, for meeting the conditions.

Unconditional Approval: Even in the happy case of unconditional approval, a follow-up meeting of student and chairperson is very desirable. Almost always, there are incidental details that can be clarified by discussion between the two.

Presuming that the outcome was positive, the student has reached the close of one very important phase and is about to start a new one, the conduct of the study itself. Many of the same principles that guided the proposal phase apply also in carrying out the investigation. The next chapter is devoted to the operational stage of the T/D. It illustrates further application of the principles just alluded to, plus others.

Formal Topic Approval

Some faculties ask that the topic be presented and agreed to in a regular faculty meeting prior to the overview proposal preparation and the formal appointment of a committee. When that is the case, an outline form like the one in Fig. 6-2 is useful. In some cases, the formal

Student:_______________ Check: Honors___ Masters___ Doctoral___

Advisor:____________________________ Presentation date:_________

Topic:____

____

I. Background of topic: (approximately 150 words to set the stage and, if necessary, define terms and topic focus)
II. Description of study: (approximately 200-word nontechnical statement on what will be done in conducting the investigation)
III. Study rationale: (approximately 100 words indicating the professional/academic/scholarly significance of the topic)
IV. Professional or academic relevance of the study: (approximately 150 words on what impact the results might have on theory or practice, i.e., relevance in terms of application)
V. Relevant background of investigator: (how the student's training and experience provide preparation for this kind of T/D)

Figure 6-2 Presentation for topic approval by faculty.

Presentation for Topic Approval by Faculty form includes a statement about the relevant background of the advisor plus a list of the proposed committee members and the reasons for their selection. If desired, that information can be added to the form shown in Fig. 6-2.

From the student's perspective, the formal topic presentation has advantages. It heightens pressure at exactly the point that is crucial: settling on a topic. It gives the student and the advisor an immediate objective, in a formal sense, that precedes the preparation of a proposal.

The topic approval ought not be confused with T/D approval. They are quite separate, with topic approval being a kind of official endorsement for moving ahead with preparing a T/D proposal. However, the fact that the school or department approves should be a powerful stimulant. Also, the practice entailed in getting a brief summary together should prove helpful when writing the full proposal.

A number of instructors who conduct T/D seminars have remarked on the value of the type of topic approval form shown in Fig. 6-2. They use such forms to give seminar students guided practice in putting together topic elements in very short preliminary form. We encourage students to include this step in personal time line construction.

SUMMARY

This chapter emphasizes T/D work leading to the approval of the study plan. The interactions of chairperson, student, and committee members are highlighted. The purpose of the study plan and the characteristics of an acceptable study plan are pointed out. Eleven items to be included in every overview approval are listed. It is shown that assessing their adequacy plus the adequacy of the student to implement the study constitute the common agenda outline for every overview committee meeting. Preferred practices before, during, and after the overview committee session are described.

7

Conduct of the Study

TIME

Leading researchers discipline themselves when they conduct a study by setting specific, short-term objectives to be accomplished at given times. Students can employ that same action principle through the use of a "to do by . . . " list (Fig. 7-1). We recommend that students use the list, or one similar to it, in connection with the time line proposed in Chapter 1. The list guides movement from one point to the next one on the time line. Also, it is a convenient place to record and schedule items on your computer that require attention and might otherwise be overlooked or forgotten. A list of this kind should be *routinely checked and updated every morning* or at some other regular time each day. An advantage of doing it first thing in the morning is the assistance it gives in setting the day's schedule.

We put great store on the importance of self-management and independence of action on the part of the investigator. Advisors are usually pleased to help students in formulating their goals. It is good

Item	Projected date	Completed date
Make backup of computer files	______	______
Next progress report to advisor	______	______
Next progress report to committee	______	______
Final revised and approved proposal to advisor	______	______
Update and record notes on computer	______	______
Questionnaire to be printed	______	______
Questionnaire to be mailed	______	______
Conference with archivist on	______	______
Other	______	______

Figure 7-1 "To do by . . . " list.

to work out the starter list with one's advisor. Also, from time to time, it is useful to bring one's list (and time line) along to a conference and to review them in the advisor's company. *Self*-sufficiency and *self*-direction should be an overriding goal for the student. The advisor wants to see those qualities grow, too. One of the places that personal autonomy in research conduct becomes most evident is in the careful use of time.

Time and the Individual

For an individual, time is a limited resource. There is no way to purchase additional time; the amount available is finite. However, it is possible to use time wisely, to get more out of a given amount of time than other persons. That means to waste less time.

Our major point is simple: If completing the T/D is a very high priority, then recognize it and admit that many other profitable and enjoyable experiences will have to be postponed or missed. Honestly face the question of commitment. Is the T/D worth all the time and effort it will take? If it is, we have some suggestions for using time wisely and guarding it jealously.

Using and Guarding Time: When the overview is successfully completed, there is a dangerous tendency to relax and lose momentum. The approval of the overview is the signal to accelerate, to press oneself to renewed effort directed at getting on with the study itself. We have found that the best way to get started is simply to get started. It is surprising how clever we are in thinking up excuses and rationalizations, all very plausible and reasonable, for avoiding a start. Often, we are not even conscious of the tricks we play on ourselves. There is always something more important, more interesting, more urgent to do than the act of getting started.

In getting under way again, save your time by using others' time when possible. One illustration is in physically preparing the final copy. Few students are expert enough to justify doing their own. A professional typist is faster and more accurate and probably knows more about style and format than students or professors. There are secretaries at the university who moonlight and who know precisely the typing requirements and style system of your school and university. A few well-directed questions can usually turn up an excellent person. Preparing a final copy of one's own chapters usually turns out to be penny wise and pound foolish.

Students have turned computer technology to their advantage by using the computers to store typed material in the computer's memory, display it for revision at any time, edit it, proofread it, rearrange it, make insertions and similar changes, import or construct tables and figures, and prepare contents, footnotes, bibliographies, and other matters all without committing them to paper until one wishes. With the help of a skilled secretary, students can save hundreds of hours while gaining the advantage of almost mistake-proof storage and reproduction in printed form on demand.

Other ways to get help are through the use of graduate student assistance, fellow students, and university printing, duplicating, and mailing services. Some of these services can be obtained at little or no cost.

University libraries offer free or low-cost services that can save time, such as hard-copy duplication of important documents found through on-line searches. Libraries also can help with searches, and they usually provide free interlibrary loan services for important works. Computer searches of many large databases are often offered at no cost or for a small fee. For example, the Center for Research Libraries (home page http://www.crl.uchicago.edu/) is a not-for-profit consortium of colleges and universities that make available scholarly research resources to faculty and students of the major research libraries of America. The collection includes over 5 million volumes of research material that is often unavailable in individual libraries.

ISI Web of Science (http://www.isinet.com/isi/products/citation/wos/) offers citation reports, documents, proceedings, and news in the world of science. ISI Web of Knowledge (http://www.isinet.com) offers citation products, such as the *Social Science Citation Index*, specialized content, evaluation and analytical tools, information management tools, and document delivery.

EBSCO (http://www.epnet.com/) offers biographic and full-text databases designed to meet the research needs of academic, biomedical, governmental, and public libraries. It also is a good source for articles from magazines such as *Time* and *Newsweek*.

The Internet Public Library (http://www.ipl.org/) is an initiative of the University of Michigan School of Information. It offers on-line texts, Web searching, references, magazines and serials, as well as newspapers.

Specialists in the library (bibliographers, archivists, reference specialists, to name a few) are powerful allies and thoughtful and skillful helpers both in technical and in substantive matters. We urge students to explain their research ideas and needs to members of the library staff and to consider them as valuable professional consultants.

Another university service that is often available is advice on the conduct of the study. To assist with questions relating to research design, measurement, and statistical analysis, the service staff personnel and advanced assistants are often made available from the university research library system or from research departments within the university.

Sometimes, this advice is available through an office of the university, but increasingly help is available on line, either to the public or to authorized users at the university. Many of these services are offered through the university library system. Some examples are the University of Minnesota site (research.UMN.edu) and the George Washington University (gwu.edu/-litrev/). Mark Leone of CMU has a number of helps for the dissertation process, and typing in his address (retrieved September 28, 2002, from http://www.2cs.cmu.edu/afs.cs.cmu.edu/user/mleone/web/how-to.html) leads to valuable links to other university sites, such as City University of New York, Duke, Michigan State, Northwestern, Nottingham University (United Kingdom), Ohio State, Purdue, University of California at Los Angeles (also Berkeley), University of North Carolina, University of Southern California, Universidad Nacional de Lujan (UNLU) in Argentina (in Spanish), and the University of Wisconsin. Learner Associates (learnerassociates.net) offers valuable guides in English, Portuguese, and Spanish to assist in the process of writing and defending a graduate school thesis or dissertation.

Also, in the reference section of this work, there are a number of entries for research library home pages that offer help and advice in the conduct of dissertation and thesis writing and research (Florida Community College, 2001; University of Kentucky Computing Center, n.d.; University of Miami Libraries, 2001; University of Minnesota Libraries, 2002).

There are also fee-based services that may be worth checking out. One example is Thesis and Dissertation Advisors—On Call, an international network of higher education faculty, published authors, and editors (dissertationadvisors.com). They offer help with editing, research, proposal development, writing, formatting, statistical analysis, and consulting. Another example is doctoral-dissertations.com, which provides similar services and even offers a free dissertation guide. Elfin Forest (elfin.com) strives to provide timesaving software to students for help in writing, referencing, and statistical needs. Another service is the Dissertation Doctor (dissertationdoctor.com), which provides advice on, among other things, getting started, preparing the proposal, and boosting productivity.

Using these on-line resources can save you a lot of time and wasted effort. Also, always ask your research librarian for help in finding appropriate Web sites, as well as for help in using the resources of your college or university library.

Simulation and Pretesting

Often, the results portion of the study can be written with probable outcomes or simulated data before the actual information collection stage, with surprisingly useful consequences in terms of clarity of the writing, accuracy of the simulations, and the helpfulness of the questions faced beforehand. If the results chapter cannot be simulated with projections of dummy data, the question is raised whether the chapter can be written based on the real facts or opinions one intends to gather.

Simulation and pretesting are useful to ascertain the relevance of the proposed data and the adequacy of data-gathering instruments. One purpose of a pilot study may be to pretest an instrument. The instrument is pretested for a number of reasons.

First, bugs appear in procedures, especially with newly developed instruments. If intended for live subjects, use of a small group like the intended respondents can tell the researcher what may be wrong with the instrument. If the instrument is for inanimate information retrieval, a trial run on real sources can detect defects. For best pretest results, develop a system to collect and heed the formative evaluative comments of those who take part.

Second, the data received or simulated in the pretest should prove conceptually sufficient to respond in some clear way to the hypotheses or research questions. If not, it is a danger signal. Perhaps the wrong questions are being asked, the wrong facts collected, or the wrong subjects used. Whatever the problem, correct or avoid it before the real data collection phase starts.

Selective Data Collection Advisable

Be parsimonious about the amount of information gathered. The search for data should be focused and explicit. Students who gather a mountain of material often end up under an avalanche. The amount of data should be just enough to deal thoroughly with the matters raised in the proposal. Selectivity in quantity plus high standards of quality are sound guidelines.

Using Available Data

Finally, here is some advice about available data: The world is full of information, much of it there for the asking. Schools, businesses, newspapers, government units, health and welfare agencies, laboratories, test publishers, archives, stock markets, and many other sources have been collecting and banking information for years. The material may be in any form, from very limited, primitive filing systems to highly sophisticated technology exemplifying the most advanced storage and retrieval capability. *Do not waste time* generating data that are already available.

A clinical psychologist we know produced a dissertation based on the analysis of patterns of responses to dozens of items on an individual intelligence test administered to several hundred subjects. It would have taken two years just to administer the tests if the data had been generated that way. Instead, permission was obtained to use existing test records from two large city school systems. That approach allowed an even more controlled management of the population, too, since it could be drawn from the larger universe to suit specific preset criteria. The data were gathered in two weeks of concentrated effort, not two years.

Graduate students are usually well aware of the many sources of data available in their discipline, and it is not possible to list such a great variety of sources here. But, it is possible to indicate the riches of general references on line or on disk, references like the *Encyclopedia Britannica* (www.britannica.com), the *Oxford English Dictionary* (OED) on disk and Oxford Reference Online (www.oxfordreference.com), and the *World Book Encyclopedia*. Public libraries, in addition to academic libraries, also provide free access to databases. For example, the New York Public Library (www.nypl.org) provides access to encyclopedias as well as a number of specialized databases. The Los Angeles Public Library (www.lapl.org) provides access to the OED. Some other general sites are biography.com, which provides thousands of biographies of famous persons, and the CIA's (www.odel.gov) *World Factbook*, which provides data on almost every country in the world. The Census Bureau (www.factfinder.census.gov) provides a wealth of demographic, social, and economic information about the United States. Links to a number of on-line reference sources are available at nytimes.com, the *New York Times on the Web* site.

These suggestions are just the beginning. A few hours spent following leads in the university library will turn up a great deal of data that have been gathered, checked, verified, and published. Use of available knowledge can have a major impact on the time and energy devoted to the conduct of a study.

Systematic Data Recording

Accurate, systematic notes are essential to every investigator. Figure 7-2 provides a format with broad applicability. Each individual takes and uses notes differently, but there are some experience-based principles that should be considered.

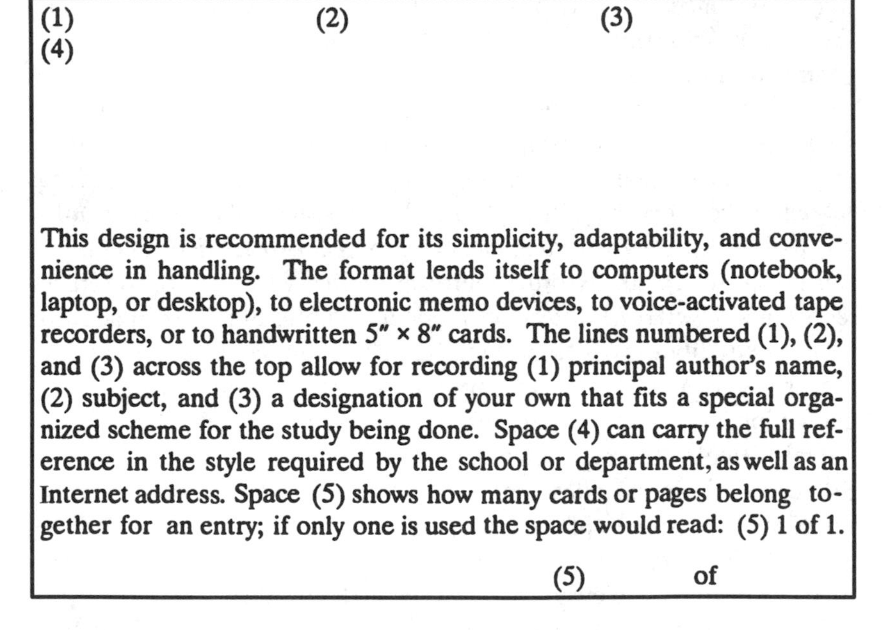

Figure 7-2 Recommended note-taking format.

Notes can be arranged in various files (we recommend computer files) and then can be sorted according to categories depending on current need. After use in one chapter or study, some can be recycled for later chapters or related studies. A common filing method is alphabetical, but one may want to file alphabetically by chapter or within categories of publications such as journals, books, and newspaper articles. Notes can also be rearranged into subject areas. In fact, the possibilities are great as long as there is a way to identify categories quickly. Some common codings that scholars use are author, subject, key word, or identification number written in the upper left-hand corner.

The usual way of categorizing notes on a literature search is alphabetically by author's last name. This is consistent with many indexing systems investigators use, such as *Readers' Guide to Periodical Literature*. Style manuals also commonly require that footnotes, in-text references, bibliographies, and reference notes be listed alphabetically by author's last name.

Select a Bibliographic Style: Our recommendation is that the reference and bibliographic style be selected before note taking begins. Then, the notes will contain the precise bibliographic reference needed ultimately in the T/D. This reference should be near the top of the front side of the note. One reason is that the source of the note is then always at hand. Many of us have taken notes thinking we will surely remember the source, only to forget it when we finally get around to using the material. Also, placing the complete, accurate bibliographic reference in the correct style on notes means that the bibliography is ready for final typing when that time comes. Furthermore, a note should contain all the information needed for any source footnote. Try to capture succinctly the points made, use an outline, and write complete thoughts, not a word or two. Finally, the notes, properly edited, could constitute an annotated bibliography that may prove publishable.

Students should become familiar with the accepted style manual in their discipline and use it consistently. Knowing the style system for citations in scholarly papers will save a great deal of time when preparing papers and reports in graduate school. The APA style manual is commonly used in the social and behavioral sciences. The APA home page (http://www.apa.org) will help writers in understanding and using APA style in writing papers and articles. There is also help (APA, 1999, 2001) on how to format references, citations, headings, statistics, tables, and Internet citations. An excellent text publication to help new writers is *Mastering APA Style: Student's Workbook and Training Guide* (Gelfand and Walker, 2001).

Read the first and last part of the work first, unless it is clear beforehand that the work is central to the study. The most relevant material for notes can often be found at the beginning and end of the cited work. Many scholarly journals require an accurate and detailed summary at the beginning of a journal article. If the main ideas are noted in outline form, they can be summarized without fear of repeating material verbatim from another author—assuming, of course, the proper credit is given in the text. Putting page numbers next to ideas on the note is a helpful practice. In footnotes or in-text references, it is proper to refer the reader to a specific page in the cited work. If a thought simply must be quoted on the note, be sure to include the page number and to use quotation marks. Following these rules helps avoid bad writing habits as well as ethical problems with regard to the use of the work of other authors.

We list the call number at the top of the note when we have used a library reference. One is always surprised, usually unpleasantly, at the number of times it is necessary to return to the same work in the course of writing. The call number will save hours of time.

Some investigators expand their category-filing scheme by printing or photocopying the notes and filing copies in different ways, even using them in different, but related, studies.

These ideas are also applicable to notes on which other types of relevant material can be recorded. Information about subjects in a study, such as test scores and socioeconomic data, can be recorded and even number coded to preserve confidentiality. With such data, subgroups of subjects can be identified and quickly pulled from a large computer file or files, and needed data can be obtained directly. Such handy, informative recording can be developed for many different units of measurement or classes of information.

Computers have opened opportunities for keeping notes, files, and records in an orderly way on a disk. All that is said above can be applied to computerized notation, and portable computers make it possible to take notes on site at a library or other data source.

Computers are an excellent tool for searching, reviewing, and storing data for notes. Databases can be searched by computers. Such searches use search strategies that often depend on the intersection of key words. For example, if one were studying German colonial influence on Papua New Guinea, key words might be *Papua New Guinea*, *colony*, *Germany*, or *colonial history*.

Researchers who do their own database searches can quickly find out if the strategy turns up references and, if so, how many. If no references are found, then one can immediately try other likely key words—in this case, for example, *New Guinea*, *German colonialism*, *World War I*, *Germans*, and so forth until a hit is made.

Focus the Search: Computer searches vary. Some will show titles, authors, and subjects. Others, such as ERIC, also provide annotated references. Thus, one can quickly peruse the screen to determine the relevance and usefulness of what has turned up. This ability to screen references quickly is critical if the problem is not a lack of references, but a surfeit of references.

Too many references may mean that the search strategy is too broad or the parameters are poorly defined. Too many references can also mean that the topic is too broad. Some researchers find that expressing research interests in terms of questions helps guard against reference overload. Looking for answers to specific questions rather than general information on a topic can narrow the scope of a search.

Outline and File: Once the search is narrowed to the most useful and relevant citations, they and their abstracts become candidates for notes and possibly for the literature review. The data may be imported to your own computer by importing a data file. Otherwise, a hard copy of the citations is printed and can be entered in the researcher's computer file either by keyboard or by a scanner or be filed in paper copy.

However entered in the computer file, a system can be devised to make access to a large amount of data possible. One way is to think of the note card system and, in a sense, emulate it. For example, use your outline software to create an outline of your project (e.g., your paper, overview proposal, or review of the literature). Making an outline forces you to think through what you want to say logically. The software will carry you through step by step. You will arrange material in orderly fashion, grouping related topics and establishing a subordinate and superordinate relationship if appropriate. In general, you will arrange your ideas in some rational relationship (e.g., chronologically, inductively, deductively, or in conformance with a classification scheme accepted by your discipline). A common outline system looks like this:

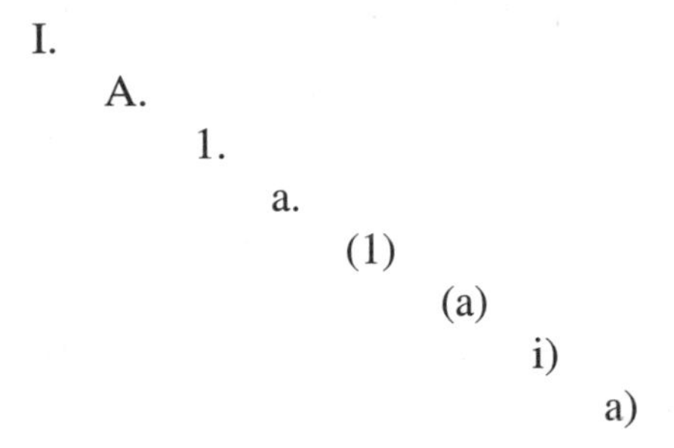

I.
A.
1.
a.
(1)
(a)
i)
a)

There are Web sites that present outline samples and assist the student in developing outlining skills. For example, Purdue University Online Writing Lab (http://owl.english.purdue.edu) has sample outlines; information about writing research papers; search engines; search helps; help with grammar, spelling, and punctuation; reference materials and resources; and professional writing aid.

Once you have an outline, you can create a program folder or file and name it for each part of the outline, then fill the file with sentences, notes, paragraphs, and thoughts that you want in that section of the outline. Eventually, the file will become the prose file, fleshing out the outline—perhaps a subpart of a chapter with its own heading.

We wrote elsewhere about breaking up a chapter with major and minor headings to make it easier to read and to help guide the logical thought flow. Consider that each heading in an outline could be the name of a file, and the headings that are grouped together in your outline could be a chapter. The headings (computer file names) that make up your chapter could then be grouped in a logical sequence to make up a directory in your program, and the directory could be named for the chapter (e.g., Introduction or Chapter 1). The example of an outline above is an appropriate size for a chapter. The files that make up the directory would then be about the right size for the purpose of working on them—to add, delete paragraphs, move, import, replace, cut and paste, and so forth.

You can use the Internet to find examples of outlines that may help you think through the contents of a dissertation or thesis proposal. A simple way to find outline help is to enter *outline* (*outlining*) or *outlining skills* into a search engine (e.g., google.com) and find a site like ActionOutline (www.greenparrots.com). This is software that lets you organize your bits of information in an outline form. This software is for sale, but there is a free trial download.

As you fill in the outline with information, some of the material will need a citation. Word-processing programs can help you mark the text where the citation belongs, allow you to enter the citation, and even display the citation on the page or at the end of the file. Some programs will even help you display the citations in an alphabetized list of references in any common style format you choose (for example, EndNote, Reference Manager, ProCite). Trial versions are available at the ISI Researchsoft home page (retrieved May 19, 2002, from http://www.isiresearchsoft.com/).

Another useful feature of some word-processing programs is the document summary. This makes it easy to find material when working on a large paper such as a thesis or dissertation. Each file, no matter how large or small, can have a summary prepared by you that pops up when you ask for it, briefly listing the file name you gave it, the date, author, and comments that you insert to identify and summarize the file briefly. This is a very quick way to find pieces of a large document scattered among hundreds of files, some of which you created years ago and perhaps have forgotten, but still are important to keep. This summary is hidden in the document until you ask for it, and it does not print out with the document on file or hinder you from working on the document whenever you wish.

Writing-Aids: Finally, software programs can help you write correctly. They will check your spelling against a word list of tens of thousands of correctly spelled words. You can add words to the list, and programs will also check grammar and make suggestions for improvement. There is also a thesaurus, which helps you find an appropriate phrase as you are writing, and it provides synonyms and antonyms for thousands of common words, not only providing you with choices, but also defining words when you are not sure of their meaning.

Writing and Presenting Your Thesis or Dissertation, by S. Joseph Levine of Michigan State University (http://www.learnerassociates.net), was created to assist the author's graduate students in thinking through the many aspects of crafting, implementing, and defending a thesis or dissertation. It is an attempt to share some of the many ideas that have surfaced over the past few years that definitely make the task of finishing a graduate degree so much easier. This guide looks at many of the quasi-political aspects of the process. Such topics as how to select a supportive committee, making a compelling presentation of your research outcomes, and strategies for actually getting a paper written are discussed.

Above, we suggested using a secretary who really knows the system to do the final document. The cost may well be less if you can provide a disk with your overview or T/D on it, already prepared, even in rough form. And, if you are really interested in seeing how close you can come to the perfect document, you can set all the margins and spaces required by your university for the T/D; generate a table of contents from your chapter headings and subheadings; and generate footnotes, reference lists, and bibliographies, alphabetized and correctly formatted. Many who begin to work with a word-processing program get so interested, and so good at it, that soon they are turning out documents that appear to be prepared professionally.

COMPUTER USAGE

Some of the growing number of uses of computers in T/D studies are for planning; for data collection and filing; for literature searches; for data analysis; for instrumentation in certain educational, psychological, business, and management research; and as the substantive content of research in such professions as library and information science and engineering. One important use of computers in the research context is to search the literature related to a given topic.

University research libraries, and thus the university community, have access to thousands of databases. Most are available without cost to students through the library's on-site license. Even if this is not so, often the vendor offers a free trial for perusal. An example would be LexisNexis (http://www.lexisnexis.com/), which provides publications on line in the fields of law, public records, company data, government information, and information from academic and business organizations. It has a searchable directory of on-line sources.

ERIC (http://www.eric.ed.gov), sponsored by the U.S. Department of Education, is a bibliographic database of education literature consisting of two files, *Resources in Education* and *Current Index to Journals in Education. Resources in Education* covers documents, consisting of research reports, curriculum and teaching guides, conference papers, and some books. *Current Index to Journals in Education* covers published journal literature from over 700 publications in the field of education. ERIC is free to users.

H. W. Wilson (http://www.hwwilson.com/) offers an information retrieval system for the World Wide Web, including search tools to access records in science and technology, art, corporate data, and full-text article-form journals in the general sciences, social sciences, and humanities.

Universities usually have their own guides and policies for literature review. Be sure to check your university's guides and requirements with regard to literature review before investing too much time in your draft. Once you have done that, you can find a lot of information on-line that will be helpful.

By typing *literature review* in the search engine, you can find a wealth of Web sites that will give you ideas, directions, and examples of literature reviews. One example is the University of Toronto Health Sciences Writing Centre's section, "Writing a Literature Review in the Health Sciences and Social Work" (retrieved August 23, 2002, from http://www.utoronto.ca/hswriting/lit-review.htm). This site explains the objectives and skills of the literature review, and it has "Questions to Ask Yourself About Your Review of Literature" and "Questions to Ask Yourself About Each Book or Article You're Reviewing."

Another site, at George Washington University (retrieved August 24, 2002, from http://www.gwu.edu/~litrev/), provides tools for preparing scholarly reviews of the literature. This Web site is helpful in teaching how to use research literature from the social sciences in a scholarly and professional manner. It is intended for master's and doctoral degree students in all the social sciences, although particular emphasis is given to the fields addressed by George Washington University's Graduate School of Education and Human Development. This site includes advice on the following:

1. Searching for research literature efficiently, finding what you need quickly, finding the full text on line when available, and avoiding an avalanche of irrelevant references.
2. Assessing individual reports of research literature to determine whether their findings and conclusions should be relied on or are likely to be misleading.
3. Integrating the various studies on a topic to make the best assessments of what is known about the topic, to identify promising future research, to improve conceptual frameworks for research, and to determine the advantages and disadvantages of previously used methodologies.

UMI Dissertation Abstracts (www.lib.umi.com) lists doctoral dissertations and master's theses in all fields. UMI/ProQuest Digital Dissertations is one of the most authoritative databases for information regarding doctoral dissertations and master's theses from over 1000 graduate schools and universities. Coverage of dissertation information began in 1861 with only reference citations. However, since 1980 it has included searchable abstracts of doctoral dissertations and since 1988 has carried abstracts of theses. Full texts of more than 1 million dissertations and theses can be ordered in paper or microfilm, and some are available for free download.

Dissertationsandtheses.com (www.dissertationsandtheses.com/) provides a searchable database of research papers. This Web site lists more than 25,000 research papers, experimental studies, and examples of entire theses to review, download, and possibly cite in your own thesis or dissertation.

If you want to find literature review examples on the Internet, try typing *literature review* or *literature review example* combined with your field of interest into the search engine (e.g., altavista.com, google.com, or overture.com). Many disciplines and fields of interest can be found using this strategy.

Another source of information is the multitude of mainframe list servers related to various fields. The research librarian is the best source of help in finding what you need. For example, there is a list directly related to higher education, with categories such as *academic*, *administrative*, and *student*. There are many listserv addresses in each category. A related subject listserv (http://www.gseis.ucla.edu/heri/journal.htm) lists journal articles using CIRP (Cooperative Institutional Research Program) data on college students. Such lists are often searched by research librarians and are made available to the university community through the library system's home page.

The home page of other organizations may also offer a great deal of information to the dissertation writer. For example, there is the Library of Congress home page (http://www.loc.gov/homepage/1chp.html), which provides access to legislative information, copyright forms and information, and the library catalog.

Another illustration is the publishing system of the National Science Foundation (NSF). This offers convenient, fast, and often free access to NSF publications, which includes a broad array of investigative studies, research reports, and policy papers. There are a number of ways to access the system, and NSF encourages electronic dissemination of its documents. The home page (http://www.nsf.gov) provides access to publications available in electronic format. This system allows you to search by document type, NSF publication, form number, or key word. There is also a customized news service, which allows you to receive NSF information on a periodic basis. This is an E-mail and Web-based alert service. For those unable to download documents, many publications can be sent electronically via E-mail (getpub@nsf.gov). Although many NSF publications are available only in electronic format, some may also be ordered in hard copy by mail.

The examples above are a sample of what is available. New sites come on line periodically. Ask your research librarian for help, and be specific about the thesis, honors paper, or dissertation topic you wish to research. In addition, search a topic yourself. There is no substitute for spending hours on your computer following leads, opening new searches, and trying new search engines to find information on your research topic.

An extension of the database search is the search of material on CD-ROM. These disks are attractive to libraries because they can store an enormous number of pages of printed material on one disk. In addition, these disks can store the database material, thus providing the search and retrieval capability of an on-line database without the on-line connection to a remote location. The disks provide the same retrieval methods and search strategies that are used in the counterpart remote database search. With a printer connected, a disk search can result in a printed bibliography or list of reference notes. ERIC, *Psychological Abstracts*, and *Dissertation Abstracts International*, among others, are available in disk form.

These forms of searching the literature not only are faster, but they can, at times, search literature not otherwise indexed, or at least not indexed in a form easy to find. As newer search techniques become more widely available, research libraries are dropping the printed form when it is duplicated by the library's purchase of a disk or on-line database search service. Thus, the researcher will be forced to learn to search via computer.

Another innovation of importance to the researchers is the on-line library catalog. Universities have now developed such catalogs, and students and faculty now have access to the library's holdings via computer terminals. Usually, the libraries themselves have terminals permanently connected to the on-line library catalog, and the catalog may be searched by title, author, or subject, with step-by-step instructions provided on the terminal screen.

Some systems allow for truncation, enabling the searcher to retrieve references to a word in its singular, plural, or other variant forms. Consulting often with reference librarians will prevent a student from concluding that everything has been found that there is to find when good material may have been missed.

All catalogs have limitations. It should not be assumed that all the holdings of a library, with bibliographic information, are in the on-line catalog. In summary, searching the catalog by computer is fast and convenient and can give the researcher a good overview of what is available in the library and where. It is often possible to print a copy of a search.

Computer-Aided Data Collection and Analysis

For observational research, there are software packages for collecting and analyzing data on behavior or events. Operating on site with a laptop computer, there are programs that allow the researcher to collect and store data as it appears. The same software can then generate frequency and duration tables and reliability tables and summarize what has been done. Part of the package is also an analysis program able to produce event analyses, time-based analyses, interactions between them, plus others. Moreover, tables created are ready to be imported into programs like SPSS-PC or SPSS-X for additional analyses. University research libraries often have Web sites that will help by making these programs available and by walking the client through the calculations. An excellent example of a university Web site that does both is that of the University of Minnesota. It also has links to additional assistance, such as Bill Trochim's Web site (Stempner, 2001; Trochim, 2002).

To search for appropriate software, one can also use search engines such as Yahoo, AltaVista, or Google. For example, the Association for Survey Computing home page (http://www.asc.org.uk/) leads to more than 170 software packages with attributes and suppliers and has a built-in search faculty. Information includes statistical design, design analysis, sample size in survey research, multilevel statistical models, and survey sampling routines. You can also search for appropriate software using search engines and entering *buyer's guide* and choosing *Internet software*. These sites often assist the user in the statistical computation and provide an array of computational options. Some have links to other sites for data analysis.

By inputting *analysis of data* or *data analysis* in search engines, you can find software for data treatment, such as the Internet version of *The Data Analysis BriefBook*. The *BriefBook* is a condensed handbook (or an extended glossary) written in encyclopedic format; it covers subjects in statistics, computing, analysis, and related fields. It strives to be both an introduction and a reference for data analysts, scientists, and engineers (retrieved September 26, 2002, from http://rkb.home.cern.ch/rkb/titleA.html).

Another example is SDA (Survey Documentation and Analysis; retrieved September 26, 2002, from http://csa.berkeley.edu:7502/). SDA is a set of programs for Web-based analysis of survey data. There are also procedures for creating customized subsets of data sets. This set of programs is developed and maintained by the Computer-Assisted Survey Methods (CSM) Program at the University of California, Berkeley.

Try also the Dismal Scientist (retrieved September 26, 2002 from http://www.economy.com/dismal/). There are free economic data and analysis (regional and national) of the U.S. economy by nationally recognized economists.

The Bureau of Economic Analysis (retrieved September 26, 2002, from http://www.bea.doc.gov/) examines national, international, and regional economic data and includes survey forms and employment information.

On-line survey and on-line data collection are also available by typing *on-line survey* or *on-line data collection* in a search engine. Some examples of what is available are the Web-based survey software of ObjectPlanet (objectplanet.com). ObjectPlanet offers Surveyor, Web-based survey software that can produce and publish surveys on the Internet and allows instant publication of on-line surveys, reports and analyses.

Another example is the PsychData.net Online Data Collection Made Easy (retrieved September 26, 2002, from http://www.psychdata.net/). PsychData.net is specifically designed to help faculty, students, and social science researchers conduct on-line surveys and academic research in a professional environment.

Finally, there is AskThemOnline (retrieved September 26, 2002, from http://askthemonline.com/). This service collects data from assessments, surveys, or any on-line form via the Web. The software can then be placed on a local server, and information collected is stored in csv (comma separated value) format and therefore is available for spreadsheets.

USE OF PRIVATE INFORMATION

Confidentiality

To obtain data, it is often necessary to promise confidentiality. This is a serious promise; breaking it is an inexcusable breach of ethics. We recommend several procedures to maintain and safeguard confidentiality of data. First, if possible, collect data anonymously. Second, roster data by number rather than name; destroy names and their connections with data as soon as possible. Third, if data are gathered by questionnaire, the questionnaire can be destroyed, returned, or identifying information cut out as soon as there is no further need for it. Fourth, keep sensitive files out of sight and under lock.

Internet Privacy

When an individual computer owner visits a Web site, that visit may activate, plant, and store a signal in the hard drive of the user's PC. The Web site's owner or agent may then locate and enter the visitor's PC and retrieve information by retracing the stored signal, all without the knowledge or permission of the visitor. That information may then be used or sold to advertisers or others without the true owner's awareness or consent.

No protection exists against information harvesting by Web site operators. Growth in the market for personal data about Internet users parallels the steady proliferation of Internet shopping and junk E-mail sources (Hafner and Lyon, 1996).

We caution researchers to store personal, confidential, and privileged information so that it cannot be accessed surreptitiously.

Obtaining Needed Permission

Permission is needed in many areas of proposed T/D research. It is not a simple concept; check, if in doubt, with the research advisor concerning the need to ask permission concerning the specific materials to be used or steps contemplated. The need to request permission may stem from custom, common courtesy, or legal rights. Whatever the source, ask permission when in doubt. Some important areas for which a need to obtain permission exists include

1. Permission to use children or persons incarcerated or under guardianship as research subjects, including permission to contact such individuals as jailors, physicians, employers at a business, teachers or principals, or armed service personnel or to gather data systematically in work, recreation, health care, and education settings for research.
2. Permission to use instruments for data-gathering purposes if such instruments were designed or developed by others, whether such instruments are copyrighted or not, unless in the public domain.
3. Permission to examine, for research purposes, personnel records, student records, and other records containing personal data when such data are not part of the public domain and therefore open to everyone.
4. Permission to use long passages, charts, tables, and other material from the work of others, whether copyrighted or not, unless such material is in the public domain or unless blanket permission to use it, or reproduce it with credits, is printed on the material in such a way as to indicate that the author and publishers intend the material to be used freely.

Permissions should be obtained in writing, should specify their purposes and limits, and should be signed by a person in authority. A useful procedure is to send a letter to the responsible individual with a copy to countersign and return; with the letter should contain the simple statement: "The permissions requested in the above letter have been granted." This, signed and dated, can be valuable insurance as well as a "pass" for use with individuals who have direct custody of the persons, records, or materials to which access is needed.

OBLIGATIONS TO HUMAN SUBJECTS

Researchers have obligations to protect human subjects in their research and to report on their procedures to do so. Because these obligations are legal and bureaucratic, one may at times forget that they are also ethical in nature. Thus, a bit of historical context is in order.

Historical Context

Moral principles of civilized peoples and nations have for centuries contained general prohibitions against harmful experimentation on human beings. Although the moral issue may not be new, it burned itself anew in the consciousness of civilized persons during the Nuremberg Trials after World War II. In the transcripts of the trials, we find testimony that human beings in Auschwitz and elsewhere were put through agonizing and maiming experiments (and eventually killed) while under the control of physicians who claimed to be doing medical research. Out of this horror came a number of steps to attempt to prevent a recurrence, including the *Declaration of Helsinki* (as cited in World Medical Association, 1964); it contains specific guidelines for physicians doing research on humans.

While America shared in the horror of the concentration camps, most in the United States saw the medical research issues as distant ones, not actually touching our lives. However, in 1972 when the Freedom of Information Act opened certain government files, the public learned for the first time of the Tuskegee Study in 1932. At that time, the U.S. Public Health Service began an experiment on 399 men in Macon County, Alabama. The subjects were black, poor, and semiliterate. The aim of the experiment was to track the effects of syphilis on untreated black males. To encourage participation, the subjects were led to believe they were being treated, but in fact they were not. Their symptoms were recorded at periodic physical examinations, and autopsies were performed after death (Jones, 1993).

Gradually, U.S. governmental and professional bodies took more seriously the notion that policies were needed to govern the practice of research, with special emphasis on the ethical requirements of doing research involving human subjects. No doubt outrage at the Tuskegee experiment played a role in the increasingly strict regulation of research on human subjects that developed in the 1970s.

Another experimental study that brought to the attention, especially of the academic community, the need for guidelines was the famous Milgram study, described in the *Journal of Abnormal and Social Psychology* in 1963. Although the Milgram study has many defenders as well as detractors, the study is noted here not to take sides in the argument, but because it contributed to the enlargement of the arena of debate. After Milgram, it became clear that not only medical research needed regulation, but also other scientific and academic research.

By 1982, the American Psychological Association published its *Ethical Principles in the Conduct of Research with Human Participants*, the Society for Research in Child Development issued a statement on "Ethical Standards in Research with Children," and the American Educational Research Association published a strong editorial in the February 1973 issue of *Educational Researcher* calling researchers' attention to the need for ethical guidelines.

During this period, agencies of the U.S. Department of Health, Education, and Welfare (HEW) issued regulations requiring increasingly strict review of research proposals when federal funds were requested. By 1974, the National Research Act extended such reviews to all research on human subjects if done at institutions that had HEW research funds. By 1978, the recommendations of the National Commission for the Protection of Human Subjects of Biomedical and Behavioral Research were published in the *Federal Register*, and after comments were received, the secretary of HEW published a proposed list of recommendations in 1979; after extensive dialogue, final regulations were published in 1981. For more detailed information on federal guidelines and regulations for protection of research subjects, refer to federal policies effective December 13, 2001 (http://ohrp.osophs.dhhs.gov/humansubjects/guidance/45cfr46.htm; retrieved May 19, 2002).

While federal regulations apply to DHHS grants, in effect they have encouraged universities to set up committees or boards to review all research involving human participants; the research includes theses, dissertations, class projects or assignments, nonfederally funded research, and institutional research. University home pages often have information about their policies, guidelines, forms, and training sessions. Examples are those of the University of California at Los Angeles (http://www.ucla.edu/), Stanford University (http://www

.stanford.edu/), and the University of Minnesota (http://www.umn.edu/). These home pages were reviewed on May 19, 2002.

There are good reasons for this extended coverage. First, if the regulations are appropriate in federally funded research, then logically they should apply equally when the funds come from some other source. Second, if inappropriate procedures entail legal liability for the student, the advisor, and the university, that liability would appear to remain whatever the source of funds. Third, with respect to T/D research or any other research done by students, training and insistence on proper and ethical procedures would seem to be an essential part of any university program.

Procedures for Review of Proposed Research with Human Subjects

The first decision a researcher must make is whether the proposed research must be reviewed under university human subject guidelines. Research not subject to review by this procedure would be research that is not concerned with human subjects—for example, an examination of texts for readability levels, research confined to historical documents (such as a history of the Harmonist Society of the 19th century), or research that is restricted to library resources or the use of publicly available documents on or about humans. Note, however, that research using data *on* human subjects *does* constitute research *involving* human subjects and, although possibly involving minimal risk, is subject to the review process (Pincus et al., 1999).

Under the DHHS regulations, each institution is required to set up an institutional review board (IRB) to review research for human subject protection. The IRB has two purposes: first, to ensure that a system of continual review and safeguards will be maintained and, second, to ensure that responsibilities will be discharged for protecting the rights and welfare of human subjects of research conducted at or sponsored by the institution, regardless of the source of funding.

Several IRBs may operate at an institution; for example, one for the social and behavioral sciences and another for medicine, but each must follow careful written procedures, spelled out in the DHHS regulations. These regulations also permit expedited reviews by IRBs, reviews designed for certain kinds of research involving no more than minimal risk and reviews for minor changes in already approved research. Expedited reviews are designed to be faster and less detailed and to require less complicated and lengthy documentation than full reviews.

Researchers are encouraged to study the regulations promulgated by DHHS, as well as their own university's regulations for full explanation of the requirements of the various reviews. Such regulations should be readily available in several places, including the library, at any research university or institution.

The IRBs also oversee the protection of human subjects in another category of research: exempt. Exempt research is the category most likely to apply to T/D research. The concept of exempt research does not imply that such research is exempt from review or regulation, but rather that such research is so benign, so nonintrusive, and so commonly accepted that there is little risk of harm to subjects if proper procedures are followed. Examples would include research conducted in established or commonly accepted educational settings, involving normal educational practices; research involving survey or interview procedures; research involving the observation of public behavior; and research involving the collection or study of existing data. Exempt research at institutions is usually reviewed by subunits under the general supervision of the IRB. Even exempt research must contain provisions for the protection of human subjects.

Under certain conditions, T/D research that might otherwise appear to be exempt research can take on additional risk when involving human subjects. Examples include research involving children, prisoners, or incompetent adults; research involving deception; and research that records responses or observations that, if they become known beyond the researcher, could reasonably place the subject at risk of criminal or civil liability or damage the subjects' financial standing or employability. Again, it is our advice to refer to competent authority and to the federal and institutional regulations for guidance.

The concept of informed consent applies to any investigation involving human participation. Informed consent means the exercise of free power of choice on the part of the human participant, without coercion, deceit, promise of future benefits, or other forms of influencing the participants to act against their better judgment.

Informed consent is one of the most important aspects of necessary permission in the conduct of studies that involve human subjects. Past abuses, chiefly in medical or psychological investigations on human behavior or disease, have resulted in a fresh look at the issue. This is why research institutes and higher education institutions now commonly require that all research on human subjects be approved in advance by an institutional review board or ethics committee.

Humans subjected to research procedures have a right to know what the procedures are, what the purpose of the research is, the risks and benefits (if any), and costs and payments (if any), and they have the right to refuse or end participation. The subject has the right to know if the results of the study will be published and to what extent information will be treated confidentially.

The subject also has a right to know what will be done with data after the research is completed. If the subject is receiving some benefit, it should be clearly stated that the benefit will not be withdrawn or changed because of refusal to participate or withdrawal from participation in the study.

Formal, signed consent forms, when appropriate, should be submitted with the T/D proposal. Human subjects have a right to a copy of their signed consent form.

In some cases, separate signed forms are not needed, as in certain mail surveys or personal interviews for which the subjects are competent adults who are evidently fully free to refuse participation. In such cases, the respondent, as long as he or she is fully informed, may be presumed to indicate consent by returning the survey or by responding to questions from an interviewer. This concept of presumed consent depends, however, on the provision of enough information to the subject that tests for *informed* consent can be satisfied. For example, one would want to tell the respondent who the researcher is, the purpose of the research, the provisions to protect anonymity if anonymity is promised or implied, the degree of confidentiality with which the data will be treated, how the data will be used, the plans for publications resulting from the study, what will happen to the data after the study has been completed, and a description of the voluntary nature of the responses.

Federal agencies, notably the Department of Education and the Department of Health and Human Services, as well as professional organizations such as the American Psychological Association have promulgated formal statements and guidelines for both practitioners and researchers. These are periodically updated, so it is advisable that students, professors, librarians, and administrators be alert to the most recent views of such significant groups on this important matter.

An example of an informative home page that deals with human and animal subjects is the one maintained by the Office of Human Subjects Research (OHSR), National Institutes of Health (NIH) (http://ohsr.od.nih.gov/). There is also the Office for Human Research Protections (OHRP), formerly called the Office for Protection from Research Risks. OHRP is organizationally located in the Office of the Secretary, DHHS. OHRP is charged with interpreting and overseeing implementation of the regulations regarding the Protection of Human Subjects codified at Title 45, Part 46, of the *Code of Federal Regulations* (45 CFR 46) promulgated by the DHHS. Also, OHRP is responsible for providing guidance on ethical issues in biomedical and behavioral research.

The difference between the OHSR and the OHRP is that the OHSR's activities are limited to the Intramural Research Program at the NIH, while the OHRP has oversight and educational responsibilities wherever DHHS funds are used to conduct or support research involving human subjects.

The U.S. Department of Energy, Office of Biological and Environmental Research site (retrieved September 26, 2002, from http://www.er.doe.gov/production/ober/humsubj/) is also informative. The goal of the Human Subjects Research program at the Department of Energy is to ensure that the rights and welfare of human research subjects are protected while advances in biomedical, environmental, nuclear, and other research continue to lead to discoveries that benefit humanity.

The University of Minnesota Research Subjects' Protection Program site (retrieved September 26, 2002, from http://www.research.umn.edu/subjects/) explains the function of the research subjects' protection program. It reviews all research, including human (IRB) as well as the work of the Institutional Animal Care and Use Committee (IACUC).

ANIMAL SUBJECTS IN RESEARCH

The use of animals in research has attracted increasing attention from individuals and groups concerned about animal welfare. To a certain extent, this movement has paralleled the heightened interest in the rights of humans who participate in studies as subjects.

Obviously, animals are unable to assert their views or preferences as readily as humans. Further, they lack any direct recourse to legal protection.

Yet, common decency and respect for all forms of life are distinguishing characteristics of human civilization. So, it should not be surprising that researchers are expected to be attentive to the health and welfare of any animals, from primates to mice, with which they work.

Universities and other centers that do research that involves animals ordinarily have well-defined policies and practices covering such work. An Institutional Animal Care and Use Committee (http://www.iacuc.org/) monitors compliance with federal, state, and local laws and regulations. Students whose plans for T/D work might involve using animals, even in the most casual way, should become fully familiar with the IACUC of the institutions and publications of the IACUC.

MATERIAL AID FOR STUDENT RESEARCH

Significant changes in support for student research have been in progress in the second half of the 20th century. They were accompanied by equally significant alterations in how research is conducted. Both the changes in funding and procedures have important implications for student research (W. G. Bowen and Rudenstine, 1992; CGS, 1990b).

1. Projects have become larger and more complex. For instance, some have subject samples as large as 5% of all the nation's

youth of given ages. As projects become more complicated, they involve more variables and more styles of data analysis.

2. A research team is more often used as opposed to a single researcher. A staff of 5 to 10 persons is not uncommon on one investigation. The principal investigator of a major project devotes increased time to management and administration, with less time for direct research.
3. Two or more institutions may form a consortium to conduct one study.
4. Investigations frequently extend from three to five years and sometimes longer.
5. An increasing proportion of research is developmental, case study, evaluative, historical, and survey in contrast to experimental.
6. The cost of individual studies has mounted, often being in excess of a million dollars.
7. Universities, corporations, pension systems, unions, defense departments, school systems, health agencies, and state social service agencies have established offices to facilitate the search for funds to support studies. These agencies maintain central accounting staffs to monitor the use and flow of research funds.
8. In universities, the proportion of faculty members with "research" prefixed to their professional titles has increased, creating a faculty subculture distinguished by being outside the tenure stream and carrying few teaching or student advisement responsibilities.
9. More graduate students are supported in their advanced studies by working on research studies conducted by faculty members.
10. Funding agencies set and publicize substantive and methodological priorities for the research they will consider supporting. They also usually require that proposals, progress reports, and final reports be prepared in a prescribed format.
11. Sites often are scattered rather than centralized. Agricultural schools, churches, hospitals, libraries, highways, laboratories and other research locations distant from one another frequently contribute data and research talent to the same project.

12. Authorship of reports is increasingly multiple, with consequent spread and dilution of individual responsibility for both facts and interpretation of results.

The total amount of money available for research related to the academic disciplines and the professions tends to increase gradually. This means that every year new money is added from public and private sources to that already available. Also, the 12 points just stated constitute important parameters with respect to the flow and the utilization of that money. T/D advisors and students face the challenge of finding ways to tap into that potential wellspring of support. Any probes made in the major stream of funding need to start with two qualities: a focus on a relevant problem and a clearly written, succinct proposal embodying a methodology that promises to get nearer to the heart of the problem.

To obtain material support it is essential, first, to know where to look and how to look. Your librarian can help you find funding sources, like directories of foundations. Your computer can also help speed your search for sources of support that match your research interest. Use the Web sites listed in the reference section; many of them link to sources that may lead to support, official recognition, or collaboration in your research. The U.S. Air Force Office of Scientific Research (http://afosr.sciencewise.com) supports basic research in the life sciences. For another example, members of the American Psychological Association have free access to an electronic bulletin of research funding announcements from a wide variety of federal agencies and private foundations. Register on line from their home page (http://www.apa.org).

Using a common search engine such as Yahoo or Google, you can type in words or phrases such as *doctoral dissertation, grant,* or *doctoral fellowships* and do a computer search of organizations in your field of studies or discipline. Look for organizations that might fund doctoral research, that might offer research help or fellowships or that might provide links to resources that can be used to further your dissertation research. Organizational Web sites that might be helpful would include the sites of federal and other governmental organizations, foundations, universities, other scientific and academic organizations, and professional organizations related to your academic or professional discipline. We provide just a few examples below.

The American Association of University Women Educational Foundation offers fellowships and grants oriented to women and minorities (http://aauw.org).

The American Educational Research Association has an excellent home page, which will lead to fellowship information (http://www.aera.org).

The Ford Foundation dissertation fellowships are focused on members of minority groups whose underrepresentation in the professorate has been severe and long-standing. Much information can be found through their home page (http://www.fordfound.org/).

The National Association of Purchasing Management (NAPM) has a doctoral dissertation grant program, which can be accessed through their home page (http://www.napm.org/).

The National Endowment for the Humanities also has grants. Information can be obtained through their home page (http://www.neh.fed.us).

The National Science Foundation also offers graduate research fellowships in various academic fields (http://www.nsf.gov).

Fulbright and related grants for graduate study and research abroad are also available in various academic fields. The home page (http://www.iie.org) is a good place to start for information.

Ask your advisor and other committee members if they have specific suggestions about where and how to look for aid with your particular topic. Keep in mind, too, that if your T/D proves to have outcomes that suggest the need for additional research, you will have a firm basis for seeking support to extend your research efforts into a long-range program.

T/D Work as Part of Funded Projects

Sometimes, students have opportunities to do their studies as parts of projects being conducted by faculty members, projects supported by local government, state, federal, or private agency grants or contracts. These can be excellent opportunities. They often grapple with real problems. The investigations have social, theoretical, and professional significance, and it is possible to establish truly collegial relationships with the project staff and the faculty members leading the work. At the same time, there can be sticky problems in such situations for both T/D advisors and students to consider (LaPidus, 1990). Some of the potential complications are the following.

Whose Problem Is It? One desirable characteristic of T/D work should be that the student has the major role in generating the problem to be studied. That may be difficult to achieve if the matters to be investigated are largely predetermined by the language of the funded proposal that was written by someone else.

Time Pressure Can Arise: Most funded research is committed to a time frame. If it coincides with the student's projected schedule, all may be well. An interruption in the student's work can ordinarily be accommodated. But, if there is a tight linkage to a strict project time sequence, there is much less flexibility to adjust to other factors. Any protracted time out for the student, even if necessary, might mean the student would have to abandon the partly done study to allow its completion by another project staff member.

How Independent Is the Investigation? Funded projects of any major proportion tend to operate by distributing work such as data collection, data analysis, and short- and long-range planning among a number of staff members. In such instances, care must be taken to ensure that the student has and does exercise the level of independence in such activities that allows the committee to properly assign accountability to the student for the thoroughness and quality of these aspects of the conduct of the study.

What Format Is Followed in Reporting? There can be differences between the school's T/D writing format and the reporting style required by the project. Sometimes, the school is flexible about such matters. If not, the student may be contracting to prepare two different reports.

Student research done on funded projects can have advantages. Perhaps the most significant point on the positive side is its realism. If all of the objectives of T/D instruction can be attained on a funded project headed by others, and if the independence and integrity of the student and the T/D project itself can be maintained in the context of the larger project, advisors can be expected to encourage their students to make increasing use of that route to the goal.

Specific T/D Funding Support

State, federal, and international agencies, a number of foundations, and many universities give direct financial and other material support to T/D projects. The specific procedures vary among organizations and agencies, but they tend to have these general operating principles in common:

1. The student completes an application form or drafts a letter to the potential funding source, providing specified information.
2. A summary of the proposed investigation is required.
3. The amount of money or other material help being requested is indicated, usually with details as to how the assistance is to be used.
4. If a source external to the university is approached, an indication that the university will accept custody and accounting responsibility for the fund is required.
5. There is a limit on the charge the university can make for managing the funds and providing facilities for the proposed study.
6. The funding source specifies how its name may be used in connection with publications and reports arising from the project.
7. A full-time faculty member accepts responsibility for coordinating, directing, or monitoring the work, with the T/D student being named principal investigator.
8. There are deadline dates for submission of applications for assistance.

Advisors sometimes keep files of potential funding agencies to share with students. Some universities maintain offices that are on the alert for such resources. In a number of cases, these same university offices offer consultation on the mechanics of proposal preparation, processing the proposal for official university approvals, and expediting communication with the agency to which the application will be directed. In some research seminars, students are required to select a potential funding source and to prepare a mock (or real) proposal in the format of the funding source as a class assignment and to subject it to evaluation by a group of fellow students and the instructor. We commend practices like this as excellent exercises leading to independence on the part of the student.

The use of specific T/D funding support has few problems associated with it in contrast to its evident advantages. There is the added work of finding a source and making the application. Timing, in relation to both the application and the wait for a response, can be crucial. But, the experience, plus the material support that results if the application is successful, usually more than compensates. It is anticipated that more and more students will try to avail themselves of opportunities for help in this way.

STUDENT DROPOUTS IN THE RESEARCH STAGE

Robertson and Sistler (1971) concluded alarmingly that "the most cited reason by administrators for students dropping out of doctoral programs was 'inadequate personal financing' and the evidence pointed to an increase in this direction rather than an alleviation of the position" (p. 60). As they turned to a discussion of the need for more information, the same writers said, "There needs to be further study to determine the extent of finance as it bears upon the pursuit of the doctoral degree in Education. Part of such studies would include investigations of sources for the implementation of such programs" (p. 72).

We believe that the situation is common. "Money problems" is an oft-cited reason given by students for stopping graduate study, either permanently or temporarily. It no doubt has validity, but we suspect it may be a contributing problem as often as it is the primary problem. The widespread occurrence of money problems and the socially and emotionally neutral tone of the matter may make it a fine cover for the more personal and potentially stressful real reasons that may actually prompt dropping out (W. G. Bowen and Rudenstine, 1992; CGS, 1990b; Lovitts, 1997; Monaghan, 1989a; Pearson, 1997).

The loss of a student who has reached almost the end of a training sequence is a serious matter. For the student, it means that major financial and personal time investments do not bring the hoped-for returns. Sacrifices by the student's family often go into that investment, too. Personal and academic or professional life also are sometimes materially altered in undesirable ways. For example, one former student is avoided by close friends of an earlier time because they do not wish to listen again and again to the inevitable diatribes against university faculty members the student feels were unfair when they invoked a statute of limitations. Another former student has adopted a personally awarded doctorate, encouraging subordinates and new acquaintances to use it as part of everyday address. That same former student periodically threatens to sue the university and individual faculty members for denying the degree. Both students actually dropped out of school while in the dissertation stage and did so despite encouragement to complete the work they had begun. The true dynamics behind their dropping out and their later behavior is not understood. We do not suggest that these illustrations are typical. The problem is that we do not know what is typical, and we should.

There is an institutional loss, too, when student dropouts occur. It has financial aspects. No student pays fully for instruction. Thus, there has been an institutional investment in the student from tax funds, endowment income, and other nontuition sources, and that investment has not achieved the expected return. Add to that the fact that irreplaceable faculty time has gone into the student's program in many ways, from advisement to small-seminar and individual instruction. Faculty time is the institution's most precious resource. Even when a student drops out, it can be hoped that not all that has been done is wasted. But, that is a faint hope. When the doctoral process, for example, is left without its capstone, the dissertation, the result is at best a very limited success.

We asked the faculty members we interviewed at the University of Pittsburgh what their estimates were as to the proportion of doctoral students they knew who completed all course work but never started dissertations. Forty-three answered. The responses ranged from negligible to 40%. The mean was 19%, or about one of five. We then asked faculty members for the same information about students who started dissertations (had approved proposals) and did not finish. The range of estimates was again wide, from negligible to 50%. The mean of the estimates was 15%, or about one of seven.

When we asked faculty members why some students completed all course work and then did not begin dissertations, their answers were of five kinds. In the lead as a cause, they said, were student personality traits such as lack of self-discipline, procrastination, failure to set priorities, indecision, and fear of failure. Such characteristics are amenable to change. The guidelines set down by advisors can often produce positive alterations in such behavior.

The second most frequent cause clustered around a group of factors that would clearly be influential, though external to the situation. These included economic factors, such as the need of the student to work to keep body and soul together, family problems, and illness. Once a student leaves the university, the impression of the faculty members we interviewed was that the chances of return to study were slim.

Program inadequacies made up a third significant group of factors in the faculty members' opinions. They were most critical of program discontinuity, that is, the lack of developmental stages and smooth transitions between one and another program phase. If the student has been accustomed to course work with the instructor making decisions, that is poor preparation for a sudden shift to the almost total independence of the dissertation stage.

Inadequacies in the cognitive domain took fourth place as a dropout reason. It was argued that some students who lack enough intellectual ability or who find the rigors of scholarship too demanding cannot readily be located until they are faced with independent study outside the support system of a class or a seminar. Faculty members also felt that there is another group who simply have not learned enough about how to originate, propose, and conduct research. Theirs is not a lack of potential, but a lack of achievement, which could be corrected.

Though the least in frequency, almost 10% of the total of comments dealt with failures of advisors and other faculty members. When a student did not locate a faculty member to identify with, the stage was set for a dropout. The student would find too little help with problems of the kind that should have a legitimate claim on faculty attention, such as discussion of the student's research ideas. It was suggested, also, that some faculty members may be thrust into T/D advisement without themselves having sufficient background and skill in helping students either to define research problems or to plan and execute investigations.

At present, it is not clear how many students drop out just prior to or during the course of dissertation work. If the reasons offered by the faculty members we asked are accepted, many of the causes of dropouts can be eliminated or sharply minimized by the faculty members themselves, either through changes in their own advisement procedures or by repair of program inadequacies (W. G. Bowen and Rudenstine, 1992; CGS, 1990b, 1991b; Lovitts, 1997; Pearson, 1997).

SUMMARY

This chapter is about the conduct of the study. The sensible use of time is emphasized. The resources and commitment needed to conduct the study are explored. Technological advances (i.e., word processing and computer usage) are pointed out. Suggestions are made for systematic data recording. Major sections explain the obligations the researcher has toward human and animal subjects. Also, specific suggestions are made for relating to the advisor and for finding financial support. Finally, causes and remedies for T/D dropouts are suggested.

8

Writing the Manuscript

QUICK REFERENCE TO ANSWERS TO SPECIFIC QUESTIONS

Sooner or later, the time comes when the advisor and the student agree that a draft of the entire document should be prepared from title page to appendices and bibliography. From our experience, the earlier that first complete draft is written the better.

THE THESIS/DISSERTATION FORMAT

One of the first things a student wants to know is what a thesis or dissertation looks like. To determine that, both students and faculty members first need to know if there is a distinctive format associated with their kind of study or with their department or school.

In a more general sense, both students and faculty members are recognizing the importance of and the need for some skeletal structure around which to assemble their ideas, the data, and their conclusions. The desirability of a well-planned outline is emphasized by Martin (1980):

> Probably no other aspect of writing so quickly distinguishes between the professional and the amateur writer than the emphasis on structure. The student writer, for example, frequently starts writing at the beginning of Chapter 1 of a dissertation with the hope of working his/her way to the end of the chapter with little more in mind regarding structure than the three or four most important points. Such a neglect of structure is the primary cause of the situation most feared by all writers—sitting for an hour in front of a blank piece of paper trying to compose the first sentence. (p. 38)

The most difficult decisions at the full first draft stage of writing have to do with the internal organization of chapters, the structure that supports the flow of thoughts. Special attention is paid to that in this chapter.

A Table of Contents as a Guide

Over many years, patterns have emerged for the T/D proposal and for the final document. The final document expands and extends the proposal text. Much of the same patterns characterize both thesis and dissertation (G. B. Davis and Parker, 1997).

Usually the T/D proposal (see Chapter 4) becomes the first four chapters of the dissertation. Only tense changes and other minor alterations will be needed if the conduct of the research is as closely tied to the proposal as it should be. This underscores the importance of a clear and carefully thought-out proposal.

The table of contents in Fig. 8-1 incorporates a step-by-step excursion through a widely applicable skeleton structure of a T/D. Note that it is an extension of Fig. 4-1, and that it is a generalized outline. Outlines illustrative of other types of studies are in Appendix B.

Not every student's study will need every heading. For example, some reports may need no tables or appendices. Some students, on the other hand, may need to add headings not mentioned here or subdivide some of these. It may prove useful to combine, omit, or mix features of the outlines in Fig. 8-1 and Appendix B. As stated, there is no standard outline that all research reports are required to follow.

I. Introduction
II. The problem
    A. Rationale, significance, or need for the study
    B. Theoretical framework for the proposed study
    C. Statement of the problem to be investigated
    D. Elements, hypotheses, theories, or research questions to be investigated
    E. Delimitations and limitations of the study
    F. Definition of terms
    G. Summary
III. Review of the literature
    A. Historical overview of the theory and research literature
    B. The theory and research literature specific to the topic
    C. Research in cognate areas relevant to the T/D topic
    D. Critique of the validity of appropriate theory and research literature
    E. Summary of what is known and unknown about the T/D topic
    F. The contribution this study will make to the literature
IV. Research procedures
    A. Research methodology
    B. Specific procedures
    C. Research population or sample
    D. Instrumentation
    E. Pilot study
    F. Data collection
    G. Treatment of the data
    H. Summary
V. Findings
    A. The plan of the study
    B. Procedures
    C. Elements, hypotheses, research questions
    D. Evidence found that supports or fails to support each of the elements, hypotheses, or research questions
    E. Unanticipated results (findings)
    F. Summary of what was found
VI. Conclusions and implications
    A. Conclusions
        1. Conclusions to be drawn based on the findings
        2. Alternative explanations for the findings
        3. Impact of the study in terms of what was learned
        4. Strengths, weaknesses, and limitations of the study

Figure 8-1 Table of contents for theses and dissertations.

B. Implications
    1. Implications for professional practice or decision making
    2. Implications for a scholarly understanding of the field
    3. Implications for theory building
    4. Implications for future research studies
C. Recommendations
    1. Recommendations for further research or for changing research methodology
    2. Recommendations for changes in academic concepts, knowledge, or professional practice
    3. Recommended changes or modifications in accepted theoretical constructs
    4. Recommendations concerning changes in organization, procedures, practices, behavior
D. Summary

Appendices
    Appendix A . . .

Bibliography

Figure 8-1 Continued

AN APPROACH TO THE FIRST DRAFT

Organizing for Writing

Organizing for writing is something only the student can do. Advisors and committee members, though, may offer helpful suggestions. The preferred organizing process starts with establishing a writing schedule (i.e., a certain time each day, with projected objectives to be accomplished by certain times) and sticking to that schedule. Also, organizing for writing means arranging notes, references, and data in systematic and readily accessible form. At this point, an ounce of order is worth a pound of clutter (Lester, 1999).

Finally, organizing for writing calls for arranging for a place to write, preferably one that will not have to be moved and can be left as is when work is interrupted and returned to later. Often, that can be accomplished at home by staking out just enough out-of-the way area for a computer and other technical equipment, a table, a straight chair, a good light, and storage shelves and boxes for materials and supplies. However it is done, for most people organizing for writing is fundamental if the manuscript preparation is to progress effectively and efficiently.

Using a Model

Editors and experienced writers recommend constructing a "dummy," a life-size blank model of the finished document. Start with the front cover and tentative title. Insert pages with titles at the top in the order in which material will probably appear, then rearrange, add to, or otherwise change as progress dictates.

We have found the way that works best for us is to create folders in the computer program (e.g., Microsoft Word), with several files in each folder. For example, one folder might be the bibliography, another folder the research topics, a third folder the dummy pages, and a fourth folder might contain the chapters of the thesis or dissertation, numbered from 1 to the last chapter. Label the folders and files clearly so that when you start work each day, you can find your way around the draft in a short time. Also, well-marked folders and files will help you to insert new data or information in the appropriate place without having to search all over the document; the other side of this point is that when you go to find something inserted weeks before, you will be able to go right to it.

The Approved Overview Document

A comprehensive and detailed overview paper pays off first in the project approval stage. Second, it proves of benefit as a guide to conducting the study. Now, in the first full-draft writing stage, the third major value of a sound overview appears. With minor additions and modifications, it becomes the first several T/D chapters.

Style and Other Local Requirements

Costly mistakes can be avoided by an early re-review of the university and school regulations about style, required kind of paper, and other details. Some requirements that applied to the proposal may differ for the T/D document. Also, consistency in style makes for a smoother and more rapid narrative flow. In the unusual case for which no mandated style or preference is expressed by the advisor, two options should be considered. First, if it is anticipated that the T/D might be published in whole or in part as a book or in a journal, choose the style of that particular publisher or journal. If that is not feasible, select one of the numerous published style manuals and follow it. Abide by one style and pay close attention to it to preclude expensive adjustments later.

Copyrighted Material

The most common location for quotations in the T/D is the chapter in which literature is reviewed, although the words of other writers may be cited elsewhere also. An overarching principle to guide researchers in quoting (or otherwise displaying) anything of someone else's is this: The owner of the copyright has the exclusive right to use, market, or otherwise employ his or her material in any form. It is essential, therefore, to stay with accepted practices for quoting and to obtain permission whenever there might be a use of copyrighted material that goes beyond the standard rules and limits. One's advisor, the graduate office, and the university library are good sources for determining the rules and limits on quotations that apply to T/D writing. The work of Gorman (1987) is an excellent source for both the history and the rationale for protection by copyright.

There are "fair use" guidelines for employing copyrighted material in CD-ROMs and other multimedia settings. Current fair use provisions in U.S. copyright law allow portions of copyrighted material to be used without the owner's permission if done for educational, research, or commentary purposes (C. D. Long, 1997a). The guidelines set limits for what may be construed as "reasonable" for those purposes and give examples, such as the lesser of 10% or 30 seconds of a copyrighted musical work. The guidelines have widespread endorsement and approval from relevant professional and governmental groups. Key documents can currently be found at the Stanford University Libraries Web site (Stanford University, n.d.). It is an excellent source of information about copyrights and legal concepts, such as fair use. It also links you to related and important information.

Studying Other T/Ds

Useful hints about what to include in the dummy and how to present the final manuscript for maximum effect can be found by examining previously approved T/Ds on closely related topics. Some may have been read earlier as part of the literature review. Their procedures and findings may be summarized and critiqued in that chapter. Now is the time, though, to look at those T/Ds for another purpose. How are they organized? How do they present their material? How can their good qualities (and their mistakes) be helpful in preparing this one? These and similar questions ought to be foremost now as previously completed research reports are reexamined.

Studies Previously Directed by the Committee Members

Every faculty member has favorite student research reports that stand out as especially well written. It is perfectly proper for students to ask their advisors and committee members about these and to use them as illustrations. In fact, some faculty members commend such memorable illustrations to their students as models. Truly superior academic, professional, and scientific writing is not easy to find. Well-regarded and time-tested guides are available, however (Barzun, 1985; Strunk and White, 1979; van Leunen, 1979). Students certainly should take every opportunity to review works that their advisors and committee members judge to be exemplary specimens.

Uniqueness

Advisors emphasize the value of building on the experiences of others and of using guides and models (LaPidus, 1990). This can be very valuable. Yet, it must not be allowed to override the essential specialness, the one-of-a-kind quality, every student investigation should display. Thus, we urge students to strive for balance. On one side are stylistic and organizational patterns adapted from the best that past experience can offer. On the other side are freshly minted forms of expression, some perhaps newly invented to illuminate the particular contributions of this specific study. Harmoniously weighted, these can blend to foster the simple elegance of writing and illustrating that characterizes printed communication of the highest quality.

"One picture is worth more than ten thousand words" is cited as a Chinese proverb. Turgenev is credited with writing (in *Fathers and Sons*): "A picture shows me at a glance what it takes dozens of pages in a book to expound." Whatever the source, the principle is both sound and useful for researchers.

Illustrations can help greatly as visual descriptions and explanations for the devices, concepts, ideas, processes, and data in proposals and reports. Informational graphics, both in images and statistics, promote clarity and foster insight for both writer and reader. Particularly useful resources are the example-filled three volumes by Tufte (1990, 1997, 2001). They range from 16th century depictions through computer simulations and computer interface design.

USING ADVICE AND TECHNICAL ASSISTANCE

An old saying has it that advice is the easiest thing in the world to give and the hardest thing in the world to take. As far as we know, there are no old sayings yet about technical assistance, but if we were to coin one, it would probably be to the effect that it too often tends to be heavy on the technical side and light on assistance. We hope to show, however, that both advice and technical assistance can be very useful in this first full-draft writing stage, and that there are ways to stockpile each so they can be drawn on when needed.

There is a real distinction between advice and technical assistance, as the terms are used here. Both, of course, involve communicating useful messages from one person to another. But they differ on these four dimensions:

Advice may be broad and general or pointed and personal; technical assistance is always focused on a scientific, academic, or professional situation.

Advice is frequently unsolicited, offered gratuitously; technical assistance is almost always in response to a request on the part of the person receiving it.

Advice tends to be directive, with the strong implication that it should be heeded; technical assistance is supplied with the understanding that the receiver will consider it, but will feel there is no implicit or explicit requirement to act on it.

Advice is frequently, if not generally, oriented to what to do in a given situation; technical assistance emphasizes how to analyze situations and how and why to evaluate possible solutions.

Thus, while there is considerable overlap in meaning between the two expressions, the way they are used here plays up the differences rather than the similarities. The next several paragraphs offer suggestions about roles certain associates of the student might play in supplying both advice and technical assistance.

Other Students as Resources

Other students most frequently advise, although occasionally they also are sources of excellent technical assistance. The experiences of other students with typists, with individual faculty members, with the staffs of various university offices, with library or computer services, or with style guides are valuable resources that can be mined for profit. Fortunate, indeed, is the writer who finds a student, friend, or acquaintance with skill and interest in academic, scientific, and professional writing in the same or an allied field. The nature and the degree of help that can be expected is, of course, a personal matter to be settled between the two individuals. We consider student-to-student advice and technical assistance to be both appropriate and desirable, and we encourage it. Both parties can learn and practice important skills in the process. Such interaction between and among colleagues is recognized as valuable in the real life of the learned professions.

Two cautions, however, must be observed. First, the manuscript must be the student's own work; advice and technical assistance from others must stop substantially short of their literally writing the T/D. Second, advice and technical assistance that have a significant bearing on the concepts, format, or writing of the document should be explicitly acknowledged, either in the preface or by suitably placed footnotes.

The Chairperson as a Primary Consultant

The *committee chairperson* is usually a primary source, in this as in other parts of the research process, both of technical help and of information about where to get such assistance. Students have the right to expect this. The chairperson, too, has the burden of deciding when to take on technical assistance consultation directly and when to refer the student elsewhere. To make that decision responsibly, chairpersons need to know and acknowledge their own limitations. They also must be aware of the competencies of other committee members and the strengths of other faculty members who may not be on the committee.

A chairperson who cannot openly admit to limited knowledge about something puts the advisee in jeopardy by filibustering, bluffing, or ignoring a real need on the student's part. Equally dangerous are chairpersons so enraptured by their own pursuits that they know very little about their associates' academic and professional interests and capabilities. Such "one-person committees," when they occur, are evidence of inadequate quality-control monitoring of the T/D process by the faculty in general. In any event, students do well to initiate and maintain regular contacts with all committee members. This will be reinforced by thoughtful chairpersons who use opportunities to refer to others when students come to them and request technical assistance. As in all other aspects of the research enterprise, the committee chairperson has the major faculty role, and the way that role is played sets the tone for all the other participants.

Recourse to Other Committee Members

The *committee members*, as mentioned, are chosen with several criteria in mind (i.e., knowledge about the topic, representativeness of departmental and other university involvement, graduate faculty status, experience). It is assumed, too, that they are all willing and able to provide technical assistance of various kinds. If a committee member is expert in statistical analysis, opinion polling, qualitative research, graphic displays, achievement testing, or group dynamics observation, it is reasonable to expect that person also to be knowledgeable about preferred practices in writing about or otherwise presenting information on the same topic. Thus, the committee member who renders consultation on procedure might well give technical assistance in how the material might best be presented in the T/D manuscript.

Technical Help from the Typist

The *typist's* experience with manuscripts can be of great importance. There are many who are speedy and accurate, but not many combine these qualities with both knowledge about the special requirements that attach to T/D typing and good judgment in applying their skills and knowledge. That desirable mixture of qualifications can usually be found in two situations. One is the commercial typing, computer, and copying services that have multiplied in recent years near campuses. A number of them advertise T/D typing and printing at established rates. The other is the departmental secretary who does student papers and other contracted typing outside office hours at a per-page rate.

In either instance, two precautions ought to be considered. First, learn from students or from faculty members how satisfactory the work from those specific sources has been in the past. Second, meet and talk with the person who would actually do the typing or word processing and assess his or her understanding of what is needed for a fully acceptable product. The more care taken at this point, the more likely it is that confidence can be placed in the typist's advice as to the combination of style, format, and mechanics that will meet all regulations and present the document in the most favorable light.

THE REVIEW OF THE FIRST DRAFT

As the first draft nears completion, it is increasingly trying for the student to hold to the idea that it is merely a first draft. So much effort has gone into it, so much time and money may be invested in it, that it becomes difficult to think of making even minor alterations to it, much less major changes. Ideally, the first draft should be so complete, so accurate, so well thought through, and so soundly written that it calls for very few modifications. This is a goal well worth the student's and committee's striving. Yet, in reality it is rarely attained. So, it is good if the student maintains a "first draft" attitude, a disciplined certainty that variances, some imperative and some only desirable, will be proposed. Adjusting to those proposals and using them to make a good manuscript even better are significant parts of the learning process inherent in this stage of the work.

Critiquing and Revision

Complicated and difficult parts of the draft may be profitably rewritten a number of times. Few persons find deathless prose flowing from their pens or word processors on the first try. Good writing is closely related to clear thinking, and neither comes easily or quickly to most writers. This is especially true of scholarly, technical, and scientific writing. Readable, clear, direct prose is usually the result of polishing, correcting, rephrasing, and rewriting any number of times. It is at this point that composing, editing, and rewriting on the word processor shows its merits most clearly. Changes on the screen are easy, and the new section or sentence can be seen and revised immediately.

Some students wait for their advisor to read and critique each draft of a section or a chapter before rewriting. This is a waste of time. Any intelligent, critically thinking person can read a T/D chapter and ask pointed questions about its meaning. If it is not clear to another person of good intelligence, it is probably not fully clear to the writer nor will it be clear to the committee. At this stage, in fact, it is probably better *not* to have the proposal critiqued solely by another professional who is knowledgeable in the field of the proposal—there may be too much tolerance for the jargon and obfuscation that are the bane of the professional and academic life. It would be good to trust one or more critical readings of the draft to an acerbic veteran of 10 to 20 years teaching composition and expository writing to high school or first-year college students, a person who knows little or nothing about the subject of the proposal.

The advisor's review of the draft is important, of course, but others can suggest improvements to the draft between appointments with the advisor. This will save the advisor's time and also impress on the advisor that the visit is regarded as serious by the student, as evidenced by the grammar, spelling, wording, clarity, and neatness of the draft each time.

This is a good time to look again at Fig. 5-1, a form that is sometimes used by committees to help to evaluate a T/D. To supplement this form, we also suggest using the checklist for theses and dissertations (Fig. 8-2). It need not follow the table of contents exactly. The central point is to ensure that the document answers the checklist questions well.

Obtaining Reactions from Committee Members

The obvious way to learn what the committee members think of the material in its first full-draft form is to ask them. The quality and thoroughness of response, however, are influenced greatly by the manner in which the student makes the request. Committee members

Introduction and Problem Statement

Is the problem stated both in a general and in a specific way?

Is the purpose of the study stated?

Are the questions or hypotheses stated?

Does the reader get a general view of both the rationale for the investigation and its relationship to a supporting theoretical base?

Is there a transition to the next section?

Review of the Literature

Does it show thorough knowledge of the research, theory, concepts, ideology, and opinion related to this topic?

Is the reader made aware that the review has been selective, and are the criteria for selection and relevance explained?

Is there any critical assessment of the reviewed literature?

Does the review reveal the relation between what has previously been done by others and what is proposed in this study?

Are suitable headings used to help the reader sort out the sections of the review?

Is each section summarized?

Are transitions provided from one section to another?

Figure 8-2 Checklist for theses and dissertations.

Is there a final summary that clinches the need to do the study, including gaps in the literature this study fills?

Method or Procedure

Does it explain what was done to gather the information essential to the investigation?

Would it be possible for another person to gather data and analyze it exactly as in this study simply by reading and following the statements in this section?

Is the specific research method used related clearly to a more general design known in the research methodology literature?

If human or animal subjects are used, are they adequately protected?

Are the variables in the study identified and described?

If controls are used, are they explained in sufficient detail?

If materials or apparatus are involved, are they described, illustrated, and their history and usefulness indicated?

Is the setting of the study specified?

If any directions or explanations are given to subjects by the investigator in the course of the study, are they included?

Is debriefing necessary? If so, is it explained?

Results

Does the reader learn how information in raw form was summarized? Descriptive statistics? Content analysis? Other?

Do tables contain all essential information so they can be read without references to the text?

Does each table stand on its own, clear and self-explanatory?

Are results grouped in relation to questions or hypotheses?

Are incidental findings not immediately related to the questions or hypotheses reported? Are there unforeseen results?

Is redundancy eliminated or minimized?

Is this section free of interpretations of results?

Discussion and Conclusions

Are the meaning and importance of the results indicated?

Are conclusions drawn about each question or hypothesis?

Are the limitations on conclusions specified?

Are alternative explanations for the findings identified and discussed?

Does the reader learn how successful the investigation was and what further study might be needed on the topic?

Figure 8-2 Continued

report that they feel they can be most helpful when the student behaves in an orderly, organized way, as in the following illustration.

The student makes an appointment and delivers the document in person. This gives time for the two to update each other on their activities with respect to the project and to talk about any matters that need to be discussed.

Allowing enough time for the committee member to read the draft in its entirety (usually a week or two weeks), an appointment is made to meet again for the student to receive the reactions directly. In preparation for the follow-up appointment, the student does these things, if they are appropriate:

Asks for agreement that the meeting might be taped so it can be reviewed by the student after the meeting.

Raises specific questions about the draft and calls attention to the parts of it in which the committee member might have particular interest.

Indicates that reactions from all committee members are going to be listened to and reviewed with the advisor before final actions are taken on them.

Encourages the committee member to make notes, changes, and comments on the draft itself while reading it.

Asks the committee member what other preparations, if any, should be made for the follow-up appointment.

In ending this meeting with each committee member, the student leaves information about how to be reached (by telephone or other message) prior to the follow-up appointment if a committee member needs to have clarification of something while reading or circumstances require a change in time or place for the meeting.

Not all committee members look for precisely the same approach. There are differences in style, and students need to accommodate them. The paramount point, though, is that the conference is for the benefit of the student. It is the committee member's obligation to be constructive, to guide, and to teach. The probability that the committee member will fulfill that obligation increases if the student takes a hand in setting the stage for productive interaction by behavior similar to that illustrated in the list.

If the initial arrangements proceed satisfactorily, the follow-up session for feedback should start in an easy, yet focused and objective, way. The great bulk of the student's time should be spent in listening and observing. Notable points for the student are as follows:

Be sure to understand the committee member's statements. If uncertain, ask to discuss them.

Avoid conflict. This is not the time to argue about whether a change should be made or how something should be presented. Keep in mind that all committee member reactions are to be discussed later with the chairperson before deciding if or how they will be used.

Stay open, not resistant. The gist and the value of what is being said can escape if one is preoccupied with being defensive.

At the close of the meeting, make an oral summary of the salient points covered to be certain that nothing the committee member considers important has been overlooked.

Sometimes, more than one meeting, even a series of meetings, is necessary to obtain all the assistance to come from a committee member. Time invested at this point pays dividends and interest by reducing the number of challenges and surprises later when the T/D defense must be made.

Coordinating Committee Reactions with the Chairperson

Under an ideal condition, the student and chairperson would have little to do when reactions to the first draft come back from committee member review. That ideal condition, though, is unusual. Since committee members were seeing the work in its entirety for the first time, they were almost certain to find gaps, data analyses, or research findings that they felt were flawed or inconsistent. Moreover, the student sometimes finds that two or more committee members offer bewilderingly divergent ideas about changes that should be made in the same part of the draft.

The effective chairperson at this stage helps the student in at least three ways. These include the reconciliation of conflicting recommendations of committee members, the restructuring of the manuscript to include missing components or to make clarifications and corrections, and the preparation of a smooth second draft that embodies the alterations.

In the first of these activities, the chairperson must remember that the student may be very inexperienced in merging different points of view, especially when they are voiced by persons the student regards as superiors. Frequently, the student can be prepared for the work to be done if the advisor points out that it is the values and relationships of the ideas or concepts that are to be thought about, more than the personalities of the differing faculty members. It may then be advisable to liken the task to that faced in writing a paper in which the varying viewpoints of several authorities need to be compared, contrasted, and, if possible, related to a larger and unifying conception.

Alternatively, sometimes the student must be led to examine the conflicting expressions of different committee members and to reject one or more of them in favor of another. In that case, it is the chairperson's place to help ensure that the student is prepared to support the decision. In all of this, the student's growth in competence to handle such situations is the central concern.

The advisor intrudes or supports only to the extent necessary to achieve closure in a reasonable time. The student should feel the primary responsibility for whichever course is chosen or decision made.

If restructuring of the manuscript calls merely for the excision or rewriting of a paragraph or a sentence here and there, it is a minor matter, more an annoyance than a problem. When the recommended shifts are big ones, though, it may signal the need for a thorough redrafting of the document. Prior to embarking on such a comprehensive reformulation, it is usually advisable to arrange a conference to include the student, the chairperson, and the committee member(s) who proposed the alterations. Such a meeting can clarify for the student and the chairperson the expectations that prompted the recommended changes. Sometimes, too, such a meeting reveals that the revisions proposed are not as drastic as the student originally thought. In rare cases, the variances requested by a committee member are substantial and far-reaching, and the committee member is adamant. The committee chairperson, in that case, may need to call a full committee meeting to attempt to resolve the matter. The overriding consideration must be that the student receives fair treatment. In extreme cases, the student may need to lodge a grievance through the channels provided by the particular college or university.

A truism to which we referred above has it that an ounce of prevention is worth a pound of cure. That certainly is accurate for the writing of the initial complete draft. The more care exercised in putting the first full draft together, the easier it should be to incorporate the changes, deletions, and additions into an even-flowing document. Chairpersons tend to impress that notion on students from the outset.

In addition to the three major kinds of assistance students can expect from chairpersons during this coordinative stage, there are countless other little ways in which a spirit of confidence and support can be conveyed. Some advisors maintain an "open-ear" policy, encouraging the student to telephone to discuss any problem that may be temporarily troublesome. Others describe and explain their own effective work habits, giving students opportunities to test them for themselves. Still others deliberately reinforce productive behavior on the part of students and then discuss with them how and why they did so. Whether they employ these or other procedures, advisors who are remembered as good models are the ones who offer advice and technical assistance in connection with the review of the first draft that help the student over rough spots, who show respect for other committee members, and whose help enhances the quality of the report.

Rewriting the First Draft

Most experienced writers on professional and academic subjects agree that they can improve first drafts by laying them aside for a week or 10 days and then rereading them, editing during the second reading. Our recommendation, therefore, is to rewrite the first draft in a two-step process (if rewriting proves necessary).

First, go through and make all of the corrections and changes that were agreed to in the coordinating session with the chairperson. Then, put the material aside for a week or two. (Most students have plenty of other things they can do in the interim, such as obligations they have postponed while concentrating on the T/D.) During this time, it is a good practice to arrange a rereading by others, some of whom, as we suggested above, are expert in clear prose composition and who are not specialists in the student's field.

As a second step, after an interlude, begin with the title page and read through the entire document, editing again for clarity and accuracy. Again, we emphasize the enormous help that a good word-processing program can be in such editing. Recheck all references. Delete excess words. Check every compound and every complex sentence to ascertain if it would be more readable if broken into simple sentences. Critically examine each paragraph that takes more than half a page to see if it might better be broken into two or shortened by leaner writing. Look again at transition points from topic to topic and from chapter to chapter. If they are not present, construct short summaries and introductions as route markers to lead the new reader over the trail of reasoning that the writer can easily follow now without landmarks because it is so familiar.

Chapter 10 contains suggestions about writing style adapted from statements by editors of major professional journals. The hints are intended primarily for would-be writers for journals, of course, but they are equally applicable to T/D writing when the focus is on fat-free prose.

Finally, in the rewriting, attention should be paid to the material in the next section of this chapter. While some T/Ds must go through several drafts before presentation for final defense, the student who is alert to committee member advice and technical assistance and who approaches rewriting in an orderly way will face fewer disappointments.

WHEN THE WRITING IS FINISHED

There are really two different final drafts of the T/D. The first is the one that the student defends before the final oral examination committee. The second is the document that is accepted and entered into the school's records as part of the fulfillment of the degree requirements. The difference between the two is a function of the amount and kinds of changes that prove necessary as a consequence of the battering the study takes in the final oral session. Some emerge virtually unscathed.

Others, although ultimately approvable, may need major repairs. More is said about this when the final oral examination itself is discussed. In the meantime, what appears next can be taken as relevant to both final documents.

The Student's Standards

The standards a student shows in writing do not emerge suddenly; earlier work with term papers and the like reveal the patterns of writing behavior the student brings to the task. In some cases, an excellent foundation has been laid in prior work, but for some students, the basics of composition are shaky, to say nothing of skills essential for scholarly writing.

Obviously, it takes even more than ordinary intellectual prowess and determination for a student weak in written expression to attain acceptance for advanced study. More often than not, students with that handicap find that the overview is an almost insurmountable hurdle. It can be questioned, of course, whether sheer ability to communicate well in writing should be a determining criterion. We would want the option to make exceptions if other circumstances appeared to warrant it, but when the ability to master the mechanics and styles of high-quality written communication is demonstrably within the student's range of potential, we would argue for holding it as a requisite for T/D preparation.

Students' standards for language usage and mechanics are, as noted, predictable from earlier samples of written work. A great deal of disappointment can be avoided, therefore, if faculty members will maintain high criteria for quality of writing in all courses and seminars and simply not accept sloppy and inaccurate sentence structure, spelling, punctuation, capitalization, paragraphing, and other recognized elements of correct writing. Both carelessness and ignorance are remediable, and the process should not be deferred until research work starts.

Equally important are the students' standards for the content, the thought processes, and the arguments that should tie the T/D into a coherent, complete report of the study, from inception to conclusions and implications. These standards, too, are not likely to flower in the context of research proposal and report writing unless they were rooted, nourished, and budding during prior professional and academic study.

The standards that students internalize can be influenced by example. A direct and straightforward way to provide positive influence is to bring students into frequent contact with high-quality original research reports in all of their courses. Discussions with students suggest that a great many of them never see or touch an actual T/D before beginning work on one. Even then, they may review them principally for hints on how to set up a table of contents, chapters, and chapter subheadings.

We urge that students be introduced early to investigative studies and to the rationale for their place in preparation for roles in the learned professions. The use of T/Ds as models for scholarly writing is part of that theme. It is not a panacea, of course. Actual remedial instruction in composition may be essential for certain students before they can be fully admitted to advanced study. However, the early and consistent employment of selected, illustrative T/Ds offers students both a most promising and a readily accessible means to exemplify high standards of quality for mechanics, process, and substance in professional and academic authorship.

The Chairperson's Standards

We queried experienced chairpersons about how they acquired the standards they use in judging the merits of student research. Also, we listened to their views on which criteria ought to be applied in determining whether a document is ready to be presented for the final oral examination session.

Senior professors frequently regarded their own preparation for student research direction and committee work as less than satisfactory. It was too frequently based on incidental, spotty, and haphazard personal experience. What they learned, they said, was picked up, for the most part, from observing what other chairpersons did and by occasionally asking questions. Thus, inconsistency could be expected in standards from one to another chairperson. With recognition of the insecure basis for their views, however, chairpersons did say that they look for the following characteristics as far as student research writing is concerned:

The problem is clearly stated and well conceptualized.
Ideas are communicated in clear, readable language.
The student demonstrates significant analytical skills.
The writing is succinct, not verbose.
The presentation is well organized.
The thought processes are well defined and internally consistent.

Not every chairperson will consider these six statements to be either an essential or a sufficient list by which to assess the adequacy of T/D writing. Also, they may not be objective or operational enough, in the view of some, to form the basis for a rating scale. Yet, the odds seem to be good that most of those items will be high in the priorities of chairpersons when they judge the quality of writing, and that documents that fall short on them will be returned to the student for more work.

The advisor cannot be expected to teach the fundamentals of composition. There may be occasional basic errors the advisor will detect and correct in the student's writing. But, the ability to write plain prose that is grammatically correct seems to be a reasonable prerequisite, not something to be learned from the advisor.

Another important role for the advisor, though, consists of increasing the student's awareness of the desirability to attain high standards of quality in writing with maximum economy and precision. By economy is meant using only as many words as are necessary. We are all familiar with sentences that ramble, repeat, and trap our thoughts in a tangle of verbiage. Improved mastery of the simple declarative sentence in writing should be one of the outcomes of T/D study for students. It is well within the scope of the advisor's authority and responsibility to keep that goal before the student.

Precision in writing also calls for attention. Students who are otherwise fluent and even creative writers often need more of the discipline that scholarly writing requires. For instance, a student reports that the literature review included "reading everything that Robert Browning wrote." The student may need to be asked if the review did not actually include only "reading all of Robert Browning's known published works, as listed in [a given reference]." Another student may write that "Americans were the first to make a landing on the moon." That student may need to be shown that a more precise (an altogether accurate) statement is that "Americans were the first to set foot on the moon." This form of polishing is a very important kind of instruction the student should expect from the advisor and committee members. It extends from making the title say exactly what is intended, through creating table headings, stating the problem, writing footnotes, and drawing conclusions to the phrasing of the implications of the investigation.

The College or University's Standards

We were unable to find any statements, as such, that colleges or universities published as standards for satisfactory writing in a T/D. The same is true for professional schools. Many institutions and schools do require compliance with certain style guides. The inference can be drawn that adherence to the style guide, coupled with correct spelling, usage, grammar, and punctuation, would meet the standards for the mechanics of composition.

In a more general sense, several professional schools do exercise a form of quality control. At the University of Michigan's School of Education, for instance, a sample of T/Ds is drawn from each year's crop for special review. The selected T/Ds are sent to a jury of acknowledged leaders at other locations for assessment. The letter that accompanies the documents asks for a critical analysis of each and a rating as to its worthiness. The responses are then distributed to all faculty members, with the expectation that the faculty's future standards and actions will be influenced constructively by the reports of these annual checks. In another professional school, it was reported that one associate dean perused every T/D approved by final oral committees. They numbered over 200 per year. Aside from the almost incredible amount of reading that entailed, there were no indications that systematic feedback occurred. It may have been felt that simply the knowledge that someone in authority would look at all the products would stimulate efforts toward higher quality.

Actually, apart from either recommended or required style guides, most higher education institutions' standards seem to be no more and no less than an amalgam of the various views of the faculty members who serve on T/D committees. We found no evidence that the amalgam is analyzed to determine where it constitutes a consensus on anything. In short, the institutional criterion for satisfactory writing appears to be whatever a final oral committee approves. Neither concomitant with nor beyond the committee's positive decision did we find any other check on quality.

School and Departmental Standards

Even a casual examination of T/Ds from different units in a school will reveal some variations in what is acceptable. One expects, of course, differences in topics, and that has been discussed elsewhere in this book. There are also understandable differences in sources, emphasis, terminology, and investigative methodology from one division or department to another. Studies about very early childhood may depend heavily on more or less quantified information supplied by third parties who observe the infants and toddlers. Investigations involving teenaged youths may, in contrast, draw mainly on data generated by or from the adolescents themselves, such as autobiographies or test responses. Research on supervision may use material drawn from interaction analysis. Work in administration and management may employ actuarial information, costs, and other facts. Trend analyses in history or in political science may use library resources, primarily, although all of the above depend heavily on library facilities, too.

But, even though sharp substantive and procedural differences legitimately appear, the quality of student research writing ought not vary significantly from one school or department to another or from one document to another in the same school or department. When it does, the most probable culprit is the faculty, who failed to establish and abide by standards. The immediate losers, in that case, are the students because inferior work will not be discriminated from high-quality work. The distinguished products of excellent students will be diminished through association with the shoddy work of others. The students who offer inadequately written T/Ds will not be informed that they are weak, and the ones who could do better will not be helped to improve. The long-range losers are the school or department and the higher education institution for they, over the years, come to be judged mainly by the products of their graduates.

Thus, the generators and guardians of T/D writing standards are and should be all of the faculty members of the higher education institution. The graduate faculty, that elect group vested with the power to guide and approve, should spearhead the total thrust for superior writing.

Application of Standards with Objectivity

Ultimately, the decision about whether the T/D is in final form, ready for submission for the final oral examination, is the decision of the student. It is a decision that, ideally, should have the full concurrence of the chairperson, but that is not always the case. If the student insists that the T/D needs no further work, even though the chairperson does not agree, the student's choice should prevail. And, both the advisor and the student may feel that their view is objective.

As noted, high on every priority list of scholarly qualities is an attitude of objectivity. It includes objectivity both about one's own work and about the work of others. It is not divorced from a humane attitude, for that, too, deserves a high priority on the same list. But, objectivity is a distinct quality. It allows one to make clear decisions about the degree of credibility to be assigned to any academic or professional matter. It is behind every reasoned evaluation. Objectivity allows the weighing of variables that can make the difference between sound judgment and sheer guesswork. Objectivity is a chief determinant of the confidence one has that one's present procedures and future projections have substantial foundations. Objectivity is a necessary precondition to believability.

Surely objectivity is emphasized in many ways in the course of collegiate preparation. Many students probably possess highly developed levels of objectivity as part of their entry behavior when they start T/D work. One of the tasks of the research advisor is to determine the degree to which that quality is already present in the student and reinforce and strengthen it as needed until it is firmly established. One of the questions that should be answered in the affirmative by the committee before final approval is given is: "Has the student consistently demonstrated an adequate level of objectivity in professional and academic matters?"

The chairperson is obligated to ascertain that the student is aware of all the objective standards that may legitimately be used to measure the product. Also, the chairperson is responsible for informing the student objectively how and in what ways the proposed T/D does or does not measure up.

The usual outcome of the application of standards is a happy one in which the student moves ahead to the next step with confidence that the chairperson is fully supportive. In such cases, the confidence usually proves to be fully justified.

SUMMARY

This chapter is chiefly about writing, with suggestions about how to accomplish it with dispatch and with superior results. Writing includes attention both to mechanics and to clear exposition of thought. The judicious use of both advice and technical assistance is advocated. The significance of institutional roles, regulations, and standards is emphasized, as are the roles of various persons in providing guidance and interpretations. The meaning of objectivity and its applications are discussed. The preeminent position of the student in decision making is made clear, as is the high stake both student and institution have in the production of excellent student research.

9

Defense of the Thesis or Dissertation

QUICK REFERENCE TO ANSWERS TO SPECIFIC QUESTIONS

The research project is not finished until the student has submitted to an examination on it, made whatever adjustments are shown to be needed as a consequence of that examination, and received a signed statement of faculty committee approval. This chapter deals with those matters, how they are to be carried out, and the factors that influence and guide faculty decision making.

STRUCTURE OF THE ORAL EXAMINATION

The oral examination in most institutions is the final procedural step in student evaluation in the degree process. It concentrates on the study, the findings, and the interpretation of the findings. However, questions regarding the academic and professional preparation of the candidate may also legitimately arise.

In the historic tradition of great European universities, the rite of passage from the rank of student to the community of scholars was marked by hours and even days of examination by established scholars. Invitations would be issued to learned persons throughout the country to attend, and every visiting scholar felt obliged to ask erudite questions. The candidate was expected to respond promptly and to be able to defend the response as long as the questions were in the candidate's field of expertise. The candidate was seeking admission to the community of scholars who had already earned the high distinction of being titled "master" or "doctor" (Haskins, 1957; see also the Introduction).

Modern examinations follow the European tradition, but differ in several details. In most contemporary cases, the examining committee focuses on the evidence of scholarship before it. The time set aside for the final defense is usually too brief to allow the committee to do much more than that. Today, most final oral examinations are conducted in two- to three-hour sessions. Those present are usually limited to the candidate and the committee, with perhaps one or two guest scholars or student observers.

Another major difference between examinations in early European universities and those of today in the United States is in recourse by the student for perceived bias or injustice. There was little opportunity for that up to a few decades ago. Now, universities have well-established grievance procedures that students may invoke if they believe they have been treated unfairly.

Scenario of the Examination*

The candidate and the committee meet at a designated time in an appropriate room. Each committee member has prepared for the examination by examining the work presented and by making note of any items needing clarification or questions to be asked.

The chairperson begins the session by asking the candidate to make a brief statement about the results and findings of the research, after which each member of the committee is encouraged to ask questions or make comments. The candidate responds, when appropriate,

*This describes the bare bones of a typical scenario. Students are advised to flesh out the scenario with the advisor well before the examination date. The content of the rest of this chapter can be helpful in doing that.

to the questions or comments. At the end of the appointed time, the candidate is asked to leave the room while the committee discusses which decision it should make on the basis of a review of the document and the final oral examination, as well as any other information relevant to the academic competence of the candidate. Then, the candidate is brought back into the room, the chairperson announces the committee's decision, and a short discussion ensues concerning the conditions attached to the decisions, if any. At this point, the defense and the oral exam are considered over. The purpose of the final defense has been accomplished, namely, to establish whether the candidate has qualitatively and quantitatively met the standards of the institution and the faculty in the completion of the research and in the program of studies.

Criteria for Excellence

An excellent oral defense is one for which it is clear to the committee that the candidate has prepared well. The document presented is a good example of discursive prose. The answers to the committee questions are concise, clear, to the point, and informative. The oral presentation is tightly reasoned. The impression made on the committee is one of quiet confidence and competence. There is little doubt at the end that the candidate has the ability and integrity to carry on competent research without detailed direction from a senior colleague.

The Evaluation Procedure

Final defense committees commonly use four options in deciding which action to take after the examination. Two of the options are unusual: The committee may approve the T/D as executed, or it may deny approval. Both decisions are extreme in the sense that they seldom happen and in the sense that they have a powerful effect on the student.

The other two options are the withholding of approval until major revisions are made or approval with minor modification. These are discussed in other sections of this chapter.

Whichever option is chosen by the committee, there must be specific reasons for it, and those reasons must be stated. The committee's decision and the reasons for it should be made clear to the student and summarized by the chairperson for the committee and the candidate at the end of the session.

PREPARATION FOR THE EXAMINING COMMITTEE SESSION

Examining committee sessions require preparation and prior planning, perhaps several months in advance. Refer to the time line for compliance with local rules on this. The preparation is the responsibility of a number of persons, but the two principal roles belong to the candidate and the chairperson of the committee.

Chairperson's Responsibilities

Before a committee examination can be firmly scheduled, the research advisor must be satisfied with the draft of the T/D that is to be the basis for the final oral examination. This draft then is sent to the rest of the committee for review. It should, in the student's mind, be considered a final draft. It should include changes and should have reconciled conflicts raised by committee members in earlier draft reviews.

If the advisor at this stage seems too strict or too demanding in the eyes of the student, it is good to remember that the advisor's reputation is also at stake. Sending the draft to committee means that the advisor has reviewed it carefully and critically and believes that it is ready for committee review.

After the committee has received the final draft, the advisor sets aside a reasonable amount of time for the committee to review the document. We suggest at least two weeks if there is no specific time set in local regulations.

If the advisor has been successful in helping the student put together a well-formulated and well-written report, the committee will usually not request further revisions prior to the examination. However, one or more members may request improvements in a more formal way during the meeting of the examining committee.

Time, Location, and Notice of Examination

We recommend that the advisor circulate copies of the final draft along with a memorandum that gives notice of the time, location, and membership of the meeting of the final defense examining committee. This may be made the candidate's responsibility, but the chairperson should then oversee it. The university process for notifying students and the faculty committee of the time and place of the meeting usually includes some procedure also to notify other members of the graduate faculty and to allow them to read the T/D before the meeting. They can then attend with some knowledge of the subject and can assess the document against the standards of the institution.

Preview of Procedures for Student

It is good form for the advisor to preview procedures with the student. The student is often unaware of role expectations in the committee meeting, is unsure of preparation that should be made, and is not knowledgeable about the support or nonsupport of the advisor during the examining committee meeting. These, and any other matters raised by the candidate, ought to be very thoroughly discussed in the advisor's office. The advisor may offer some advice about the steps the candidate might take to prepare for the final defense.

The advisor should make sure that the candidate has gone through all the mechanical steps that accompany the final stages of the T/D process and eventual graduation. The two persons might again go over the limitations of the study—limitations that are unavoidable and not remediable at this point. Problems may be anticipated in this preview session, but the role of the advisor should be to make the candidate feel at ease and in control. After all, the candidate has done the best work possible, and the advisor has approved what was done; although the product may not be perfect, it is their expectation that a favorable outcome will result.

This is a good opportunity for the advisor to review the formalities of the session, how questions will be asked, how long the session is likely to be, and, as well, a description of how the advisor will chair the session, including a perception of the advisor's role as chairperson of the examining committee. Finally, there ought to be some frank talk about the role of the candidate in the session and how that role might be seen as functional to the achievement of the goal. We provide our recommendations regarding the role of the student subsequently. It is also valuable at this point to read again what we said (see Chapter 6) about the overview meeting for much of it applies.

Candidate Responsibilities

The first responsibility of the candidate is to be well prepared. The second is to be completely frank and open with the advisor about the problems and weaknesses of the study and any other possible difficult issues, from the point of view of the student, that may come up in the final defense. This committee session will have more of the atmosphere of a scholarly examination than any prior meeting of the group. Students must be ready for that and all that it implies about student-faculty interactions during the examination.

Availability of Needed Equipment

At some examining committee sessions, the candidate needs a special room or special equipment such as an overhead projector or computer-connected projector for the final defense. This may include equipment used during the overview plus additional items. Whatever the equipment required, it is the candidate's responsibility to check with the chairperson to ascertain if it is permitted in the examining committee session. If so, it is the candidate's responsibility to obtain the equipment and place it in the examining room before the session and to make sure it works. It is also the responsibility of the candidate to schedule the room with the concurrence of the chairperson of the T/D examining committee.

Freedom to Observe Oral Defense Examinations

The final defense ordinarily is publicly announced and is open to eligible members of the university community who wish to observe it. Graduate students and faculty should be especially welcome. An open and public final defense is in the finest scholastic tradition.

Use of Simulation for Preparation

Once there is a recognized structure and procedure to the final defense committee meeting, a fairly realistic simulation can be designed. Students can work together to constitute an examining committee, simulate the whole meeting from beginning to end, and even pass, fail, or amend the candidate's presentation. In a simulation, fellow students often ask harder questions and grill a candidate with less mercy than faculty in the same situation. A candidate who has been through a number of tough simulations will probably have anticipated the questions that will be asked in the real defense and will have formulated thoughtful answers.

The simulation process can be carried to a fine art. Students from the candidate's department can assume the roles of specific members of the committee, reflect their backgrounds and research interests, and predict many of their questions. Having gone through the final draft of the T/D, the student-colleagues who are playing the roles of members of the committee often should be able to perceive any weaknesses in the study and anticipate the queries expected of faculty examiners. Simulation is also educational for those who help. These students will then have an opportunity to model their behavior on a colleague who may be a little more advanced.

We recommend beginning simulation sessions early in the final writing stages. If unanswered questions or gaping holes in early drafts become evident, they can be repaired before the document goes to the committee.

In summary, the best preparation for the final defense is a document written and argued so tightly that there is very little room for embarrassing questions. Committees like such T/Ds because they are well done and because the committee can spend most time during the defense exploring the implications of the study and looking to the future research needs it reveals rather than tinkering with errors in grammar, style, research design, or methodology.

CONDUCT OF THE ORAL EXAMINATION

If there is sound preparation, it is unlikely that the final oral will hold any great threat. In many cases, the final defense is seen as a pro forma meeting. That condition prevails when the student investigator has produced an excellent study, fulfilled the promises made in the proposal, worked closely with advisors, and communicated fully with committee members. In such cases, the advisor and committee members have a common view that the graduate research was well done. The final defense then becomes what many faculty hope for in every case—a lively and informed discussion of an important problem and field of interest in which the candidate and faculty participate essentially as colleagues. The discussion focuses on the growing edge of research, explores the implications of the results of the study, examines the interdisciplinary effects of the study findings, and brainstorms new research ideas to push back the frontiers of knowledge, understanding, and professional practice. Such final orals are exciting and enjoyable for everyone; in the best of circumstances, they become the focus of interest and intellectual excitement of a much broader circle of scholars than just the committee. In our view, this is a state of constructive intellectual ferment to be sought at colleges and universities that aspire to be "great" or "excellent."

Role of the Chairperson

If the chairperson is also the research advisor, there is some role conflict inherent in the examining committee session. The advisor has worked very closely with the candidate and finally approved the work in a form to come before the committee. Hard as one may try, it is impossible to be completely disinterested in the outcome of the process. For many advisors, the candidate's product becomes almost a part of the advisor.

The committee chairperson role has expectations that are somewhat different from those of the research advisor. The chairperson is expected to conduct the session in an impartial way. The role is not one of defense of the candidate or defense of the chairperson's own deep involvement in the work of the candidate. The role is rather that of an impartial judge, who assures a fair and open hearing for the candidate, and for each member of the examining committee, even the most junior. The chairperson has the obligation to set the conditions and guide the process so that all the participants can come to a fair, equitable, and reasoned decision as to the best course of action under the circumstances.

Balanced Participation

The oral examination should be equitable and evenhanded with respect to all parties. The person chiefly responsible for maintaining that equilibrium is the chairperson. Balanced participation means, operationally, that every person on the committee has a fair and equal chance to ask questions and make comments. It also means that the candidate has a fair and equal chance to respond to questions or comments and to put forward others when appropriate. It means that all members of the committee have the same opportunity to participate.

If the persons who have roles in the oral examination feel that the session has been partial, biased, unbalanced, or unfair, the results of that feeling may well spill over to create other committee problems and perhaps other problems for the candidate. Moreover, such feelings may well engender formal grievances.

Tone of the Session

As the convener and as the presiding university official, the chairperson is in the position to set the tone of the meeting. It is a serious undertaking, most of all for the candidate who has invested so much in the study, and the session is expected to have a serious and a moderately formal quality. The most important tone, however, is conveyed by the verbal and nonverbal behavior of faculty. The behavior should indicate that the individual faculty member cares so much, values so much, the candidate's work that no effort was spared to read it carefully, and that while the faculty member is supportive of the candidate, nothing short of excellent work will be allowed to pass the committee. It is best if this tone can be established and maintained from the beginning by the chairperson.

If there are observers, the chairperson is responsible for arranging seating for them that separates them physically from the candidate and the committee members. Also, the observers should be addressed by the chairperson before the examination begins to explain that comments, questions, or other forms of participation or expression by them are to be reserved while the examination is in session.

Clarification of Questions

The chairperson is also looked to for clarification of technical or substantive questions on the T/D and on the examining committee process. For example, if the student's work has been part of a larger program of investigation directed by a faculty member, the degree to which the student has been able to maintain independence would be a reasonable area of inquiry. As another example, suppose the student has made significant use of a consultant from another university. What kind of monitoring has that consultant's participation had from committee members? For a third example, what if the candidate is deaf and will be using an interpreter to facilitate communication during the committee examination session? How can one be certain of accurate interpretation?

It is essential to anticipate such questions and to have explanations readily accessible before the session if one is in the role of chairperson. In cases when the questions are clearly for the candidate, the clarification role of the chairperson may be simply to supply a communication link between a faculty question and a student's attempt to understand the question. In any case, the role of the chairperson does not include answering faculty questions clearly directed at the candidate concerning either the investigation or what the candidate has learned through the program.

Signaling Completion of Examination

There is no magic number of minutes the session is required to last. Based on our data, the total time, from calling the meeting to order to notification of the candidate of the outcome, typically ranges between one and one-half and two and one-half hours. After every faculty member has had a chance to ask questions of the candidate, and the candidate to respond and ask questions, the chairperson should be able to sense that the time for ending the examination is drawing near. The chairperson should then try, without being arbitrary, to bring the session to a close. There are always individuals who may find it difficult to stop talking; dealing with those individuals within the context of an oral examination is the responsibility of the chairperson.

Committee Member Roles

The role of the committee member is to be a judge of quality. Specifically, it is to ascertain if the quality of the T/D is sufficient to admit the candidate to the ranks of those holding an honors, graduate master's, or doctoral degree. In our view, this is the essential element of the role. It is carried out in a number of ways.

The oral examination certainly does give the committee a chance to ascertain the quality of the document and the quality of the student's work. If judgments that influence the outcome go beyond that, the committee is treading on thin ice.

The candidate's lifestyle, political orientation, or championship of popular or unpopular causes all are beyond the purview of the final defense committee with respect to the mores of present-day academia. The issue may seem different, however, if the candidate is known to be engaged in dishonest, unprofessional, or illegal activities. But, even here, committees are reluctant to make judgments, *in this situation*, on anything very much beyond the written and the oral presentations. They tend to see such judgments as outside their role unless the activities have to do with the research itself.

Committees do assess the depth and range of the candidate's knowledge about the document at hand and the methodology used to do the study. If the candidate cannot answer detailed questions about his or her work, including the review of the literature and the methodology, committee members should delve deeper to ascertain reasons for this apparent ignorance.

One important thing the committee members look for is the congruence between the promises made in the proposal and what appears in the final draft of the study. The committee exercises approval over any changes the student makes in the study plan after the overview committee has met and approved the proposal. If the approved proposal has the attributes of a contract, then *both* parties must adhere to it. Therefore, the committee will be looking at the final draft to determine if the approved proposal has been carried out in the conduct of the study.

Students sometimes assume that the acceptance of the final draft by the committee for the purpose of the oral examination signals its acceptance as a document of sufficient quality to meet all the requirements of the university and the committee. This is a false assumption. What the committee action means, in fact, is that the members individually have reviewed the draft carefully and are satisfied that it is good enough to provide a basis for an oral examination. Problems that remain with the final draft will be brought out at the examination. They may or may not be communicated to the student or the advisor beforehand. That depends on the time constraints on the individuals, whether there is good communication among them, and whether the problems were actually identified earlier. Some issues do not surface until there is the interplay of minds during the examination itself. In any case, the problems that remain in the draft that goes to the committee will be worked out in committee and may become a part of the substantive revisions that must be made before the document is finally approved.

Role of the Candidate

Preparation is the key to success. The final oral examination is the culmination of a long preparation process. The candidate has been guided in pre-T/D study by an academic advisor, a person who is usually a member of the committee. The candidate has thoroughly reviewed the literature, designed the methodology, and conducted the study under the guidance of the advisor and committee. Finally, the T/D was written with the advice and consultation of the whole committee. Every committee member had a chance to see it and comment on it before the final defense meeting. With all that background, there should be no great surprises, and the final defense should go smoothly.

Yet, it is not uncommon to find important problems at the end. Why? We have made a list of three main reasons reported by colleagues and from our own experience.

1. The advisor has been misled about how much of the work—the design, the literature review, the data gathering, and analysis (including the knowledge base from which these are drawn)—was really done or understood by the candidate. Because of that, seri-

ous weaknesses come out at the final oral examination and then are pursued by the committee, often to the point at which it becomes acutely embarrassing and uncomfortable for everyone.

2. The advisor errs in allowing the candidate to come to the final defense before the research is thoroughly and carefully done and before it represents a work of excellence. Sometimes, the candidate is convinced that he or she is ready for the final defense and convinces the advisor of this when, in fact, there is a good deal more work to do. Often, there is pressure of time, such as a statute of limitations, a baby due, an upcoming job in another city, or a tenure decision to be made on the candidate who is a faculty member at another institution. Sometimes, there is simply a factor of fatigue, when the advisor and the student have revised the work over and over again and, in effect, throw themselves on the mercy of the committee.
3. Occasionally, the candidate is unrealistic in assessing personal skills, ability, commitment, or the amount of time and detailed work required to complete the T/D, and the advisor is unsuccessful in communicating with the candidate about the problems. The advisor then decides to bring the full force of committee rejection to bear to convince the candidate.

The role of the candidate in the final defense meeting is important. In our view, the role is one of *openness*, *honesty*, and *mature* expertise. Openness about the data and problems of the study is the only ethical way to approach this final test. Honesty is the one most important attribute of a researcher. Maturity motivates candidates to do their own work, accept the responsibility for all that was done in the study, live up to the promises made at the time of the proposal, and treat colleagues in an ethical and unbiased, objective manner.

Responsiveness of a positive, constructive kind is another essential attribute. The final defense is not the place to become "defensive." It is a time for calm, reasoned responses to questions or suggestions. When a response is appropriate, a direct, to-the-point answer is usually best. There is nothing fatal about a straight "I don't know" when that is the simple truth, either, although that response often should not be necessary. In most cases, the candidate's thorough knowledge of a fairly specialized subject area means that the candidate has the most expert knowledge in the committee room. There is no reason, though, for the candidate to flaunt that knowledge. Such behavior is unnecessary and dysfunctional. The time for the candidate to expound with great erudition and wisdom is (if at all) after the awarding of the degree, not during the defense of the research for the degree.

In addition to responding to questions and comments of the committee, the candidate's role includes that of note taker regarding changes suggested by the committee during the oral examination. Sometimes, this responsibility can be delegated to a fellow graduate student who is sitting in on the oral examination. The chairperson and committee members take notes, too. In any case, the responsibility lies with the candidate to see that, in one way or another, the job is done. Remember, too, that not all changes proposed during the examination survive the critical appraisal of the full committee during the committee's end-of-session deliberations. It is what is conveyed to the candidate by the chairperson after the examination that really counts as far as required changes are concerned. It is the candidate's role to raise any question if suggestions for change agreed on in committee are not clear. It is also within the student's role to defend against suggested changes in the T/D that seem unfair, inconsistent with the promises of the research proposal or overview, unethical, or untenable in light of the research. Of course, one would want to be very careful in resisting suggested changes, and perhaps substantial reliance on the views of the chairperson would be appropriate at this point. In our experience, however, there have been very few cases in which a final defense committee suggested a change that was not also seen as desirable by the candidate.

All the above chores are simplified if a voice-activated tape recorder is switched on during the examination. It may be under the control of the chairperson, with the tape remaining in that person's custody. It could then be listened to by the candidate afterward for the purpose of ensuring that the committee's requirements regarding changes and additions are clearly understood and verified.

DECISION MAKING REGARDING THE ORAL DEFENSE

Applying Criteria for Approval

The criteria for approval the committee uses should be made explicit. The T/D evaluation form (Fig. 5-1) was designed to help achieve that purpose. It is useful both at this point as a last-minute check before the final defense and earlier in the T/D process as the draft version is being written. *It seems essential* to us that *all* criteria that have significant weight be stated on the T/D evaluation form. The committee owes that to the candidate, to the institution, and to themselves.

Ambiguities and hidden agendas create misunderstandings and disputes; clarity and openness help to prevent them. We recommend the T/D evaluation form at this point as a summative evaluation form as we recommended it for formative evaluation throughout the preparation phases.

Conditional Approval

There are two forms of conditional approval. If the document is acceptable but minor revisions are needed, the committee will simply indicate where changes should be made and rely on the candidate and the research advisor to make the alterations. Under these circumstances, the candidate makes the minor revisions, submits them for a final review by the research advisor, and then circulates the corrected copy to the committee. Committee members sign and the chairperson sends the document to the appropriate university office.

The second level of provisional approval is much more tentative. It may be used with a final draft that has major problems, but ones that the candidate understands and can probably clear up in a reasonable time. In this case, the candidate is instructed to carry out the major changes and to bring the complete T/D or the altered portions back to a committee meeting or for approval by individual members. This form of provisional approval is short of failure, but if the revisions are not a sufficient improvement over what the committee reviewed at the oral examination, the candidate simply does not pass.

The process of getting back to the committee varies, but in any case, the responsibility is on the candidate to make the substantial revisions on a timely basis and get them to the advisor and, after advisor approval, back to the committee. In such cases, individual committee members do not sign the approval form until completely satisfied that the revised document reflects credit on the candidate, the advisor, the committee, and the university.

Formal Voting

Practice varies from institution to institution, but usually a final oral committee is comprised of an odd number of members, which implies that a vote, if taken, should not be a tie. Usually, only members of the graduate faculty may vote, although others, even from outside the institution, may serve on the committee. Whether the chairperson votes depends on the institution, as does the issue of whether a passing vote must be unanimous, simply a majority, or a specified number of votes.

Our experience and research indicate that there is seldom an issue about the vote. The committee tends to work as a group and, with the help of the chairperson, arrives at a consensus acceptable to all. If one member, or a minority of members, is adamant about a point or decision, usually the committee hears all the arguments, weighs the issues, and comes to a conclusion that seems fair.

A committee can be persuaded to take an action by one member if that member's arguments are good enough and if those arguments support fairness and the concept of high quality in graduate research standards. Usually, the committee chairperson knows what the formal votes will be before passing the official approval form around because agreement on the wisest course of action has been reached by voice vote in committee. When the committee members sign the formal approval form, they are, however, casting formal votes that become a matter of record and for which they are accountable.

Notification and Interpretation to the Candidate

At the end of the oral defense, the candidate should clearly understand the decision of the committee. Sometimes, that decision has to be interpreted to the student. The situation may be stressful, or the student may simply not understand the implications of the decision.

A common point of misunderstanding, we have found, is when the committee is calling for major revisions and the student hears the call in terms of minor modifications that can be accomplished in a short time. Committees usually remain calm and quiet, at least in front of the candidate, and speak in low tones and short sentences. The atmosphere of the final defense session may mislead the candidate to believe everything is going well when in fact it is not.

The research advisor ought to make clear to the student at the end of the meeting the decision of the committee. A good procedure is to have the candidate recount what was decided and what changes are being required in the draft. Further sessions should also be scheduled with the advisor and, if advisable, with individual committee members to check progress. This keeps the candidate focused on the future rather than on rehashing the committee meeting. Some self-pity is natural and human, particularly if the final oral examination did not go well, but it is dysfunctional. It is best for the candidate to start immediately on what remains to be done.

FOLLOW-UP AFTER APPROVAL OR DISAPPROVAL

Usually, the follow-up period is one of extremes of feeling on the part of the candidate. If the study is approved, the candidate may be so happy that it is easy to forget to make the revisions and do the other procedural things that are necessary before graduation is a reality. If the results of the oral examination seemed disastrous, the candidate may understandably exhibit avoidance behavior with respect to the whole process and everyone attached to it. Neither extreme is functional or task oriented with respect to reaching that difficult, time-consuming goal everyone agreed to at the beginning. The thing to do is to start picking up the pieces immediately.

Candidate and Research Advisor's Roles

Whatever happened at the defense, the advisor's role is to help the candidate calm down, reassess, reevaluate, and redirect toward whatever it takes to reach the goal. Failing the oral defense is not necessarily irretrievably final.

Candidates have renegotiated with their committee and redone the same or different research with success. It takes more time. Sometimes, it means learning new skills, taking additional courses, and the appointment of a new committee, but it can be and often has been done.

On the other hand, it may be that the candidate cannot muster the resources, cannot take the time, or is too discouraged to begin again. In that case, the advisor has a counseling role to help the candidate arrive at a realistic self-perception. It may also be possible for the candidate to do better in another department or another university or school.

Even when the T/D has been approved, there are usually some revisions to make, and sometimes these are substantial. All of the rules of the university, too, concerning the filing of abstracts, corrected copies, and binding as well as rules concerning the mechanics of actually becoming a graduate of the university, have to be followed after the successful examination session. Both the candidate and the advisor have to guard against the temptation to let things slide because the major work has been done. For both, whether the time is one of sadness after disapproval or happiness after approval, this period is one that should be devoted to reexamination of original goals, the determination of the relevancy of these goals in light of the final defense committee's decision, and, if appropriate, the renewed determination to reach the goals.

Disseminating the Results of the Study

In major universities, dissertations are copyrighted, microfilmed, and indexed in *Dissertation Abstracts*. There is a fee attached to these services. The copyright is designed to protect the author's work from use by others without permission. Microfilming and indexing the document through the University Microfilms process makes it available to other scholars and to libraries for review and even purchase. In using University Microfilms, the author agrees to permit these uses and, under certain circumstances, receives a royalty. The author is often offered the opportunity to have the dissertation listed in the survey of earned doctorates awarded in the United States, and these forms are available at universities that grant earned doctorates.

University Microfilms will make available to authors printed copies of the abstract of the dissertation written by the author. These abstracts can be used effectively to disseminate the results of the study. In some cases, a dissertation will be accepted for inclusion in one of the storage and retrieval systems mentioned above. This can bring wide dissemination. Abstracts may also be sent to professional societies having a professional interest in the subject of the dissertation for printing in their publications.

Professional societies provide another dissemination opportunity. In almost every case there are annual meetings where authors read papers. There are journals and reviews of research that publish not only some of the papers given at the annual meetings, but also manuscripts submitted for review by the journal. While a journal would rarely publish a whole thesis or dissertation as such, it may be happy to publish an article or chapter from one. For publication, revision is usually necessary to make the work fit into the style and format of the journal.

We recommend using the professional societies for dissemination purposes because the process not only makes the study available to others, but also contributes to the recognition, security, and standing of the author. In fact, we recommend that the advisor and candidate explore the possibility of sharing findings, when appropriate, even before the completion of the T/D. For a student to give a paper at an academic or professional meeting is a great learning experience. Often, the help of the research advisor is critical to providing the opportunity.

Finally, there are some investigations that by their nature lend themselves to publication commercially. Historical studies, for example, sometimes find their way into a book or a number of articles. If the work has enough general interest or is topical at the time of publication, it may be successful commercially. This means it will sell as a general work, as a textbook, or as a professional work of merit. In this case, the author may be on the way to more publications and some success as a writer. All of these possibilities are addressed in more detail in the next chapter.

SUMMARY

This chapter explains the process of T/D defense, including the oral examination, suggestions for preparing the examining committee session, and the conduct of the oral examination. The kinds of decisions and how they may be arrived at are discussed. Finally, the need for follow-up after the final defense and the need to disseminate results are described.

10

The Completed Thesis or Dissertation and Future Growth

QUICK REFERENCE TO ANSWERS TO SPECIFIC QUESTIONS

Faculty members believe students should do theses and dissertations for future-oriented reasons. Some are

To add to the body of knowledge necessary to solve the many problems with which academics and professionals now grapple, like undereducation, job dissatisfaction, unemployment, crime, accidents, and others

To establish the ability to write about professional and academic discipline data in ways understandable to people who need such information

To prepare the student for participation in research as part of a career

Plainly, the faculty members who told us those things in interviews or through their writing envisioned links between what might be learned during the completion of research and certain tasks students would need to perform during their future careers. Also, there was a clear indication that the results of research ought to lead to possible resolutions of current or future problems. The question, then, is not whether there should be a tie between student investigations and future work, but rather the question is how best to encourage that viewpoint and to implement it actively.

Myers (1993) says it well:

> What is needed is serious contemplation of the achievement, thoughtful consideration of what changes the achievement will bring to the self-concept of the student, and reinforcement of the sense of ownership of both the product and the process just completed. Without dedicated attention—largely on the part of the sponsor—to the final step in this developmental task, the meaning of the enterprise can be lost. (p. 336)

AFTER THE RESEARCH IS APPROVED

The last four decades brought marked changes from the days when completed T/Ds were simply covered and sewn together by a local bookbinder. Distribution then included a copy for each committee member's office shelf and two for the institution's library. A national list of T/Ds was published occasionally, and interlibrary loan was the only means of wider dissemination.

Now, almost all dissertations and many theses find their way onto microfilm and can be obtained readily at a modest cost. Also, many are referenced in databases that can be searched by computer. Storage, search, and retrieval resources and procedures are as common now as library card files have traditionally been. With access so convenient, why go to the trouble of revising the document for another form of publication? There are several widely acknowledged reasons.

Learning to write for publication is valuable in itself for it develops a set of skills that can enhance all written communication. Members of the academic disciplines and the professions must be able to write material that is well organized, clear, and interestingly stated. Memoranda, directions, reports, letters, evaluations, policies, proposals, regulations, lesson plans—the list of styles and forms of written expression in which scholars must perform well is almost endless.

Security and recognition are often tied to publication productivity. In higher education, one of the criteria for continuation of employment and ultimately for permanent tenure relates to the quality and quantity of authored articles and books. (It is important to remind oneself here that sheer publication does not give assurance of job security. The published material must be of high quality, there must be enough of it, and other characteristics such as teaching ability are weighed, too. But, publications are essential if the criterion of quality and extent of published work is to be assessed at all.) It is also true that initial and continued employment and promotion in research and development centers, state and federal agencies, and other public and private positions can be influenced positively by growth in one's own list of scholarly writings in print.

Career exploration and direction, opportunities for testing new paths, can be significant outcomes from reworking the T/D for possible publication of a book, article, or monograph. Some learn for the first time that they enjoy editorial activity, and that they have hitherto unrealized capabilities for it. Others, during the rewriting, find their interest kindled or quickened in planning a programmatic set of investigations based on the research already done. This may be only one step from seeking and obtaining financial backing for a several-year research-and-development effort. Also, others are turned in new directions by job or consultation offers that come to them because of the interest generated in prospective employers by initial and follow-up publications stemming from their research.

The Internet offers a world of resources whether one is actively seeking or simply thinking about career moves on completion of the doctorate. One of the good places to start is a Web site called Careers and Jobs, and it is free (http://www.starthere.com/jobs/). It is one of the most exhaustive sets of databases available. It includes academic posts, and it has links to other Web sites. If college and university teaching or administration are the primary concerns, try the Chronicle of Higher Education site (http://chronicle.com/chronicle). Search can be either by field of interest or geographical location. Both Web sites were retrieved and reviewed on May 17, 2002.

Contributions to knowledge may, of course, be found directly in the research reports themselves by anyone who searches them out, but it is the nature of the T/D that it is phrased very carefully. Committee members tend to counsel restraint both in what is said and in how it is phrased. Some committee members may urge the candidate to cut loose in the final draft, particularly in the section on implications. By that time, though, the candidate is writing with such ingrained caution that boldness is out of the question. Thus, a journal article may afford the first real opportunity to be more daring, to point out more explicitly how the results and conclusions might be used to add to wisdom and to improve practices. Appearance in the forum of public print also invites comment and discussion, so important to the weighing and balancing that ought to take place before new concepts or changes are fully accepted.

Dissemination of new information still lags. Great gaps yawn between where knowledge is located (e.g., in T/D pages) and where that knowledge ought to be if it is to be used. Publication is one way to narrow those gaps. In addition to the conventional print forms, the delivery of papers or participation in panel discussions is another means of dissemination. Writers who cite relevant T/Ds in their own publications are aiding in dissemination, too. (It was mentioned previously that publication could reinforce academic and professional security and recognition. The same is true of citation. A large number of citations of a scholar's work in the publications of others suggests that their work has extraordinary significance.) The T/D supplies an excellent database from which to disseminate new ideas, information, or concepts, whether through print, oral presentation, or via citations. Committee members and other faculty members who encourage students in those directions are making a contribution to both the students and to their professions.

WRITING FOR PUBLICATION

Few thrills match the first acceptance of an article for publication. It is a great feeling for the author, and it can rightly be a prideful event for the faculty members who tutored and encouraged the author. Surprisingly, relatively few publications about professional or academic publication appear in any field's literature. Etzold's (1976) article is one of the rare ones to address the matter seriously. It provides a tightly knit and thought-provoking process guide to the writing, submission, and acceptance of scholarly manuscripts. It offers practical assistance that can benefit both beginners and experienced writers.

Guidelines on Writing

A brief set of guidelines on writing for publication follows. It draws in part on Etzold's (1976) suggestions, in part on our own experience, and in part on what colleagues told us. The outline has two major components, one dealing with writing the article and the other with getting the article published.

Writing the Article: Writing the article calls for particular attention to three procedures.

First is deciding on the form in which the content will be presented. Journals tend not to employ the conventional T/D format for articles. They prefer shorter pieces; they often merge the problem statement and the literature review, and in many other ways, journal articles have organizational qualities of their own. What they have in common, though, and what successful manuscripts require, is a systematic sequence of content that enhances communication of concepts. The structure (outline) decided on ought to reflect one's scheme for proceeding in an orderly way with the different components and facets of the topic. Preplanned organization should be flexible. Some excellent ideas occur while writing, and it should be possible to fold them into the article's outline as they occur.

This is the time to review your computer files, checking each one for items and ideas you think could be worked into the article you have in mind. Also, this is the time to start a new outline to fill in and store in your computer, this time an outline for an article.

Second, the article should begin with and maintain a firm fix on its main theme. Every paragraph or larger section ought to move that same theme ahead, building on the foundation of the earlier paragraphs or sections.

William Strunk Jr. (Strunk and White, 1979) said it best in *The Elements of Style*:

> Vigorous writing is concise. A sentence should contain no unnecessary words, a paragraph no unnecessary sentences, for the same reason that a drawing should have no unnecessary lines and a machine no unnecessary parts. This requires not that the writer make all his sentences short, or that he avoid all detail and treat his subjects only in outline, but that every word tell. (pp. ix–x)

Anything that deviates from the main line of development should be reexamined to bring it into the main current of the article, to justify it as a necessary side step, or to eliminate it. One can help oneself to monitor the forward movement of the text by posing these questions: Does the first sentence of every paragraph stick to the core theme of the article? Does it follow sensibly the first sentence in the immediately preceding paragraph?

Third, make absolutely sure that all grammatical, spelling, and other mechanical and structural composition details reflect preferred practice in contemporary usage. Quality of expression and correct usage can be upgraded for almost everyone by taking advantage of the standard features of most word processor programs. These not only can call the attention of the writer to such basics as correct spelling, but also can offer synonyms and even check a manuscript for overuse of trite phrases. All of that help, and more, can be had almost automatically if the proper commands are entered into the keyboard.

Correct language cannot make an otherwise weak article into a good one. But, few factors can distract an editor from the positive qualities of a manuscript as quickly and as emphatically as sloppy and inaccurate writing.

Successful authors reach out for the counsel of friends, associates, previous teachers, and others who promise honest and energetic criticism plus suggestions to remedy the defects they detect. It is extremely unusual that the first draft of a manuscript turns out to be the one that ought to be submitted to a journal editor.

Achieving Publication: The article, once written, calls for tuning in on a number of conditions that influence editorial acceptance. Three of the main variables are discussed briefly.

First, pick a periodical to match your topic. Ask your committee members to make suggestions. Journals that cater to social work studies seldom find room for reports of studies in engineering or business.

If a paper has a focus on a matter of interest to professionals only in one state or only in one region (i.e., the Nebraska Association of School Psychologists), then a journal that deals mainly with that state or region's concerns would be the target of choice. If the article is a theory, opinion, or development piece, it would be better aimed at a publication that is known to carry many such articles rather than at one with an annual index of titles that shows only statistical studies. One good source of information on the characteristics of publications is the *Directory of Scholarly and Research Publishing Opportunities*, carried in most public libraries.

Another way to find opportunities is to use your search engine, enter *publishing opportunities*, and follow leads. Also, review journals, in hard copy or in electronic format, to find topics and areas in which they publish. Often, this is done quickly on the computer by searching, using key words that describe your dissertation. Once you find the journal articles that appear to be close to your topic, you have found journals that may be interested in publishing on that topic. Then, look up the journals and find their requirements for publication.

Second, find out what author guidelines, if any, the chosen journal provides. If the information does not appear in each issue of the journal itself, write or call the editor and make an inquiry. Henson (1993) reviewed the practices of 54 journal editors. He reported:

> Few beginning writers realize the importance of making their manuscripts fit the requirements of the target journals. Put bluntly, the editors will not alter their journals to fit your manuscript. (p. 801)

We have adapted and constructed in the section following this one a sample set of notes that might be supplied to prospective authors by a simulated journal.

Third, be ready to try another journal if the first choice rejects the manuscript outright. Peters and Ceci (1980) offer evidence from a cleverly designed and executed investigation that rejections are often the result of differences in judgment on the part of editors rather than lack of merit in a proposed article. We believe that it is a rare topic that cannot be matched sooner or later with the publication interests of more than one journal. Usually, too, whether the rejection is outright or conditional, the author is given the main reasons for the decision. By taking those reasons as constructive criticisms, it is often feasible to prepare an improved draft that may be accepted on a second go-round.

There is a great deal of competition for journal space. Editors of high-quality periodicals annually receive many times the number of articles that they can publish. Standards for acceptance grow in rigor each year as more and more journals state their criteria more explicitly. An increased number of journals use a referee system that screens potential articles through groups of volunteer associate editors who are specialists in the journals' domain of special interest. Achieving publication, therefore, depends in large measure on doing a superior job of putting together a well-composed, tightly organized manuscript and directing it to a periodical, the style and publishing interest of which match the article's content.

Scholarly Publications in Electronic Format

A number of scholarly, refereed journals now publish electronically, and that number increases each year. Paper remains the major venue and will not disappear any time soon, but good reasons support the growth of the electronic medium. Therefore, it may be to the advantage of today's T/D students and their mentors to make inquiries about how one prepares and submits to editors who govern electronic journal publications.

If you wish to publish articles in electronic journals, you can use electronic journal aggregators and services to find sites and publishing information. Many university library home pages have lists of electronic journals and how to access them. An example is the Johns Hopkins University's project MUSE home page (http://muse.jhu.edu), which provides access to over 100 journals in the humanities, social sciences, and mathematics.

Research libraries increasingly have access to full-text recent issues of scholarly journals. For example, the University of Pittsburgh University Library System (ULS) has electronic, full-text access to recent issues of the following Carfax titles:

African Studies
Arabic and Middle Eastern Literatures
Cambridge Journal of Education
Compare
Counselling Psychology Quarterly
Defense Analysis
European Planning Studies
Journal of Latin American Cultural Studies
Journal of Pacific History
Journal of Southern Europe and the Balkans
Labor History
New Political Science
Open Learning
Pretexts: Literary and Cultural Studies
Prometheus
Regional Studies: The Journal of the Regional Studies Association
Research in Science and Technological Education
Studies in Higher Education
British Educational Research Journal
Bulletin of Hispanic Studies
Debatte
The European Legacy
Global Society
Journal of Contemporary China
Journal of Further and Higher Education
Journal of Iberian and Latin American Studies
Journal of Political Ideologies
Strategies: Journal of Theory, Culture and Politics

These journals may be accessed through the Electronic Journals listing on your university library's web site. They are available to the entire university community.

At the same time, keep in mind that a group of publication-related issues like copyright, full-text presentation, fair use, library marketing, and reprint policy may yet remain unresolved in connection with this format.

Illustrative Guidelines for Articles or Papers

We have simulated guidelines that could have relevance for all who are trying to write for professional journals. They cover guidelines for manuscript preparation. They will not fit every journal, but study of them will help illustrate the similarities and differences between T/D style and article style.

These guidelines are useful, also, if you want to prepare a paper for distribution at a conference or to colleagues. Following them will help to produce an article that reads well and is a consistent, unified publication.

1. Select the *time perspective*. Write in the present tense or in the past or future, but be *consistent*.
2. Write in the active voice: "Jones believes that clear enunciation helps to communicate well" *rather than* "It is believed by Jones that . . . ."
3. *Keep sentences simple, short, and logical.* (Rambling, convoluted, page-long sentences turn people off.) Write with known peers in mind—not abstract "scholars."
4. Employ subheads to break copy into readable segments and to guide readers in making transitions. One subhead per three typed pages is a minimum rule.
5. Avoid quotations unless they are essential or unique in style. Identify the fact and the source. Provide copyright permission for quotations of 50 or more words and for charts or figures or models.
6. Make use of the graphics capability of your computer both to present concepts and to clarify procedures or methods used. Consult key sources for displaying data and for showing very complex theoretical constructs (Tufte, 1990).
7. Extract the *most quotable brief statements* (for use as highlights at tops or sides of pages), at least one for every three pages.
8. Keep footnotes to a minimum. Put them at the end of the manuscript in the order in which they appear. They are appropriate to acknowledge the basis of the study (e.g., doctoral dissertation, paper presented at a meeting, and so on); a grant or other finan-

cial support; scholarly review or assistance in conducting the study or preparing the manuscript.

9. The *reference* list cites only works that are referred to in the article. Every work cited in the text must be listed in the references. A *bibliography* cites other works for background. Do not duplicate items on the reference list in the bibliography.
10. State the names and correct titles of institutions of all *authors*. List them in author order on the last page of the manuscript.
11. On a separate cover page include professional biographical information: name, title, unit within larger institution or organization or legal name of the institution or organization, and mailing address.
12. Prepare the *manuscript double spaced on one side*, with margins of at least 1.25 inches. Do not reduce. Send the original and one clear copy.
13. If human or animal subjects have been used in the study, include a statement (or a photocopy) indicating that the investigation was approved by the appropriate human or animal subjects review committee at your institution.
14. Identify specifically any computer programs and any individual consultants employed in statistical analyses reported in the manuscript.
15. Copies of signed, dated, and witnessed release forms should be included for any photographs of humans to be used, and care should be taken to conceal identities.
16. In your cover letter to the editor, offer to provide a disk copy of your manuscript. This often speeds reviews by readers and facilitates technical editing to the journal's requirements.
17. If you have the copyright to your material and wish to retain it, make your desire clear immediately to the editor. Many journals insist on receiving assignment of the copyright as a precondition for publication. It is appropriate and ethical to negotiate for the arrangement you wish *prior* to review of your manuscript.
18. A dissertation or thesis is considered a publication. Thus, any article based on a dissertation or thesis should cite the dissertation or thesis in the article's text and reference list.

These directions illustrate the principle that journals have their own preferences for mode of expression. Guidelines, on the one hand, help publications to maintain and express their own journalistic styles and, on the other hand, offer assistance to the author while the manuscript is still in the early stages of composition. The guidelines for periodicals may vary markedly, one from another, as reflections of their differing editorial policies and purposes. Thus, it is advisable to obtain and to work directly from the guidelines of the particular publication to which the article will be directed.

IMPROVEMENT OF ONE'S PROFESSIONAL OR ACADEMIC DISCIPLINE

Part of the rationale for requiring research projects is that students who complete them are, as a consequence, better prepared to bring about improvements in their fields. The same rationale holds that the studies themselves, if disseminated and applied, can influence change for the better.

Research and Professional Improvement

Guba (1967), in analyzing the relation of educational research in general to educational improvement, said the following:

> Ideally, research develops the basic findings, the "new truths," the empirical data, upon which improvement decisions should be based. In education we have been singularly shortsighted in the past in constructing mechanisms by which research products are moved into practice. (p. 12)

While Guba's sentiment applied to educational research, it seems to us to have relevance for investigative studies in general. The new truths, also, may arise as a result of taking new looks at old data, seeing things from changed perspectives. Students, while still engaged in the research process, should be guided by their advisors to think of the possibilities of weaving the results of their work into the fabric of their field's future. That task ought to be kept before students as a responsibility. Now, students and advisors too often tend to close the door on research activity as if it is a completed episode that stops with the faculty committee signoff after the final oral examination. Instead, students should be guided to see their approved theses and dissertations as points of transition, not simply ends in themselves.

There is solid evidence that journal publication does follow shortly after the dissertation is completed for many graduates. For example, Schuckman (1987) studied publications by recent Ph.D. recipients in psychology and biology. It was not uncommon for three to five publications per student to appear within four years after graduation, although a substantial number did not publish at all in that same time period.

Schuckman also produced evidence that the number of postdoctoral publications per student was not related to gender. Not only was there no significant relationship between frequency of publication and male or female gender, but also it did not seem to matter whether the student's advisor was male or female. In other words, Schuckman's (1987) study provided no evidence for the belief that the sex of the graduate student's advisor had a significant impact on the student's publication rate following graduation.

The encouragement of publication by graduates is a major responsibility of advisors and committee members according to the professors we interviewed. Many advisors wished graduates would ask them to help in moving the dissertation, or a study based on it, into the mainstream of journal articles.

Translation into Theory and Practice

We emphasize, again, the obligation to put the findings of both T/D and other research and development into the hands of potential users. That obligation includes the analysis, interpretation, "repackaging," and dissemination of research results and other pertinent information for a variety of specific, nonresearch audiences. The main purpose is to provide operating agencies and individuals with a sound and growing research and development information base for evaluating and modifying current programs or planning and implementing new ones.

Students amass data of various kinds in the process of their research. Some are about people; some are about things like books or other objects, about procedural policies, or about schedules. Still more are about interactions of people and things, such as how new planets are born, how teachers design individualized education programs, the attitudes of citizens toward public welfare and taxes, or the dynamics of collective bargaining. Taken together, enormous quantities of data are collected and processed in some way annually. For the most part, the information is seldom used again after serving its function once in a T/D.

Yet, if it is accessible, it has many additional potential uses. Accessibility is becoming less and less a problem, with increases in the understanding and the technology necessary for easy and inexpensive data storage and retrieval. Knowledge availability systems have burgeoned with computers, modems, on-line search capabilities, fax machines, and a large variety of software becoming common as part of the library service and in schools, homes, offices, businesses, and other public and private organizations.

Thus, one of the significant contributions of student research may well be found in the data collection itself, quite apart from the specific use to which the information may have been put in the particular T/D for which it was gathered and processed. The contribution is ready, low-cost access to significant amounts of the raw material for inquiry, concept building, hypothesis testing, and decision making.

While it is still uncommon, a related and preferred development in student research is to build into the process itself an appreciation for the importance of what Guba (1967) called a "linking mechanism" between the T/D and practice. This calls for enlarging greatly on the implications section of the document and devoting an entirely new section to a presentation on the potential applied significance of the investigation's outcomes. After the development of the implications material, the student is almost certain to feel a greater stake in building on the scholarly insights and know-how engendered during the design, conduct, and reporting of the research itself.

FOLLOW-UP STUDIES BASED ON T/D RESEARCH

Completion of the T/D can bring relief from taut nerves and a strong temptation to turn away from the tension source. Sensitive committee members, aware of that syndrome, prepare advisees to recognize and to think about other, more positive ways to glide from student-researcher to researcher-student, a more mature form of the scholarly species. That transition can be fostered by guiding the advisee to prepare for questions in the final oral examination that bear on which follow-up investigations the findings ought to stimulate. It is only one step from that to helping the advisee to sketch procedures that could be used to pursue the suggested studies.

Potential studies that capture and hold students' interest after the T/D is finished vary in kind. Three forms of follow-up do kindle more than ordinary interest: those that replicate, those that expand, and those that refine instruments.

Replication is a great research need. The literature is replete with one-shot studies, many with possible significance but with sample, locale, or other limitations that minimize generalizability. Even with results of investigations that are broadly applicable, replication is usually needed in additional settings to create a critical mass capable of firing an adoption of changed mood in the enormous bodies of scholarly community and business systems. There are, of course, some studies that, by their nature, cannot be replicated. For them, closely related, companion investigations are needed to confirm and extend the credibility of the originals.

Expansion presses the original research work outward to new horizons. It answers questions like, How much further will this principle reach? Where else can what has been found have influence? What other professional practices are amenable to study and analysis in this way? How does what has been uncovered in this study link to other scientific laws or academic concepts? Expansion carries the implication of a programmatic approach to additional inquiry stemming from the T/D findings and motivated by them.

Instrument refinement is a possibility for further study when the student research requires the use of ratings, scales, questionnaires, tests, observation schemes, interview protocols, apparatus, formulas, or other tangible data collection aids. Sometimes, too, the study itself may not involve instrumentation, but it may unearth reasons why existing tests, scales, or similar items should be improved.

Replication, expansion, and instrumental improvements are only three directions that follow-up studies can take. Whether one or more of these paths or others seem feasible, it cannot be overemphasized that committee members have the obligation to try consciously to engage the creative imagination of their students in thinking about follow-up. This needs to be done early in T/D work, too, and reinforced frequently if it is to carry the student through the typical tendency to let down after final approval.

REINFORCEMENT FOR FOLLOW-UP

Two of the most effective motivators for degree-seeking students are financial support and faculty approval. Strategic patterning of these can create powerful forces that foster continued research activity subsequent to T/D completion. The following is a list of a number of possible ways to join reward systems to follow-up activities on the part of students:

When financial support is given during research, whether as tuition remission, job opportunities, or outright grants, include in the application and the award statement language that indicates expectation that follow-up will be done.

Establish as standard practice a post-T/D approval committee meeting that is devoted to consideration of possible follow-up work. The agenda could include

- Student ideas about possible follow-up activities
- Governmental or private foundation resources
- Suggestions about journals for submission
- Organizations or agencies interested in the kind of investigation done by the student
- Identification of other faculty members doing related research
- Practical suggestions for making a start on follow-up

Hold competitions for best T/Ds. Provide for a sufficient number of categories, with several awards in each category, to ensure that all truly meritorious studies receive recognition. Include students as judges.

Arrange for student presentations about their completed research to local audiences of other students and of faculty members. Presentations can range from class or seminar discussions to formal papers at colloquia or in faculty meetings. In all cases, make it a requirement that at least one-third of the presentation deal with potential or planned follow-up activities.

Publish a school periodical that contains summaries of completed student investigations. A necessary part of each summary may be the student's projections about possible related continuing research activity.

Hold an annual school or departmental event (luncheon, dinner, one-day conference) that highlights graduates who have published articles, presented papers, or carried on studies that built on student research they completed in the recent past.

One of the most frequently voiced concerns of advisors is that too many students have become discouraged from continuing research by the time they complete the T/D. Some end up embittered by the experience, rendered hostile to anything that relates to research. Approximately 40 years ago, James (1960) made the essential point this way:

> It is important to keep the candidate . . . in mind. Some candidates are treated so harshly that, for them, research study in later years is something carefully to be avoided. . . . It is of major importance that the candidate's efforts to identify a problem, to plan and carry out the research, to present the results, and to defend . . . results among . . . older professional colleagues should constitute a "success experience," and not a passage through purgatory. (p. 148)

We carry James's notion a step further by emphasizing the potential positive impact of thoughtfully designed end-of-mission activities. It is to be hoped, of course, that pleasant experiences will predominate all along the student research trail. If there are substantial difficulties, it is to be expected that committee members will help students work their ways through the difficulties objectively, without abrading feelings in the process. Finally, we encourage the deliberate employment of reparative and rewarding professional acknowledgment and encouragement to enhance the likelihood that the solid satisfactions of inquiry and investigation will remain dominant in those who complete T/Ds.

FUTURE TRENDS

During 1973 and 1974, the Educational Testing Service (1974) reported on the trends in graduate education in its report *Flexibility for the Future*. Significant for T/D study were these summary recommended actions:

> That the practice of evaluating all graduate schools and their faculties in terms of research be re-examined;
> That all doctoral students spend time doing off-campus work related to their major fields;
> That efforts to recruit women and minority group members for faculty positions be intensified;
> That faculty be allowed more time for seeking solutions to society's major problems; and
> That institutional policies governing such matters as student residency and fellowships be made more flexible. (p. 63)

Each of those recommendations remains as fresh today as when they were first made. Without exhausting the possibilities, these are some examples. About the first recommendation, one could ask what role *student* research has and should have in that reexamination. As for the second, to what extent might that recommendation be instrumental in promoting student studies in off-campus settings, with attendant influence on the nature of T/D topics? The third recommendation not only opens the way to studies of women and minority persons' recruitment itself, but also promises to bring more subjects of concern to women and minority groups into the pool of potential student research topics.

The fourth recommendation focuses on faculty time for addressing the world's chief problems. For the professions, that immediately suggests investigations that attack such national problems as aging, union-management relations, education for literacy and values, and studies about population control, to name only a few. The academic disciplines have at least as urgent an agenda.

With regard to the last of the five recommendations, two difficult problems for T/D students are embedded in it: residency and financial support. Residency usually refers to the time spent in study while on the campus. It is increasingly difficult for students to continue in residence (so defined) while conducting research, particularly dissertation work, because of the extended period of time often entailed. The chief problem is financial support for the student and the student's research during that period. Moreover, when financial support is available from the higher education institution, it is usually in exchange for performing some task other than the T/D work. Thus, the student is the captive of the job for which the payment is given; that captivity effectively limits the range of action of the student to investigate certain potential topics. More flexibility in residency requirements and financial support are objectives worth pursuing.

SUMMARY

This chapter begins to chart some of the largely unexplored terrain beyond the formal completion of graduate research work. The contributions of such investigations to the growth of the individual student are discussed on the one hand, and on the other hand, the functions of the T/Ds in the development of the professions and academic disciplines are considered. Suggestions are made for how faculty members and students may further their own development by means of intelligently planned activities coincident with and following the conclusion of the officially prescribed research process.

Appendix A: Suggested Proposal and Project Guidelines

The following outline suggestions supplement material that appears in the text about structuring proposals for either qualitative or quantitative research theses and dissertations. It is possible to combine parts of these outlines, to add or delete parts, and, of course, to create new outlines. As we have said, there is no fixed recipe for outlining research projects. There is no substitute for thought. These are examples, only, of ways to structure thought and problems.

The outlines illustrate ways to set up frameworks for thinking through various types of problems or issues of significance to the professional and academic disciplines. It can be seen that they all have a common theme: the identification and specification of some matter for study and the orderly process of working toward a solution. Students are encouraged to adapt these, and others that appear in the text, to suit the particular studies they wish to address.

Example A: Empirical Investigation Outline

I. Statement of the problem
   A. The general concern that makes this a matter of significant and current interest.
   B. The specific practical problem that needs to be researched to enhance practice or understanding, design policy, or determine action.

II. The theoretical framework
   A. Name(s) and brief description(s) of relevant theory(ies) to be utilized in approaching the problem.
   B. Review of major concepts and their interrelationships derived from existing theoretical work.

III. Review of literature
   A. Discuss how the theoretical framework or its components have been used in existing empirical studies.
   B. Relate the literature review to the utilization of concepts in the current study. Show how existing literature points to the need for the specific investigation proposed.

IV. Methodology
   A. The research problem—the statement of a relationship to be tested (general hypothesis). In some cases of exploratory research, it may not be appropriate to formulate hypotheses. Instead, state precise research questions with a specification of variables to be included.
      1. Specification of variables: Give objective definitions of each variable that will be controlled, measured, or manipulated.
      2. Specification of interrelationships between variables: The dependent variable(s) (goal or result), the independent variables (factors that relate to the goal or result), and the intervening variables.
   B. The specific working hypotheses.
      1. Break down the general hypothesis and state specifically the exact type of relationship expected between the independent and dependent variable(s).
      2. State the exact type of relationship expected between each of the identified subpopulations and each of the subresults expected. (How will the introduction of intervening variables affect the general results?)
   C. Operational definitions: Define each term in the statement of the relationship to be tested so that it is carefully delimited. This includes each of the variables of concern and the population under study.
   D. Limitations and delimitations: Specify each under the appropriate subheading.

E. Procedures.
   1. Procedures for collecting data.
      a. General plan: State in words and provide a diagram, if feasible.
      b. Population and sample: Indicate how selected and criteria used.
      c. Data and instrumentation: Include all relevant data and instruments.
      d. Mode of analysis: Describe both the techniques and their application.
      e. Time schedule: Utilize a time line or PERT (program evaluation and review technique) format.
   2. Pretest and results.

Overview takes place here.

V. Collection, analysis, and interpretation of data
   A. Collection of data.
   B. Processing and tabulation.
   C. Carrying out appropriate tests for analysis.
   D. Interpretation of data.
VI. Summary and conclusions
   A. Generalizations from research results to theoretical framework.
   B. Serendipitous findings.
   C. Practical implications of research results (professional development, for practice, for policy, for action, and so forth).
   D. Limitations of the study.
   E. Implications for further research and practice.

Example B: Policy Analysis Investigation Outline

I. Statement or definition of the problem
   A. The general concern(s) that make(s) this a significant problem of current interest.
   B. The specific point(s) of focus of this proposed study within the general concern(s).
II. Conceptualizing the problem for analysis

A. Outlining the dimensions or the parameters of the factors of concern.
B. Demonstrating the interrelationships of these factors for a general framework of approach.

III. Relevant literature: Discussing sources, including theories and principles, from which the problem conceptualization was derived, including any studies that have been used or can be related to the problem conceptualization or some aspect of it

IV. Specifying the process of analysis
A. The specific questions or propositions to guide the analytic effort.
B. The concepts or variables that will be used systematically in the analytic effort.
C. Operational definitions of concepts.
D. Strategy or design for making inferences about data.

V. Procedures
A. For collecting evidence or data.
1. General design.
2. Sources of evidence or data.
3. Instruments or techniques for collecting/extracting evidence or data.
4. Mode of analysis planned.

Overview takes place here.

VI. Collection and analysis of evidence or data
A. Carrying out the library and/or field research.
B. Carrying out the specified mode of analysis.
C. Analysis and interpretation of findings.

VII. Summary and conclusions
A. Relating the findings to the original conceptualization of the problem.
B. Serendipitous findings.
C. Specifying the implications of the study for the policy concern.
D. Suggesting further efforts in policy analysis with some specific reference to limitations of the present study.

Example C: Theoretical Synthesis Investigation Outline

I. Statement of the problem
   A. The general concern(s) that makes it relevant and desirable to attempt a synthesis of a particular body of knowledge or theory or of two or more related theoretical or conceptual perspectives.
   B. Describe the specific points of focus of this effort within the general concern(s).

II. Developing a framework for theoretical synthesis
   A. A concise but comprehensive overview of the major concepts in the knowledge, conceptual, or theoretical body (ies) of concern.
   B. Specification of the perceived problems or gaps in knowledge, conceptual, or theoretical coherence.

III. Relevant literature: A preliminary review of existing conceptual and theoretical work in the area of concern(s), including key empirical studies employing relevant concepts and theoretical constructs

IV. Methodology
   A. Specifying the problem for synthesis.
      1. Identifying the specific dimensions to be addressed in the synthesis (e.g., conceptual confusion, conceptual conflicts, conflict in research findings relevant to theory).
      2. Operational definitions.
         a. Of major concepts.
         b. Of variables standing for concepts as used in research.
      3. Strategy or design for synthetic efforts (identifying the relevant population of sources and how they will be sampled, if appropriate).
   B. Procedures for collecting and analyzing relevant information for synthesis.
      1. Sources of analysis for conceptually and theoretically relevant material.
      2. Sources of relevant research to shed light on concep-

tual or theoretical adequacy or to assist in resolving conceptual or theoretical conflict.
3. Techniques for extracting systematic information from secondary sources.
4. Planned mode(s) of analysis.

Overview takes place here.

V. Collection and analysis of information
   A. Carrying out the library and related informational source research.
   B. Carrying out the specified mode(s) of analysis.
   C. Analysis and interpretation of results of inquiry: Toward a conceptual and theoretical synthesis.
VI. Summary and conclusions
   A. Presenting a new model for conceptual or theoretical approach(es) on the basis of the inquiry.
   B. Specifying the implications for the further study of professional problems or issues under the guidance of the new model.
   C. Suggesting the implications for further concept or theory building with specific reference to limitations of the present study.

Appendix B: Course Outline

This course outline is designed for faculty who teach or plan to teach courses on thesis or dissertation research and preparation. The outline below is the result of years of development by several faculty members with many classes and students.

This course outline is designed for faculty who teach or plan to teach courses on thesis or dissertation research and preparation. The outline below is the result of years of development by several faculty members with many classes and students.

Students are expected to be important contributors to the seminar learning process and thus are required to review critically their own work, the work of their peers, and dissertations completed by others. The experience of the authors has been that the overwhelming majority of those who successfully complete the course successfully defend the overview proposal in committee.

RESEARCH SEMINAR DEPARTMENT OF ADMINISTRATIVE AND POLICY STUDIES APS 3090

Term: Fall
Time: 4:30–7:10 Wednesday
Place: 5P51 WWP Hall
Instructor: James Mauch, mauch@pitt.edu
Telephone: 648-7104

Seminar Objective and Content

The objective of the instructor is to help students use research as a tool in developing theses and dissertation proposals.

The seminar is concerned with the problems of designing and conducting dissertation research. More specifically, the course is designed to assist the student with the following:

1. A critical review of selected studies.
2. Identification of the trends in the body of research to become familiar with current concerns as well as to point out research needs.
3. Identification and formulation of researchable problems.
4. Development of a research design that employs appropriate methodology for dealing with the formulated problem.
5. Experiential learning through a simulated presentation of the overview to a committee comprised of class members and the instructor.

Who Should Take the Course

The seminar is appropriate for students who are nearing the end of required graduate study and who are ready to begin serious work on thesis or dissertation proposals. Thus, the instructor assumes that each student

1. Has successfully completed the required courses in research methodology and disciplined inquiry.
2. Has identified a research topic that is acceptable to the research advisor.
3. Has established a schedule that will make it possible to be in frequent contact with the research advisor about the topic as it develops.
4. Has established a schedule that will permit concentrated work over the time of the term, having as a firm goal the completion of the overview proposal in draft form by the end of the seminar.

Evaluation

This seminar is designed for graduate students who are prepared to engage in serious and scholarly preparation of a research proposal.

Students in this course are expected to assume a collegial role, and their substantive and methodological contributions to class discussions and colleagues' work are expected to be substantial, scholarly, and informative.

Given the above, and the fact that grades are required, evaluation will be based partly on the quality and relevance of class contributions, including evidence that members of the class have read, understood, and are able to critique the readings.

Therefore, it should be clear that a commitment is necessary. Student presence and contribution is important and is required for a successful class. Students should not waste the time and money of others by coming to class unprepared or by failing to be present to contribute insight into the work of colleagues. Unexcused absences are evidence of lack of commitment to study. Absences and incomplete work will be part of evaluation and may result in an incomplete or failing grade. If a student cannot make the commitment or is unwilling to undergo the discipline of class requirements, the first meeting of the class is the point at which it is appropriate to drop the class.

Each student will be asked to demonstrate computer proficiency or attend a computer workshop designed to demonstrate the uses of the computer in the development, design, writing, and execution of the proposal. Those who are already computer literate will be expected to learn to use software designed to help write proposals and scholarly papers.

An acceptable research proposal must be submitted before the course is successfully completed. This means that a proposal draft, acceptable to the research advisor, must be submitted to the instructor before a letter grade is awarded.

Text

Mauch, J. E., and Birch, J. W. (1998). *Guide to the successful thesis and dissertation* (4th ed.). New York: Marcel Dekker.

In addition, each student is asked to have available a style manual acceptable to the university, school, or department. Students will be required to conform to *one* style manual in completing class assignments. The following style manuals may be used:

American Psychological Association. (2001). *Publication manual* (5th ed.). Washington, DC: Author.
Turabian, Kate L. (I 996). *A manual for writers of term papers, theses and dissertations* (6th ed.). Chicago: University of Chicago Press.

Course Assignments

Assignment 1: Describe your topic to be developed as an overview proposal. It should be one page or less, single spaced. Include name and date, title, problem statement, and proposed methodology. Prepare sufficient copies to be distributed to the class for the discussion. Each seminar participant will provide written comments to the writer of the description. Each person will be given a short period to discuss the project during the seminar and to receive additional feedback from the other participants.

Assignment 2: Each student will be required to attend a workshop designed to provide experience in using the computer to search the university on-line library catalog, which contains over half a million citations. In addition, during this same class, students will have the opportunity to do computer searching of a bibliographic database programmed for retrieval.

Assignment 3: Based on comments from class, prepare the introduction and problem chapter of your proposal. This is a draft. Concentrate on writing clearly what you want to tell the reader in three or four pages. Substance and clarity are more important than format. Avoid "big" words; use your own language. Make enough copies for class so all can read and critique.

Assignment 4: Based on comments from class, continue, as above, with the review of the literature. This could be 20 pages easily, but more important than length is the submission of something for colleagues to review.

Assignment 5: Review and evaluate three theses or dissertations relevant to the chosen topic. Prepare a written critique of each, one or two pages in length. Be prepared to present this in class. You may find the evaluation Fig. 5-1 on pages 145–147 useful.

Assignment 6: Based on comments from class, continue as above with the research design.

Assignment 7: Based on comments from class, continue as above with the preparation of the reference list.

Assignment 8: Develop a research proposal (overview) to be presented to a simulated overview committee composed of class members. It should be a minimum of 15 pages, maximum of 25. Copies should be available one week prior to the presentation to the committee. Follow the overview outline in the text.

Each student will be assigned to serve as a research advisor and as a committee member for other students. Research topics should also be discussed with student advisors as soon as possible.

Assignment 9: Review of the literature, research design, and bibliography. When the parts have been put together, revised, and shared with the research advisor, they become the draft overview.

The dates of assignments may vary with the scheduling of instructional resources.

RESEARCH SEMINAR SCHEDULE

Class	Meeting dates	Content/assignments
1	8/27	Introduction, objectives, assignments. Read Chapters 1 and 2 for next class. Begin library search for Assignment 5.
2	9/3	Description of proposed research. Assignment 1 due. Read Chapters 3 and 4 for next class.
3	9/10	Research sources. Assignment 2.
4	9/17	Introduction and problem statement. Assignment 3. Chapter 5.

	9/24	Review of the literature. Assignment 4. Chapter 6.
	10/1	Dissertation critique. Assignment 5. Chapter 7.
	10/8	Critiques, continued. Assignment 5. Chapter 8.
8	10/15	Research design. Assignment 6. Chapter 9.
9	10/22	Reference list. Assignment 7. Chapter 10.
10	10/29	Completion of draft research proposal to share with class. Assignment 8.
11	7/5	Assignment 9, simulated overviews: 1.______________ 2.______________
12	11/12	1.______________ 2.______________
13	11/19	1.______________ 2.______________
14	12/3	1.______________ 2.______________
15	12/10	Class evaluation and review.

Bibliography

Adler, A. G. (1991). How should we cite references—or should we? *American Psychologist, 47*, 424–425.

Allen, G. R. (1973). *The graduate student's guide to theses and dissertations: A practical manual for writing and research.* San Francisco: Jossey-Bass.

American Educational Research Association. (1973). Editorial. *Educational Researcher, 2*(2), 2–3.

American Psychological Association. (1982). *Ethical principles in the conduct of research with human participants.* Washington, DC: Author.

American Psychological Association. (1997). Task Force on Statistical Inference identifies charge and produces report. *Science Agenda, 10*, 9–10.

American Psychological Association. (1999, August 9). *Electronic reference formats recommended by the American Psychological Association.* Retrieved May 16, 2002, from http://www.apastyle.org/elecref.html

American Psychological Association. (2001). *Publication manual* (5th ed.). Washington, DC: Author.

Asher, W. (1990). Educational psychology, research methodology, and meta-analysis. *Educational Psychologist, 25*, 23–28.

Association of American Universities and Association of Graduate Schools in the Association of American Universities. (1990). *Institutional policies to improve doctoral education.* Washington, DC: Author.

Atkinson, R. C. (1990). Supply and demand for scientists and engineers: A national crisis in the making. *Science, 248*, 425–432.

Bangert-Drowns, R. L., and Rudner, L. M. (1992, December). Meta-analysis in educational research. *ERIC Digest*. ED339748. Retrieved May 16, 2002, from http://www.ed.gov/databases/ERIC_Digest/ed339748.html

Barzun, J. (1985). *Simple and direct: A rhetoric for writers*. New York: Harper and Row.

Barzun, J., and Graff, H. F. (1985). *The modern researcher* (4th ed.). San Diego, CA: Harcourt Brace Jovanovich.

Bogdan, R., and Bikler, S. K. (1982). *Qualitative research for education*. Boston: Allyn and Bacon.

Bowen, C. W. (2000). A quantitative literature review of cooperative learning effects on high school chemistry achievement. *Journal of Chemical Education*, *77*(1), 116–119.

Bowen, W. G. (1981). *Graduate education in the arts and sciences: Prospects for the future*. Report of the President. Princeton, NJ: Princeton University Press.

Bowen, W. G., and Rudenstine, N. L. (1992). *In pursuit of the Ph.D.* Princeton, NJ: Princeton University Press.

Castetter, W. B., and Heisler, R. S. (1980). *Developing and defending a dissertation proposal*. Philadelphia: University of Pennsylvania.

Chronicle of Higher Education (Online, 1992, March 11). p. A18.

Clarke, M., and Oxman, A. D. (Eds.). (2000, December). Cochrane reviewers handbook 4.1.1. *The Cochrane Library* (Issue 4, 2000). Retrieved April 14, 2002, from http://www.cochrane.dlk/cochrane/handbook/start.html

Clifton, C. (1993). *A silent success: Master's education in the United States*. Baltimore, MD: Johns Hopkins University Press.

Cook, D. L. (1966). *PERT: Program evaluation and review technique applications in education*. Washington, DC: U.S. Government Printing Office.

Cooper, H. M. (1998). *Synthesizing research: A guide for literature reviews* (3rd ed.). Thousand Oaks, CA: Sage.

Cortada, J. W., and Winkler, V. C. (1979). *The way to win in graduate school*. Englewood Cliffs, NJ: Prentice Hall.

Council of Graduate Schools. (1990b). *The doctor of philosophy degree.* Washington, DC: Author.

Council of Graduate Schools. (1990b). *The doctor of philosophy degree.* Washington, DC: Author.

Council of Graduate Schools. (1991a). *International graduate students.* Washington, DC: Author.

Council of Graduate Schools. (1991b). *The role and nature of the doctoral dissertation.* Washington, DC: Author.

Coyle, E. (2001). Project methodology III. *Health Evidence Bulletins–Wales* (n.d.). Retrieved May 17, 2002, from http://www.uwcm.ac.uk/methodology/appendix5.htm

Davis, G. B., and Parker, C. A. (1997). *Writing the doctoral dissertation: A systematic approach* (2nd ed.). Hauppauge, NY: Barron's.

Davis, T. (2001). *Open doors.* New York: International Institute of Education.

Dillman, D. A. (2000). *Mail and Internet surveys: The tailored design method.* New York: Wiley.

Educational Testing Service. (1974). *Flexibility for the future.* Princeton, NJ: Author.

Eisner, E. W., and Peskkin, A. (Eds.) (1990). *Qualitative inquiry in education: The continuing debate.* New York: Teachers College Press.

Etzold, T. H. (1976). Writing for publication: The art of the article. *Phi Delta Kappan, 57*, 614–615.

Evans, B., and Evans, C. (1957). *A dictionary of contemporary American usage.* New York: Random House.

Fine, M. A., and Kudek, L. A. (1993). Reflections on determining authorship credit and authorship order on faculty-student collaborations. *American Psychologist, 48*, 1141–1147.

Flexner, S. B. (Ed.). (1987). *The Random House dictionary of the English language* (2nd ed.). New York: Random House.

Florida Community College. (2001). *Introduction to Internet research* (*LIS 2004 syllabus*). Retrieved May 21, 2002, from http://lscc.cc.fl.us/library/lis2004/reading.htm

Ford, L. (1997). Rigor or rigormortis: Identifying ''quality'' qualitative research. *American Psychologist, 51*, 46–47, 51.

Fowler, H. W. (1965). *A dictionary of modern English usage* (2nd ed.). Oxford, England: Clarendon Press.

Gardner, J. W. (1978). *Excellence*. New York: Harper and Row.

Gash, S. (2000). *Effective literature searching for research* (2nd ed.). Brookfield, VT: Gower.

Gay, L. R. (1996). *Educational research: Competencies for analysis and application* (5th ed.). New York: Merrill.

Gelfand, H., and Walker, C. J. (2001). *Mastering APA style: Student's workbook and training guide*. Washington, DC: American Psychological Association.

Gibaldi, J., and Achtert, W. S. (1999). *MLA handbook for writers of research papers* (5th ed.). New York: Modern Language Association of America.

Glass, G. V. (1977). Integrating findings: The meta-analysis of research. In L. S. Shulman (Ed.), *Review of research in education* (pp. 351–379). Itasca, IL: F. E. Peacock.

Glass, G. V., McGow, B., and Smith, M. L. (1981). *Meta-analysis in social research*. Newbury Park, CA: Sage.

Gorman, R. A. (1987). Copyright and the professorate: A primer and some recent developments. *Academe, 73*, 29–33.

Greenberg, B. (1987). *Using microcomputer and mainframes for data analysis in the social sciences*. Columbus, OH: Merrill.

Guba, E. G. (1967). *Educational improvement and the role of educational research*. Bloomington, IN: The National Center for the Study of Educational Change.

Hafner, K., and Lyon, M. (1996). *Where wizards stay up late: The origin of the Internet*. New York: Simon and Schuster.

Hart, C. (1998). *Doing a literature review: Releasing the social science research imagination*. London: Sage.

Haskins, C. H. (1957). *The rise of universities*. London: Cornell University Press.

Hawley, P. (1993). *Being bright is not enough: The unwritten rules of doctoral study*. Springfield, IL: Charles C Thomas.

Hedges, L. V. (1986). Issues on meta-analysis. In E. Z. Rothkopf (Ed.), *Review of research in education* (pp. 353–398). Washington, DC: American Educational Research Association.

Heinrich, K. T. (1991). Loving partnerships: Dealing with sexual attraction and power in doctoral advisement relationships. *Journal of Higher Education*, *62*, 514–538.

Henson, K. T. (1993). Writing for successful publication. *Phi Delta Kappan*, *74*, 799–802.

Hernandez, L. L. (1996, December). In search of a dissertation committee: Using a qualitative research approach to study a lived experience. *The Qualitative Report*, *2*(4). Retrieved May 16, 2002, from http://www.nova.edu/ssss/QR/QR2-4/hernandez.html

Hunter, J. E., and Schmidt, F. L. (1990). *Methods of meta-analysis: Correcting error and bias in research findings*. Newbury Park, CA: Sage.

Isaac, P. D., Koenigsknecht, R. A., Malaney, G. D., and Karras, J. E. (1989). Factors related to doctoral dissertation topic selection. *Research in Higher Education*, *30*, 357–373.

James, P. E. (1960). The dissertation requirement. *School and Society*, *88*, 147–148.

Johnson, J. M. (1996). Western Europe leads the United States and Asia in science and engineering Ph.D. degree production. *National Science Foundation Data Brief*, 12.

Johnston, J. M., and Pennypacker, H. S. (1980). *Strategies and tactics of human behavioral research*. Hillsdale, NJ: Lawrence Erlbaum Associates.

Jones, J. H. (1993). *Bad blood: The Tuskeegee syphilis experiment*. New York: Free Press.

Kavoosi, M., Elman, N., and Mauch, J. (1995). Faculty mentoring and administrative support in schools of nursing. *Journal of Nursing Education*, *34*, 419–426.

Kenny, D. A. (1999, February 24). *Meta-analysis easy to answer*. Retrieved May 17, 2002, from http://w3.nai.net/~dakenny/meta.htm

King, D. (2000, May). Specialized search engines: Alternatives to the big guys. *Online*. Retrieved May 22, 2002, from http://onlineinc.com/onlinemag/OL2000/king5.html

Krathwohl, D. R. (1988). *How to prepare a research proposal: Guidelines for funding and dissertations in the social and behavioral sciences* (3rd ed.). Syracuse, NY: Syracuse University Press.

Lalumiere, N. (1993). Comment. *American Psychologist*, *48*, 412.

Lancy, D. (1993). *Qualitative research in education: An introduction to the major traditions*. New York: Longman.

Land, B. D. (2001, July 1). *Web extension to American Psychological Style* (WEAPAS) (Rev. 2.0). Retrieved May 17, 2002, from http://www.beadsland.com/weapas/

LaPidus, J. B. (1990). *Research student and supervisor*. Washington, DC: Council of Graduate Schools.

LeCompte, M., Preissle, J., and Tech, R. (1993). *Ethnography and qualitative design in educational research* (3rd ed.). San Diego, CA: Academic Press.

Leedy, P. D., and Ormrod, J. E. (2001). *Practical research: Planning and design* (7th ed.). Upper Saddle River, NJ: Merrill–Prentice Hall.

Lester, J. D. (1999). *Writing research papers: A complete guide* (9th ed.). New York: Longman.

Lincoln, Y. S., and Guba, E. G. (1985). *Naturalistic inquiry*. Beverly Hills, CA: Sage

Lindvall, C. M. (1959). The review of related research. *Phi Delta Kappan*, *40*, 179–180.

Lipsey, M. W., and Wilson, D. B. (1993). The efficacy of psychological, educational and behavioral treatment: Confirmation from meta-analysis. *American Psychologist*, *48*, 1181–1209.

Locke, L. F., Spirduso, W. W., and Silverman, S. J. (2000). *Proposals that work: A guide for planning dissertations and grant proposals* (4th ed.). Thousand Oaks, CA: Sage.

Long, C. D. (1997a). Adventures in intellectual property rights. *Academe*, *83*(2), 8–11.

Long, C. D. (1997b). Opportunities made equal. *Academe, 83*(2), 48–51.

Long, T. J., Convey, J. J., and Chwalek, A. R. (1985). *Completing dissertations in the behavioral sciences and education.* San Francisco: JosseyBass.

Lovitts, B. (1997, September 22). Contextual factors in graduate student attrition. National Science Foundation, Division of Science Resources Studies, Professional Societies Workshop Series, *Qualitative Approaches to Studying Graduate Student Attrition.* Retrieved May 17, 2002, from http://www.nsf.gov.sbe/nsf98322/qualit.htm#research

MacKinnon, D. W. (1962). The nature and nurture of creative talent. *American Psychologist, 17*, 484–495.

Madsen, D. (1983). *Successful dissertations and theses.* San Francisco: Jossey-Bass.

Mallinkrodt, B., and Leong, F. (1992). International graduate students, stress, and social support. *Journal of College Student Development, 33*, 71.

Marchant, G. J. (1997). Issues in authorship. *Newsletter for Educational Psychologists, 20*, 3–5.

Martin, R. (1980). *Writing and defending a thesis or dissertation in psychology and education.* Springfield, IL: Charles C Thomas.

Mauch, J., and Spaulding, S. (1992). The internationalization of higher education: Who should be taught what and how? *Journal of General Education, 41*, 111–129.

Mecklenburger, J. A. (1972). ''Merely journalism'' as educational research. *Phi Delta Kappan, 53*, 202.

Meloy, J. M. (2002). *Writing the qualitative dissertation: Understanding by doing* (2nd ed.). Mahwah, NJ: Erlbaum.

Merrill, G. E. (1992). The Ph.D., upholding the sciences. *Academe, 78*(5), 24–25.

Milgram, S. (1963). Behavioral study of obedience. *Journal of Abnormal and Social Psychology, 67*, 371–378.

Miller, D. C., and Salkind, N. J. (2002). *Handbook of research design and social measurement* (6th ed.). Thousand Oaks, CA: Sage.

Mishkin, B. (1993). Fraud in science: The case for tough enforcement of standards. *Cosmos, 3*, 47–51.

Monaghan, P. (1989a, December 6). Psychologist specializes in counseling graduate students who seem unable to finish their doctoral dissertations. *The Chronicle of Higher Education*, pp. A13–A16.

Monaghan, P. (1989b, March 29). Some fields are reassessing the value of the traditional doctoral dissertation. *The Chronicle of Higher Education*, p. A8.

Myers, R. A. (1993). The 1992 Leona Tyler Award address. *The Counseling Psychologist*, *21*, 326–337.

National Academy of Sciences. (1989). *On being a scientist*. Washington, DC: National Academy Press.

National Center for Education Statistics. (1999). *Digest of Educational Statistics, 1998* (NCES 1999-036). Washington, DC: Author.

National Center for Education Statistics. (1997, November). Degrees earned by foreign graduate students: Fields of study and plans after graduation. *Issue Brief*. Retrieved May 17, 2002, from http://nces.ed.gov/pubs98/98042.pdf

National Collegiate Honors Council. (1997, winter). *The national honors report*, *17*(4).

National Science Foundation. (1996). *Selected data on science and engineering doctorate awards: 1995* (NSF 96-303). Arlington, VA: Author.

Newman, E. (1980). *Edwin Newman on language*. New York: Warner Books.

O'Connor, P. T. (1997). *Woe is I*. New York: G. P. Putnam's Sons.

On line. (1992, March 11). *The Chronicle of Higher Education*, p. A18.

Parr, G., Bradley, L., and Bingin, R. (1992). Concerns and feelings of international graduate students. *Journal of College Student Development*, *33*, 20.

Pearson, W. (1997, September 22). Research on graduate student attrition. National Science Foundation, Division of Science Resources Studies, *Qualitative approaches to studying graduate student attrition*. Arlington, VA. Retrieved May 17, 2002, from htttp://www.nsf.gov/sbe/srs/nsf9832/qualit.htm#research

Peters, D. P., and Ceci, S. J. (1980). A manuscript masquerade. *The Sciences*, *20*, 16–19, 35.

Pincus, H., Lieberman, J., and Ferris, S. (Eds.). (1999). *Ethics in psychiatric research: A resource manual for human subjects protection*. Washington, DC: American Psychiatric Association.

Pool, R. (1990). Who will do science in the 1990's? *Science*, *248*, 433–435.

Post, E. (1997). *Everyday etiquette*. New York: Funk and Wagnalls.

Pulling, B. S. (1992). The D. A., alive in Idaho. *Academe*, *78*(5), 23.

Reynolds, M. C., Zetlin, A. G., & Heistad, D. (1996). *A manual for 20/20 analysis*. Philadelphia, PA: Temple University Center for Research in Human Development and Education.

Rice, J. (1989). Managing bibliographic information with person desktop technology. *Academe*, *75*(4), 18–25.

Robertson, N., and Sistler, J. K. (1971). The doctorate in education. *Phi Delta Kappan*, *52*, 182–184.

Root-Bernstein, R. S. (1989, November/December). Breaking faith. *The Sciences*, 8–11.

Ruark, J. K. (2002, April 26). The history that may never be read. *The Chronicle of Higher Education*, p. A16.

Schalock, R. L. (2001). *Outcomes-based evaluation* (2nd ed.). New York: Plenum Press.

Schmidt, F. L. (1992). What do data really mean? Research findings, meta-analysis, and cumulative knowledge in psychology. *American Psychologist*, *47*, 1173–1181.

Schuckman, H. (1987). Ph.D. recipients in psychology and biology. *American Psychologist*, *42*, 987–992.

Seeman, J. (1973). On supervising student research. *American Psychologist*, *28*, 900–906.

Seligman, M. E. (1992). The doctorate via e-mail, or, the OKBridge Solution. *The APA Monitor*, *23*, 4.

Sellin, D. F., and Birch, J. W. (1980). *Educating gifted and talented learners*. Rockville, MD: Aspen.

Sellin, D. F., and Birch, J. W. (1981). *Psychoeducational developments of gifted and talented learners*. Rockville, MD: Aspen.

Sherman, C. (1999). The future of Web search. *Online*, *23*(3), 54–61.

Sieber, J. E., and Stanley, B. (1988). Ethical and professional discussions of socially scientific research. *American Psychologist*, *43*, 49–55.

Sigma Xi, The Scientific Research Society. (1991). *Honor in science*. Research Triangle Park, NC: Author.

Slavin, R. E. (1992). *Research methods in education*. Needham Heights, MA: Allyn and Bacon.

Smallwood, S. (2002, April 12). Bitter aftertaste. *The Chronicle of Higher Education*, p. A10.

Stanford University. (n.d.). *Copyright and fair use*. Retrieved May 21, 2002, from http://fairuse.stanford.edu/

Steggna, R. (1972). What is a university not? *Intellectual Digest*, *2*, 55.

Stempner, J. (2001, March). Library research assistance, vol. 5. *Information Technology Newsletter*. Retrieved May 20, 2002, from http://www1.unm.edu/oit/newsletter/01/0301_itn/research.html

Sternberg, D. (1981). *How to complete and survive a doctoral dissertation*. New York: St. Martin's Press.

Strunk, W., Jr., and White, E. B. (1979). *The elements of style* (3rd ed.). New York: Macmillan.

Stuart, E. B. (1979). *A manual for preparation of theses and dissertations for the school of engineering* (4th ed.). Pittsburgh, PA: The University of Pittsburgh.

Taylor, S., and Bogdan, R. (1998). *Introduction to qualitative research methods: A guidebook and resource*. New York: Wiley.

Terman, L. (1954). The discovery and encouragement of exceptional talent. *American Psychologist*, *9*, 221–223.

Trochim, W. M. K. (2002, May). *Bill Trochims's Center for Social Research methods*. Retrieved May 21, 2002, from http://trochim.human.cornell.edu/selstat/ssstart.htm

Tufte, E. R. (1990). *Envisioning information*. Cheshire, CT: Graphics Press.

Tufte, E. R. (1997). *Visual explanations: Images and quantities, evidence and narrative*. Cheshire, CT: Graphics Press.

Tufte, E. R. (2001). *The visual display of quantitative information*. Cheshire, CT: Graphic Press.

Turabian, K. L. (1996). *A manual for writers of term papers, thesis, and dissertations* (6th ed.). Chicago: University of Chicago Press.

U.S. Department of Health and Human Services. (1981). Protection of human subjects. *Federal Register*, *46*(16), 8366–8391.

U.S. Department of Health and Human Services, National Institutes of Health. (2001, December 13). *Code of federal regulations, title 45, public welfare*. Retrieved May 19, 2002, from http://ohrp.osophs.dhhs.gov/humansubjects/guidance/45cfr46.htm

University of Kentucky Computing Center. (n.d.). *Meta-analysis references and software*. Retrieved May 17, 2002, from http://www.uky.edu/ComputingCenter/SSTARS/MetaAnalysis.htm

University of Miami Libraries. (2001). *Social science data collections, data user help*. Retrieved May 21, 2002, from http://www.library.miami.edu/data/help.html

University of Minnesota Libraries. (2002). *Library frequently asked questions*. Retrieved May 20, 2002, from http://www.faq.lib.umn.edu/public/PublAccess.pl

University of Pittsburgh. (1974). *Office of Measurement and Evaluation*. Pittsburgh, PA: Author.

University of Pittsburgh. (1992). *The university honors college*. Pittsburgh, PA: Author.

University of Pittsburgh, School of Education. (1981). *Style manual*. Pittsburgh, PA: Author.

van Leunen, M. C. (1979). *A handbook for scholars*. New York, NY: Knopf.

Vartuli, S. (Ed.). (1982). *The Ph.D. experience: A woman's point of view*. San Francisco: Praeger.

Webster's Ninth New Collegiate Dictionary. (1985). Springfield, MA: Merriam-Webster.

White, P. (1991). *The idea factory: Learning to think at MIT*. New York: Dutton.

Whitehead, A. N. (1953). *Science and the modern world.* New York: Macmillan.

World Medical Association. (1964). Declaration of Helsinki: Recommendations guiding doctors in clinical research. *World Medical Journal, 11,* 28.

York, C. C., Sobel, L., Gratch, B., and Pursel, J. (1988). Computerized reference sources: One stop shopping or part of a search strategy? *Research Strategies, 6*(1), 8–17.

Zinsser, W. (2001). *On writing well: The classic guide to writing nonfiction* (6th ed.). New York: Quill.

Ziolkowski, T. (1990). The Ph.D. squid. *The American Scholar, 59,* 175–195.

Zuber-Skerritt, O., and Knight, N. (1986). Problem definition and thesis writing. *Higher Education, 15,* 89–103.

Zuber-Skerritt, O., and Ryan, Y. (Eds.). (1999). *Supervising postgraduates from non-English speaking backgrounds.* Philadelphia: Society for Research into Higher Education.

Index